The Today Show

The Today Show

Transforming Morning Television

Cathleen M. Londino

ROWMAN & LITTLEFIELD
Lanham • Boulder • New York • London

Published by Rowman & Littlefield
A wholly owned subsidary of The Rowman & Littlefield Publishing Group, Inc.
4501 Forbes Boulevard, Suite 200, Lanham, Maryland 20706
www.rowman.com

Unit A, Whitacre Mews, 26-34 Stannary Street, London SE11 4AB

British Library Cataloguing in Publication Information Available

Library of Congress Cataloging-in-Publication Data

Names: Londino, Cathleen M., 1949– author.
Title: The Today show : transforming morning television / Cathleen M. Londino.
Description: Lanham : Rowman & Littlefield, 2016. | Includes bibliographical
   references and index.
Identifiers: LCCN 2016018658 (print) | LCCN 2016032005 (ebook) | ISBN
   9781442269927 (hardback : alk. paper) | ISBN 9781442269934 (electronic)
Subjects: LCSH: Today show (Television program)
Classification: LCC PN1992.77.T6 L55 2016 (print) | LCC PN1992.77.T6 (ebook)
   | DDC 791.45/72—dc23
LC record available at https://lccn.loc.gov/2016018658

♾™ The paper used in this publication meets the minimum requirements of
American National Standard for Information Sciences—Permanence of Paper
for Printed Library Materials, ANSI/NISO Z39.48-1992.

Printed in the United States of America

To my mother, Helen (1924–2016),
and the producers of *Today*, who know how to deliver a great product.

Contents

Acknowledgments

Many thanks to my son Jonathan Londino, whose editing and language skills were invaluable to this work, and to my son Paul, whose computer skills I rely on to function in the twenty-first century. Also, much appreciation to my son James, whose actual meaningful scientific research humbles me, and to my husband, Larry, who keeps me competitive. To Mary Childers, who both identified and resolved my most pressing issues, and all the strong women in my life—Candice Londino, Tera Santucci, Joanne Johnson, Inna Katkova, Maureen Anderson, and Irene Demkiw—who never fail to inspire me.

A special thanks to Stephen Ryan, Andrea O. Kendrick, and Jessica McCleary, Rowman & Littlefield's supportive team, for all their professional service and advice. A heartfelt thank-you to Doug and Patricia Piroh, who always go above and beyond my expectations.

Finally, a special acknowledgment for the executives at NBC and *Today*, who gave me such generous access to *Today*'s personnel and historical files. Thank you to Farrin Jay, who generously provided the *Today* photos.

From a longtime fan of *Today*, thank you Pat Weaver for your inspired vision.

Introduction

I am a lifelong fan of the *Today* show, having watched the early Dave Garroway years on a tiny black-and-white television set. Along with my sister and brother, every morning while getting ready for school we watched, waited, and squealed with delight whenever J. Fred Muggs was on. My parents, like those in so many other households around America, were hooked, and watching *Today* became a regular part of our morning that stretched into years, long after the chimp departed *Today* company. I continued to watch into my adult years, not even aware that the other networks were trying desperately to woo me. For twenty-five years, from 1952 to 1977, *Today* was the most watched and most trusted morning news and information program on the air. How did *Today*, so seemingly effortlessly, bring that window on the world to millions each morning and keep their loyalty year after year? This book hopes to answer how one man's vision brought to fruition, shaped, and influenced more than six decades of broadcast history.

The major research for this book took place at NBC in New York City. Among the NBC departments consulted were News, Station Relations, and the *Today* Unit. The News Audience Research Department, which initiated studies on audience analysis, competition, and talent, supplied information on personnel and departments to contact for specific areas of research. The *Today* Unit, consisting of the producers, production team, talent, and secretarial staff of *Today*, was contacted for information on the production of the program. Executive producer Paul Friedman and producer Doug Sinsel were interviewed concerning the production practices and activities prevalent in 1977. They also made it possible to observe the live production of the program and gave permission to interview key individuals. The research itself involved an examination of memos, records, letters, interdepartmental communications, and network–station correspondence obtained through NBC departmental files and the *Today* Unit. The Program Analysis Department provided records of all *Today* programs from 1952, including information on changes of personnel and production facilities. The director of the Department of Affiliate Relations, Steve Flynn, assisted by providing files on *Today* correspondence between NBC and its affiliated and owned stations between 1952 and 1977. Such files contained information on program decisions that would affect the affiliated stations in terms of programming information, personnel, and advertising changes.

Other NBC departments were contacted and personal interviews conducted to obtain information pertaining to select historical and production aspects of *Today*. The Department of Participating Sales provided information on *Today* sales activities. In addition, Robert Conrad, vice president for participating program sales, authorized Central Files to release advertising rate cards on *Today*, and the Ratings Division made *Today* ratings and audience share data accessible. Jerry Jaffe, director of the Ratings Division, provided comparative ratings and share of audience on *Today* competition over the same twenty-five-year period. Information pertaining to news or promotion of *Today* was obtained through NBC's News Department.

The News Audience Research Department conducted specific studies concerning audience research, talent effectiveness, program content analysis, and program competition. Those unpublished research studies were used for programming decisions by the executive staff of *Today* and NBC and were not publicly available. In 1967, NBC authorized a promotional booklet on the first fifteen years of *The Today Show* distributed primarily to affiliate stations and advertising agencies in honor of *Today*'s fifteenth anniversary. It provided information on what NBC considered to be the highlights of those years. I would particularly like to acknowledge the work of former *New York Times* writer Robert Metz, whose book dealt primarily with the private lives and relationships between the talent and producers of *Today* and provided useful background on its early history as well as anecdotal material on David Garroway, Hugh Downs, Frank McGee, Barbara Walters, and other cast members.

Every attempt has been made to represent a true and fair examination of the first twenty-five years of *Today* and to conscientiously credit all sources. Errors are my own and not the responsibility of NBC.

1

Creating *Today*

Pat Weaver's Concept

During the first twenty-five years that *Today* was on the air, from 1952 to 1977, television news evolved dramatically. News informed in 1952; it didn't entertain. The typical fifteen-minute network evening news show in 1952 featured a staid, talking-face reporter. NBC's *Camel News Caravan* anchor John Cameron Swayze read the highlights of hard-news items that were only occasionally relieved by an interview with a newsmaker. About that time, Sylvester L. (Pat) Weaver, vice president in charge of programming at NBC, pitched a bold new concept: a two-hour early morning news show that would run Monday through Friday from 7:00 to 9:00 a.m. Since the networks were not then providing regular programming before 11:00 a.m., executives and station managers wondered whether there was even an audience available in the early morning hours. By developing *Today*, Weaver filled a programming void before viewers even realized there was one. Radio was then the most popular and reliable way for Americans to get their morning news. Nevertheless, he was undaunted by the challenge in creating something so innovative in scope and content: "This is in every sense a vast undertaking. We are building a program that will change the viewing habits of the nation. We want the public to be well informed, to be amused, to be lightened in spirit and heart."[1]

But the very definition of news began to change in 1952 when entertainer David Garroway was chosen as "master communicator" to deliver a folksy but trustworthy version of newsworthy events on the newly created *Today Show*. Significantly, the other factor that contributed to whetting an appetite for news was the availability of time—and lots of it—time begging to be filled with content that ranged from the serious and important (including the opportunity to cover something more in depth) to softer feature segments designed to illuminate and entertain. Over the years, Weaver's original concept underwent some tweaking and fine-tuning, but it clearly worked. The challenge for Weaver was not how to implement his brilliant idea but how to attract the audience that he suspected was out there.

In the early 1950s, when Pat Weaver conceived of *Today*, he created a revolutionary new program that appeared from the start to be destined for failure. The obstacles against the program seemed insurmountable. *Today*, unique in length, format, and hour of transmission, had not yet established that a significant television audience was available at that early hour. The morning was thought to be exclusively radio and newspaper time, but Pat Weaver knew differently:

> In spite of what people said, I knew and had known for years that there was a gigantic audience in the morning. With the *Breakfast Club*, and *Breakfast at Sardi's*, and at the CBS station out on the coast, we had these immense hits in the morning so I knew the audience was there. The question was, could I make them watch a show that was better for them than the original concept, which was to do *Rise and Shine*, you know, another gang show with funny jokes and song. The difficulty in those days from the news point of view was that you were really doing a newsreel at night so that the job of television to reach people and influence them was very difficult to do. And the *Today* show was an opportunity to really cover the world to show what, eventually, real world coverage could be like. And yet, do it in such a way with enough showmanship so you would get the major audience that would otherwise look at *Rise and Shine*. But the audience was already there. That was no secret. It was not a bold experiment there. It was based on knowledge that I had and it was available. But you know, available knowledge is rarely understood by most people.[2]

One of the most difficult tasks facing the *Today* staff was to establish a strong lineup of stations willing to carry the program. NBC was asking its affiliated stations to bear the risk and burden that was required to begin broadcasting at 7:00 in the morning for a show that probably would not last for more than a few weeks. *Today* was to be a daily program, and stations were expected to clear two hours of time each day, five days a week. This in particular seemed absurd since in 1952 even the network evening news was capsulized into only fifteen minutes. Surely, the affiliates thought, programming two hours of news per day could not be sustained for any length of time.

The incentive for stations to carry the program proved to be strong. In part, the incentive came in the form of excellent local advertising opportunities and in part from the promotion developed by *Today* executives. NBC promoted the program to its affiliated stations with the help of a specially made film. The opening sound portion, transcribed below, reveals how *Today* executives were able to appeal to "patriotic duty" to induce the affiliates to carry the program:

> *Today* is a program that must through its entertainment and its news become a national habit. It must stir imagination. It must create an informed listener public. A program like this is a magnificent view of the tool of television and its ultimate social responsibility. John Smith, American, on this program will meet the people that he must know to be an informed citizen of a free society. He will hear the voices that count in the world. He will listen to word that echoes the story of history. He will see the places of peace and the places of war. His horizons will be limited by neither time nor place. John Smith will be there. He will know. This is the real secret weapon of free men: To know, to understand, so that John Smith is ready for today, whatever it may bring.[3]

Despite the obstacles and apparent disregard for "Jane" Smith's worldly needs, Pat Weaver persevered and succeeded in developing a program that surprised the critics when it lasted more than just a few weeks. Although it struggled through prudent alterations and improvements during its first few years on the air, *Today* proved to have had enduring qualities. In fact, *Today* lasted far longer at NBC than did Pat Weaver, who left NBC in 1956. On January 14, 1977, when *Today* celebrated its twenty-fifth year and its 13,364th hour on the air, Weaver was invited back to NBC to appear on *Today*'s silver anniversary program. In an interview, he reminisced about the origination of the program and its first tenuous years on the air, refuting NBC's claim that *Today* was not successful during its early years: "The show has gotten a 'bad start' history that isn't fully deserved. It was by the end of the second year that it became the largest grosser in show biz including motion pictures. So that from a commercial point of view, it was an extremely effective smash hit from the beginning."

The early success of the program was somewhat debatable. NBC declared that *Today* was unprofitable for the first six to eight years on the air, but according to *New York Times* writer Robert Metz, it was because NBC manipulated the cost/profit ratio of the program to make *Today* appear unsuccessful. He further claimed that this type of manipulation was not peculiar to *Today*:

> In broadcasting, as in other enterprises with numerous so-called profit centers, how much a particular segment of the business earns or loses depends on how you assign *general* overhead expenses. How much of the building's depreciation and heating expenses do you assign. . . . How much of the

salaries of the NBC vice-presidents and pages, cleaning women and security guards do you lay on it?[4]

He added, "NBC must have assigned heavy news department expenses to *Today* and God knows what else, for as early as its second year the show began to develop spectacular momentum with advertisers."

The points made by Metz and Weaver claiming that *Today* was successful, financially, during its early years was substantiated in part from a 1953 article in *Variety*:

On the basis of orders already on the pad, NBC-TV's early morning *Today* show will earn more money in 1953 than any other TV show on the networks. The 7 to 9 a.m. across-the-board Dave Garroway–emceed program with its flexible sales formula will achieve an SRO status during the month of December, with $1,200,000 in sponsor order already committed for that month alone. Total annual billings for the multi-sponsored show will top the $7,500,000 mark. . . . *Today* adds up to one of the all-time major sales-programming success stories in TV.[5]

By the end of *Today*'s second year on the air, the program did in fact begin to succeed financially. *Today* became an attractive buy to advertisers in part because of two advertising concepts. Because the (then three-hour) production of the program was too expensive to be sponsored by a single advertiser, Weaver implemented "participating" advertising, which allowed several advertisers to purchase spots on the program much as they would buy space in a magazine. The other successful advertising practice was the requirement of *Today*'s program host and other panel members to deliver commercial messages. That gave the sponsors the added bonus of close talent–product identification. It was a practice that helped generate great profits over many years.

In 1958, the overall advertising structure of the program was revised. The program was divided into half-hour sales plans whereby the first and third half hours were available only for local commercial messages and the second and fourth half hours were sold exclusively by the network. This plan simplified the sales structure and financial arrangements between the network and its affiliate stations. It also made station relations a vital part of *Today*'s success. From the beginning, *Today* was forced to develop effective communications with its stations to coordinate the regular network feed with local commercials and breaks. Such communication evolved over the years to include any special information that might affect the normal program feed. Local stations were informed of whatever commercial opportunities or changes were necessary along with information concerning the coordination of the expanded time if *Today* went beyond its normal two hours.

When Weaver developed the original *Today* panel, he understood the importance of creating a congenial atmosphere where talent would hopefully be able to develop a chemistry with each other that would be attractive to an audience. His panel consisted of a host, a "second banana" supporting team member, a newsreader, and, eventually, a "*Today* girl." Weaver felt that the combination of personality types on the panel was more important than any one individual personality, with the exception of the host. Each of the positions was defined by the personality who occupied it, and when that individual left the program, it was expected that the same type of personality would fill the position. Despite the brilliantly conceived panel of personalities and responsibilities, Weaver could not have known that the addition of one new member was to be the breakthrough the show needed. It was the arrival of J. Fred Muggs, chimpanzee and regular presence on the show in the second year, that brought in steady viewers that translated into strong enough ratings to guarantee advertisers.

Muggs was certainly a beneficial addition, but it was Garroway, *Today*'s first host, whose image and leadership infused the show with a particular identity. Although *Today* was essentially a news program, Weaver emphatically desired an entertainer with a warm personality to be the program host rather than a person with a background in news. Weaver believed that the man best suited to convey information to an audience should be one who was able to establish a warm rapport with viewers. He felt that David Garroway was the perfect choice as the first host of *Today*, and David Garroway concurred: "Well, I was built to do this show. All my training had been as a generalist; to specialize in nothing and know something about everything. This show was made for me and it was my show automatically, I felt. I deserved it." Weaver believed the ideal *Today* host should possess a rare combination of human and professional qualities, which would include charm; a sense of humor; a warm, friendly personality; and a casual, relaxed manner. Both the first *Today* host David Garroway and the third host, Hugh Downs, closely embodied those qualities. They were extremely successful and well liked by the audience for a combined total of more than eighteen of *Today*'s first twenty-five years on the air.

No other position on *Today* evolved more dramatically than that of the permanent female panel member. In the first twelve years of *Today*, there were twelve *Today* girls. The title appropriately described their position as well as their responsibilities. Their duties were confined to light features that were intended to be of interest to women, and their attractive physical appearance was designed to appeal to male viewers. Then, in 1962, Barbara Walters was hired as a program writer and was soon given occasional "on-air" reporting assignments. She proved competent enough to be offered the permanent on-air female position in 1964. Producer Al Morgan, convinced of her ability to handle all types of feature material and interviews, gradually increased her responsibilities. Within ten years, Barbara Walters was made cohost of *Today. Today* gave her the opportunity to develop her position into a significant contributing role during the years when very few females were allowed to handle important assignments. With Morgan's encouragement, Barbara Walters became a model for other women who were interested in broadcast journalism. Through her demonstrated competence, she made it acceptable for other network newswomen to be given responsibilities on a par with newsmen.

One of the reasons *Today* had been successful was the flexibility in its programming that allowed it to be ever current. No other program had the opportunity to be as responsive as *Today* in terms of covering significant social and political issues and events. In 1961, when the responsibility of producing *Today* was moved from the Programming Department to NBC News, it initiated a stronger overall commitment to news as well as even more attention to social and political issues. Frequently, the program was expanded beyond its normal two hours when the importance or significance of an event warranted the extra time.

From the beginning, *Today* relied on technology to bring the world home to viewers through a set cluttered with gadgetry designed to impress the unsophisticated viewer. But technology, which made remote worldwide communications possible, was an important part of *Today's* early programming, and Pat Weaver felt that it would continue to play an important role. In 1952, much of the technology that became critical to *Today's* future was in the developmental stages, but Weaver anticipated that it would be absorbed into the programming when it became practical:

> We knew that tape was coming. We knew that lightweight equipment was coming so that was actually in the plan for *Today* . . . the show was to go out much more. It also went out through the windows, of course, in the studio in those days. It [remote broadcasts] would be picked up as the technology increased. It would be able to give you the world picture we were then getting on radio.[6]

Today kept on the cutting edge of broadcast technology by embracing and implementing new innovations into its programming. One such change in technology—videotape—nearly brought down the show. Others, like broadcasting regularly in color, enhanced it. The invention and implementation of videotape allowed NBC to tape delay the program to the Midwest and Pacific Coast stations, thereby eliminating the need for a third live hour of *Today*. Videotape had a "freeing" effect on the program, allowing many features and events that were difficult to program live to be pretaped. Ironically, it was that same technology that in the early

1960s almost destroyed the show, when producer Robert Bendick decided to tape *Today* the afternoon before and air it the following morning. But other developments, such as high-quality portable equipment and satellite transmission capability, made remote broadcasts feasible from anywhere in the world. The perfection of the minicam opened up that "window to the world" by providing the ability to access remote locations outside the studio. Jet transport, then microwave and satellite transmission, brought the world home.

It is a tribute to Weaver's vision and the perseverance and vigilance of NBC and its dedicated producers that *Today* ultimately found unprecedented success by changing and adapting to the challenges it faced. Weaver knew the importance of having the right person at the helm of the show. In *Today's* case, that was a producer or executive producer who would be responsible for overseeing every aspect of the program on a daily basis. Through the years, decisions were made with hopeful forward steps—some tentative, some bold, some ill conceived, some brilliant. *Today's* producers were responsible for all facets of the production, including the supervision of programming, production, staff, crew, and talent. Producing *Today* "live" two hours per day, five days a week, without repeats, was extremely complicated. Undoubtedly, the most difficult role for any *Today* producer was to maintain control over the program and still be responsive to the demands of the talent. Although *Today* had many producers who made individual impressions on the program, all faithfully retained the overall original concept and integrity of the program. They maintained a balance of news, information, and entertainment throughout its history. The majority of changes were those that affected the appearance of the program, such as studio origination, theme, and set. Many set changes occurred because of a need to modernize or to accommodate developments in technology. Some changes were made in an effort to attract new viewers or retain the interest of the regular audience. For the most part, producers were reluctant to make major changes in personnel and format that they felt would be disrupting to the program and disorienting to the audience. Executive producer Paul Friedman expressed it best: "It's scary to tamper with an American institution."

With *Today* having survived its first year, albeit precariously, NBC began to rack up substantial profits by selling their audience to enthusiastic advertisers, and that potential audience increased as *Today* added more stations to its lineup. The network shared revenue with their local affiliated stations that participated with *Today* in format, content, and available commercial minutes. But it was the consistency, reliability, and dependability of the talent, whom viewers trusted and liked, that led to a substantial loyal and satisfied audience. The audience that gave their time and loyalty didn't like change, and they expressed their concerns by turning on and off their television sets or by looking elsewhere. Other networks tried to lure the adventurous or disaffected away to competitive programming, but none came even close until ABC's *Good Morning America* in 1976.

For most of its first twenty-five years on the air, *Today* enjoyed the envious position of being virtually free from strong competition. One of the reasons *Today* had been so successful is that it had become a morning habit with millions of Americans. By the end of its first quarter century, 10 million viewers, including 65 percent of Congress, regularly started their mornings with *Today*. Viewers were reluctant to compare *Today* with other network offerings as long as *Today* provided the kind of programming that the audience expected and wanted. Other networks did try, however, to capitalize on the morning audience that *Today* had so clearly established was both available and profitable. Major attempts to counterprogram from CBS included *The Morning Show, Captain Kangaroo,* and *CBS Morning News*. Serious efforts by ABC did not begin until 1975, when *A.M. America* premiered, failed, and reappeared in a revised edition under the title *Good Morning America*. Except for *Captain Kangaroo,* which was aimed at children and thereby provided an alternative to *Today,* the other programs attempted but failed to duplicate the efforts of *The Today Show* in format and content. It took ABC more than twenty-five years to mount a program that would become *Today's* greatest challenger.

The vision of morning news developed by Pat Weaver more than sixty years ago probably endured far beyond his wildest expectation. Weaver's idea of a total news and information program that was both informative and entertaining set the gears in motion for an industry that would eventually provide exactly that, twenty-four hours a day, seven days a week. Channels and networks would someday be created for a worldwide audience whose appetite for news seemed insatiable. In its first twenty-five years, *Today* initiated, tested, and perfected the practices that determined its unprecedented success in broadcast history. It is worth examining those practices to determine how *Today* was able to successfully implement, adapt, and develop Weaver's original bold concept that paved the way for the future of television news.

2

✛

Programming *Today*

Mornings at Seven

ORIGINAL CONCEPT AND PHILOSOPHY OF *TODAY*, 1952–1953

The Today Show officially debuted on January 14, 1952, but the concept of the program was devised much earlier by Pat Weaver. Originally, the program was to be called *Rise and Shine* and even began under that working title. But *The Today Show* actually got its name as a result of a trip to Mexico City, where Weaver spotted the word *hoy* on many of the street corners and on the fronts of film houses. The English version of *hoy* ("to-day") became the now iconic title, *Today*.[1] That name spawned similar descriptive titles for other Weaver programming creations, such as the daytime *Home* and, later, the *Tonight* show. All three titles were alternately referred to as *The Today Show, The Home Show,* and *The Tonight Show*.

Today was an ambitious creation for several reasons. First, the network in 1952 did not feed regular programming until 11:00 a.m. Eastern Standard Time (EST), and *Today* was scheduled to air from 7:00 a.m. to 9:00 a.m. That meant that NBC-owned and -affiliated stations had to begin transmission several hours earlier than normal, requiring additional station hours as well as more personnel. Second, it had not been determined that there was a significant television audience available at that early hour. It was assumed that radio and newspapers already adequately provided whatever news or world contact millions of Americans might desire. Further, *Today* was slated to run a blockbuster two hours, five days a week. Despite those heavy odds, Weaver persevered and succeeded in developing a working production concept for the new program.

According to NBC's Program Analysis Department, the concept of *The Today Show* was both ambitious and well thought out:

> *Today*, a new concept in television programming, is primarily a news program designed for listening as well as viewing. *Today* is a service using every communication tool known to man. Dave Garroway, as "master communicator" of the program, is the central figure of this informative and entertaining show for as "communicator" on *Today*, he will be a reporter, columnist, commentator, roving editor and entertainer.
>
> News will form the core of *Today* but the show will offer other items of a "newsy" nature as well. These will include reviews of the latest Broadway openings, capsuled reviews of the new motion pictures, book reviews, discussion of new magazine articles, record reviews and interviews with authors. Guest stars of the entertainment world will stop by and be interviewed and hit recordings are interspersed throughout the program.
>
> The working format of the show is that of a newsreel theatre in that the features of the program repeat themselves about every 20 minutes or so. Garroway opens the show and repeats in cycle the top news stories in the news called "*Today* in two minutes" or briefing period. James Fleming, NBC newsman and news editor of *Today*, gives the hard news at approximately 20 minute intervals and the latest newsreels are shown in same cycle, [sic] however, if there is a big news story breaking the program will stay right with it. The international pick-ups, calling in NBC newsmen around the world by radio occurs and repeats also in the cycle.
>
> Jack Lescoulie gives the latest sports news, as well as some spot news and oddities in the news. Jim Fidler, of the US Weather Bureau in Washington (by audio only) gives the latest weather while Garroway or Lescoulie mark the map as directed, showing weather in Mid-West & East in the *Today* studio, and as an added feature each of the cities which carries the program is listed alphabetically on a chart and the current temperature in each city is listed. Newspapers from the leading cities in the US are displayed on a rack and Garroway gives the various headlines that this morning will be appearing in local papers throughout the land. The leading weekly news magazines and monthlies on their day of publication are also shown and discussed and perhaps the author will be interviewed on the program. Dramatic critics will sometimes be interviewed on their reactions to the Broadway play that opened the night before and which they covered for their paper. Mobile units make remote pickups from cities where a news story is breaking so that you have on the spot coverage by video or audio or both as the event happens. The political news when it breaks will be covered by a Washington pickup and special events or interviews with political figures will be handled by the NBC Washington staff. Top selling and popular recordings, as well as brand new issues of recordings are played at intervals throughout the program, during this time the cameras in the studio are turned on the window on the 49th Street side of the studio and passersby are picked up as they stop to look in on the show.

The program at the beginning of the series is fed to 30 cities and stations will be added along the network from time to time. The program is fed to the Eastern network from 7 am to 9 am and to the Midwestern network from 8 am to 10 am, consequently each area has a 2 hr program and various features of the program are repeated appropriately for consumption by available audience during the entire 3 hrs running time of program.

Five and ten minute segments of the program are available for sale to various sponsors and there is a local breakaway for those cities wishing to take the break at the 25 min and 55 min after the hour period. On WNBT locally this period is called *"Today in New York"* and features purely local news, weather, and classified ads from the morning papers. This 5 min local spot may be sold on a local basis. For those cities not wishing to take advantage of the breakaway the network program will continue to be fed.[2]

Obviously, the concept was quite complex and involved great coordination and commitment for the program to be as effective in actuality as it was theoretically. As *Today* approached its premiere date, there were many rehearsals designed to help the "master communicator" Dave Garroway and other panel members become better acquainted and interact more easily on the air. It also gave the technical crews a chance to solve the numerous problems stemming from the maze of communication equipment on the set. As it turned out, the original target date of January 7 was postponed to January 14, 1952.

Despite the premiere program being organized in great detail with time scheduled with careful precision, the actual on-air result appeared to be a "comedy of errors." At best, the conglomeration of communications equipment was more complex than the information that they purveyed, and the set design contributed to that effect. RCA Exhibition Hall on 49th Street in New York City was equipped with the most modern electronic communication equipment available. There were three teletype machines providing news from the major wire services, a telephoto machine with the capability of receiving and developing remote pictures in approximately fifteen minutes, four phones connected to overseas news centers, shortwave facilities to eight points around the world, and two TV monitors facing Garroway. There were also eight clocks clearly displaying the hour from various U.S. and international time zones above the world map background. "Garroway, who has always been fascinated by gadgets, stood in awe of his equipment and said so—again and again."[3] Even weather, which had traditionally been an important feature of *Today*, was an integral part of that first broadcast. The original chalkboard weather map was filled in after a phone call to the U.S. Weather Bureau in Washington, D.C., obtained the latest weather information. And the current temperature of each *Today* affiliate station was charted and broadcast.[4]

The result from this rather cluttered set sparked a review by Jack Gould in the Sunday *New York Times*:

> Thus far, *Today* has been excessively pretentious and ostentatious and unreasonably confusing and complex. . . . With all the variety of equipment around them, the Messrs.' Garroway, Fleming, and Lescoulie give the appearance of baffled fathers on Christmas morning who were intrigued with a new set of electric trains but are not quite sure how they work. . . . *Today*, in short, is the slave rather than the master of its own inventiveness and ingenuity.[5]

Most reviewers were even more critical. Many of the newspaper critics were eager to see the show fail and were predisposed to finding negative aspects about the program. They feared that newspapers would become obsolete if *Today* were successful in becoming the news purveyor of the early morning hours. In retrospect, however, it seemed that most critical attacks of the actual broadcast compared the finished product to those extravagant programming promises that were made prior to its premiere. *Variety* exposed the television-versus-press conflict and the negative coverage that resulted from a biased perspective:

> NBC firmly believes that the press in general is out to knife the show as an encroachment on the newspapers' primary function as a communications medium. Within the past couple of weeks, the web press department had been lamenting the fact that it was becoming increasingly difficult to either get into the listings or to make an impressionable dent on pictorial-editorial space, because of the show's major accent on delivering the morning news and feature events to waker-uppers. The New York City TV reviewers were practically unanimously "thumbs down" in their reaction toward the show and with but a few isolated cases, such as the one daily in Cleveland and another in Washington, the TV eds throughout the country went on a panning crusade.[6]

Although the program was off to a shaky start, Weaver pulled it successfully through its birth pains and continued to supervise it through necessary changes. It was his program concept set into practice along with innovative advertising that brought in sufficient revenue that set *Today* on the road to success. Sylvester L. Weaver came to NBC in 1949 from a position as supervisor of programs at the ad agency Young and Rubicam. From the beginning, he brought innovative and radical ideas to television. He is credited with "inventing" the television spectacular—programming that would be "special" in its content and run for an hour or more. That type of costly programming led to a change in the advertising structure for "such programs" since no single advertiser could afford to sponsor such spectacles. Therefore, it was Weaver's idea to divide the program into segments and offer the agencies a chance to "participate" in a particular program, a process similar to magazine or newspaper advertising.[7] That became the basis of the advertising structure that he developed for *The Today Show*. At the time, most programs were fully sponsored by a single advertiser, a practice that was not feasible for *The Today Show*, but participating advertising was developed to help NBC meet the enormous expense of producing the then three-hour live program. Although the production of *The Today Show* was somewhat less expensive than a single prime-time entertainment program, producing *Today* five times per week made it cumulatively very expensive. Its innovative advertising structure and the dedication of the NBC sales staff who devoted their efforts to selling *Today* partly offset that expense. Within two years, the cost of a commercial minute rose steadily from the original $2,000 to $3,861 by September 1953.[8] The other critical component in *Today's* approach to advertising was to have the show's talent available to "pitch" commercials, which gave the advertisers a direct interest in the show and its talent.

During the first few months, Weaver exerted pressure on the sales staff to sell more participating advertising that could be inserted during four five-minute time segments. Weaver suggested that the program was perfect for morning food products, such as coffee, orange juice, and cigarettes, and that the housewife was particularly susceptible to advertising for products that would guide her more easily through her housekeeping and cooking chores. From the beginning, it was that kind of projected advertising revenue that made the show attractive to affiliate stations since it held out great promise of bringing in significant advertising profits. For example, an article in *Variety* explained the early financial arrangements with NBC-owned and -operated station WNBQ in Chicago:

> Now that NBC-TV's *Today*, hosted by Dave Garroway, is off and running, it shapes up as a potential bonanza for the local outlets carrying it. To secure the best possible lineup of stations, the web obviously has patterned the ambitious two-hour morning spread so it can be used by the local plants as a lure for hometown revenue. For instance, WNBQ, the Chi NBC-TV operation can rack up a hefty maximum of $9,500 weekly on *Today* hitchhikers. That's the potential weekly tab on the four daily five-minute news segments and the 12 daily station breaks that are being offered for station sale.[9]

By securing a large number of affiliate stations that would provide local outlets for *The Today Show*, NBC was able to assure national advertisers that the program had the capability of reaching a large audience. But most important, it was necessary for *Today* to actually attract those potential viewers: *Today* had to establish a significant audience on a consistent basis to attract advertisers. It was Weaver's opinion that the *Today* audience would consist of a large turnover of viewers who would watch the show for approximately fifteen minutes. The program was designed to provide frequent repetition of newsworthy features. Ideally, he felt the show would not be too visually stimulating so that the morning audience could lend a casual ear or eye and still follow the program. On the other hand, it needed to be both visual and innovative enough to draw viewers away from their morning radio or newspaper habits. The initial concept of *Today* was for it to resemble a radio show with pictures. In a famous Weaver memorandum, he states,

> We cannot and should not try to build a show that will make people sit down in front of their sets and divert their attention to the screen. We want Americans to shave, to eat, to dress, to get to work on time. But we also want America to be well informed, to be amused, to be lightened in spirit and in heart, and to be reinforced in inner resolution through knowledge.[10]

Despite Weaver's lofty ambitions for the American public, ratings continued to be low during the early months, and it was unclear whether the show would be given a reasonable chance to catch on or be canceled. Despite thousands of unsolicited letters pouring into NBC each week lauding the program, many advertisers remained unconvinced of its attractiveness. Those early ratings clearly indicated that the *Today* audience was not yet large enough to attract strong advertising interest.

Negative reviews of early *Today* attempts ("Do yourself a favor NBC, roll over and go back to sleep"[11]) did not persuade Pat Weaver to scrap the program. Instead, he called an executive production meeting to analyze the failures of the show and to capitalize on its more promising aspects. Particularly criticized were the lame phone interviews such as that conducted with NBC reporter Ed Hasker in Frankfurt, Germany. When asked by Garroway about the news in that part of the world, he replied, "The big news is the weather . . . we had our first big storm of the year. We're really chilly." "You're not alone," said Garroway. "Good-bye, Ed." In response to that and similar kinds of activity, Weaver asked his staff to reevaluate the program and to strive for the original program idea in a less complex fashion. The executive producer of the program, Richard Pinkham, recalled, "We all knew what we were supposed to do. We knew we were pioneering and didn't expect instantaneous success."[12]

1952–1957: ESTABLISHING THE FORMAT

As modestly as *Today* began, it would eventually live up to the Pat Weaver memo that stated, "*Today* was about to inaugurate a new era in television programming."[13] The show began to improve under the talented direction of Weaver, who felt they had not been producing their best effort.

He suggested that the executives reread his original memo, which said, in part, "Mark the things that are not being done, and which you are not trying to do. Unless reported back to me as abandoned, I am expecting that these things be done."[14] Over the next five years, they worked diligently to make sure they got done.

In January 1952, *Today* was fed from WNBT-NY over the network from 7:00 to 9:00 a.m., with a feed to the Midwest network from 8:00 to 10:00 a.m. (There were no feeds to the West Coast until September 27, 1954.)[15] That meant that *Today* was actually on the air for three hours. News, interviews, and features were repeated in each hour to account for the variations in viewing and time zone differences. By the time *Today* reached its first anniversary, the *Today* talent had chalked up 718 hours of airtime, used approximately 160,000 feet of film, and entertained a large variety of animals from beagles to Francis the Talking Mule. *Today*'s news staff had put in 5,720 hours to provide the show with twenty-four-hour news coverage.[16] Gradual changes resulted in substantial improvement in the *Today* format. The set became less cluttered, Garroway became accustomed to the electronic gadgetry, the panel interacted more evenly, and the show began to approximate its original concept of news, information, and entertainment.

The original *Today* panel consisted of David Garroway as host, Jim Fleming as news editor, and Jack Lescoulie handling sports and feature segments; Estelle Parsons, who began as a production assistant, soon became a permanent "*Today* girl."[17] But it took the addition of a new panel member to provide the magic necessary to attract viewers. J. Fred Muggs, an adorable baby chimpanzee dressed as a little boy, stole the hearts of millions of viewers. Muggs joined the show two weeks after *Today*'s first anniversary and began to attract a devoted audience. Children were drawn to the program, and subsequently the parents were enticed to watch, too. Fortunately, Muggs also attracted a great deal of publicity, giving the show a hefty promotional boost. The number of stations taking the *Today* feed had grown from the original thirty-one to forty, and the chimp promised more growth. *Today* also boasted "a substantial number of advertisers but not quite enough to make the show profitable. The show had already lost $1.7 million in the first year."[18]

Although Muggs was undeniably an asset in the eyes of viewers, he was less appreciated by those who had to work with him. He seemed angelic enough with the tally lights on but was sometimes vicious behind the scenes. One *Today* executive remembered the problem with Muggs:

> The chimp was the darling of the audience, but not being housebroken, did not stand quite so high with the studio crew. Or with Garroway either. Muggs had a penchant for taking a bite out of Dave whenever possible, and

David Garroway and J. Fred Muggs.

there were occasions when Garroway had to shield his bloodied face from his viewers with one hand while cuddling—or restraining—the unlovable Muggs with the other.[19]

Garroway substantiated those comments by adding, "There were twenty-two entries in the NBC dispensary for anti-tetanus shots for chimp bites with my name on it." Muggs was also the cause of discontentment for the more seriously news minded: "Some on the show had questioned from the beginning the wisdom of having a half-tamed anthropoid on the set. It was during the J. Fred Muggs publicity build-up that *Today* show newscaster Jim Fleming, who had joined the show to work in electronic news, quit in disgust, concluding that *Today* had definitely gone ape."[20] When Jim Fleming left the show in March 1953, Merrill Mueller replaced him for only a few months, until he was replaced with newscaster Frank Blair, who served in that capacity for nearly twenty-two years (from August 1953 to March 1975).[21]

With increased audience and subsequent revenue, *Today* producers turned their focus to program content, experimenting with a variety of feature segments over the next few years to attract and retain a growing number of viewers. On July 7, 1953, according to NBC files, *Today* produced its first remote telecast from Jones Beach in Long Island, New York, and added a new program feature called *The New York Scene*:

> *The New York Scene*, Aug. 12, 1953: a new spot added to program format— (not included on any specific day or time on show)—the NBC $65,000 Cadillac Mobile Unit used for the first time at Pres. Eisenhower inaugural ceremonies,—is seen as it strolls thru the streets of New York giving viewers a view of some particular spot of interest of the New York Scene—such as Times Square–Washington Bridge–Park Avenue.[22]

By 1954, *Today* began to keep records of regular programming changes, some of which seem more like stunts contrived solely to attract viewers. One such change was *Finders Keepers*, which ran for about six weeks in the fall:

> *"Finders Keepers"* starts today—a spot occurring approximately once a week but on no definite day—during which time a glove or container containing money will be dropped on the sidewalk in any city throughout the country. NBC-TV cameras will train on the spot to see whether any passers-by pick up the glove in curiosity—if they do, they are entitled to keep all the money. First week $100 bill placed in glove—and $100 is added each week.[23]

More notable programming changes came after the expansion of *Today* to the West Coast starting on September 27, 1954:

> *Today* goes Coast-to-Coast—first time today—and hereafter. The West Coast via stations KNBH-TV, Los Angeles; KRON-TV, San Francisco; and KFSD-TV, San Diego receive the 8:00–9:00 a.m. portion of *Today* via quick kine at 8:00–9:00 a.m. PCT. This West Coast version of *Today* is under the aegis of Joe Thompson who formerly worked on *Today* in NY—Roy Neal, head of NBC-TV Hollywood News Operations assists him. The kine of *Today* shown on the West Coast will have occasional local cut-ins for late-breaking West Coast news—and up-dating of national and world stories.

In conjunction with the acquisition of those West Coast stations, *Today*'s lead-in *was* a special regional program designed especially for West Coast viewers:

> Preceding *Today* on the West Coast at 8:00–9:00 am PCT, KNBH-TV, Hollywood, will produce a regional show entitled "Seven to Eight"—heard 7:00–9:00 am PCT. "Seven to Eight" is a local version of *Today* featuring news, weather, time, etc.—and is presided over by Johnny Grant. "Seven to Eight" is carried by same three stations taking the quick kine of *Today* and is therefore a Network Program.[24]

By 1955, the West Coast *Today* feed was expanded to its full two hours. Stations KNBH-TV, KRON-TV, and KFSD-TV took the 7:00–9:00 a.m. EST *Today* program via quick kine at 7:00–9:00 a.m. Pacific Standard Time (PST). The network became aware of the increasing importance of the West Coast audience and with the initiation of Daylight Savings Time revamped the West Coast programming. Those changes made *Today* the first daily news TV show to be transmitted directly from New York to Los Angeles:

> *6:00–7:00am PPT*—KRCA-TV only, in Los Angeles, carried the 9:00–10:00am NYT *Today* origination, live with local inserts and hard regional news given from KRCA-TV.
> *7:00–8:00am PPT*—Entire Pacific Network (stations in Fresno, Los Angeles, Sacramento and San Francisco) carry a quick kinescope of the 7:00–8:00am NYT *Today* origination . . . with local regional news inserts.
> *11:00–12:00 Noon PPT*—*Today in the West*—Pacific Net station (Fresno, Los Angeles, Sacramento, San Diego, San Francisco) combine quick kinescope features of 8:00–9:00am NYT *Today* origination with live regional features. Seattle & Portland take this 10:00–11:00am PST.[25]

Today's producers continued to experiment with several new programming ideas that somehow found on-air time slots. Some ideas lasted for only a few weeks, although a seed of an idea sometimes blossomed later under more favorable conditions:

> *Vacation Travel Series*—April 5–July 11, 1955 and August 3, 1955—filmed visits to various spots suitable for vacation—different areas for different interests—with tape narration by well-known personalities who are familiar with the area.
> *Most Wanted Criminals*—October 24–November 4, 1955—program presented pictures and pertinent details about ten criminals most wanted by the FBI.
> *Author Interviews*—July 12, 1955—filmed interviews with well-known authors presented approximately once a month, occasionally more. . . . Interviews sometimes live.[26]

Since RCA (parent company of NBC) developed color broadcasting, it naturally followed that *Today* would be an ideal forum to experiment with and introduce special programming in color over the NBC network. Colorcasts became common enough that records were not kept of such segments after mid-1957. Some early examples included remote previews from Grant Stadium in Atlanta of the Georgia Tech–Miami game; the Yankees and Brooklyn Dodgers from Yankee Stadium; the University of Michigan–Iowa football game; the F-101 long-range fighter from Wright-Patterson Air Force Base in Dayton, Ohio; and the new all-color studios in 1956 from WNBQ Chicago and WTMJ in Milwaukee, Wisconsin.[27]

Today began to present social-issue segments as early as 1956 when it produced a monthly series on housing and devoted a week to career opportunities:

> *Monthly Series on Housing and Building*—Joe Michaels prepares report approx. once a month to show how America is handling housing and building problems—slum areas, etc. (usually film)—May 8, 1956, June 12, 1956, July 10, 1956, July 24, 1956. (Housing features presented subsequently, but not billed as part of his feature.)
>
> *JOBS 1956*—Daily slot this week on job and career availabilities in various field for college and high school graduates. May 28–June 1, 1956.[28]

From the beginning, sports programming had received considerable attention on *Today*, but in 1956, it became more formalized when producers initiated a daily sports series. *"Today* in Sports" consisted of a daily feature complete with filmed sports stories and interviews with prominent sports personalities. That series eventually evolved into a less formal two or three spots per week featuring various seasonal sports.

On the lighter side, *Today* debuted a regular series on fashion in the summer of 1956, although fashion segments had been used intermittently over the earlier years. It turned out to be a very popular segment that eventually led, in 1957, to the "First Annual Fashion Designers Awards" feature. By 1958, fashion was considered to be a regular part of the format.

After 1956, no further records were kept of regular segments, rejecting the staid weekly or daily feature for a more flexible approach to programming. This enabled the producers to select material by relevance rather than attempting to fit regular feature material into a fixed format.[29]

Today was also a very active political forum, covering such important topics as the controversial Supreme Court decision on school integration and the Army–McCarthy hearings. In 1956, *Today* brought the Chicago Democratic National Convention and the San Francisco Republican National Convention to its audience by remote broadcast. Because of the eastern and western time differences, broadcasting began at 4:00 a.m. PST for the Republican Convention so that it could be seen at 7:00 a.m. on the East Coast.

Today also reported such memorable events as the collision of SS *Andrea Doria* and *Stockholm*; the report included exclusive footage of the collision of the two ships. Even earlier, just three weeks after *Today*'s debut, the staff had worked through the night to rewrite the next day's program when England's King George VI died. They also fed an audio broadcast of Queen Elizabeth II's coronation, while still pictures via facsimile machine provided the visual background.[30]

By the time *Today* had reached its fifth anniversary in 1957, it had accumulated an impressive list of guests. Among those distinguishing the early morning hours with their presence were Eleanor Roosevelt, Senator John F. Kennedy, Supreme Court Justice Thurgood Marshall, former president Harry Truman, and Senate Democratic leader Lyndon B. Johnson.[31] *Today* celebrated its fifth anniversary with an entire week of programming that at one point featured a tiered cake that was particularly appealing to J. Fred Muggs. Among the program elements, *Today* reporters narrated top film stories that they had covered in 1956, including Maurice Robinson and his coverage of the *Stockholm–Andrea Doria* collision, Joe Michaels on the Middle East crisis (Israeli–Egyptian fighting), Dick McCutcheon and the Hungarian revolt, Cliff Evans and the Victor Riesel story, and Mary Kelly and the Grace Kelly–Prince Rainier wedding.[32] They also aired a film showing the best of J. Fred Muggs, and Garroway performed a poetic rendition in tribute to the 263 sponsors who had advertised on *Today*. There was also a tribute to the *Today* girls, noting among those females who had borne the title during that time period J. Fred Muggs's sister, Phoebe B. Beebe, who had served intermittently from December 1954 to the end of 1956. The actual second *Today* girl, however, was 1954's Miss America, Lee Ann Meriwether, who in 1956 was replaced by Helen O'Connell.[33]

1957–1962: GROWTH AND CHANGE

The first major format change occurred in 1958, when financial losses on *The Today Show* were so heavy (approximately $2,500,000)[34] that NBC entertained proposals for revising the show. One of the four proposed alternatives was to scrap *Today* altogether.[35] According to NBC records, three other plans were considered at the time with a discussion of the possible outcomes, but ultimately they considered a plan that would strengthen the show and retain its basic format. On August 13, 1958, at a meeting of the NBC affiliate Board of Delegates, NBC distributed a booklet detailing the new *Today* format. A part of the booklet emphasized the new *Today* programming format, which brought a change in studio origination, a time change for the local news cutaway, the addition of Betsy Palmer as a regular panel member, and attractive new programming:

New Facilities
Recently *Today* was moved to the most modern studios . . . where space and the best technical equipment afford opportunities to add features and production values not possible in the RCA Exhibition Hall. *Today* is also being produced by two alternating production units . . . allowing for long-range programming plans and facilitating the promotional exploitations of coming attractions and features.

New Format
The new *Today* will allow for clean time cutaways for affiliate use. Under this plan we suggest that the five-minute local cutaways in station half-hours be moved to a position immediately following the NBC national news. . . . This will create, for stations, a cohesive news package . . . the prestige, and power of NBC's world-wide coverage plus the impact of local news happenings.

New Faces
Betsy Palmer will be a typical new *Today* personality. *Today* will also become a showcase for talent . . . bright new people who will bring exciting freshness to the morning screen . . . as has been done so successfully on the evening *Jack Parr Show*.

New Features
Dave Garroway's homey philosophical approach will be utilized in a regular *Today* feature . . . tentatively titled, *"Garroway's Tomorrow"* . . . in which he will analyze the future in politics, science, education, health, government, etc.

Today will be a new front porch on the nation where important personalities traveling through New York will sit and chat, giving us intimate glances of their worlds.

Outstanding female guests will appear regularly to attract and influence *Today*'s large woman audience.

The entire concept of *Today* will, of course, continue to include the services that have made the programming outstanding . . . exclusive broadcasts of such features as the welcoming of the *Nautilus*, the first live television appearance of Roy Campanella from his hospital bed, and the activity in the control tower at Idlewild International Airport. *Today* will continue to be dedicated to the best in national news, weather and sports . . . serving the nation with the brightest mornings in television.[36]

That plan, adopted by NBC after the affiliate representatives approved it, became the standard format for *Today* except for minor changes in the local news cutaway time and commercial break time. As the NBC executives predicted, it did eventually solve the financial problem and contributed to *Today*'s most successful years with multi-million-dollar profits.

There were several important programming changes made during the years of 1958 and 1959. On October 6, 1958, *The Today Show* moved out of the RCA Exhibition Hall and into NBC studio 3 B in Radio City. Although the move was made so that a live audience could be brought into the studio, after the fall of 1959, NBC no longer admitted a live audience to the show. *Today* was also reduced to a two-hour format when the third hour of production was dropped because the perfection of videotape made it possible to record the 7:00–8:00 a.m. hour of the program and tape delay the feed to the Midwest network. The new two-hour format introduced several programming changes. According to an NBC Program Analysis format memo, there was an attempt to rigidly prescribe format and content that ultimately proved to be too restrictive:

> [There was] a tendency for each of the 2 hours to be programmed separately, with new materials aired in the 2nd hour, thus there has been a departure from the total newsreel concept . . . the news segments are still presented as before, as well as regular scheduling of weather & sports so these latter spots do retain newsreel aspect. Five-minute co-op spots continue to be presented regularly in each hour (as indicated on front schedule card). Attempt was made to have the first 30 min of each hour devoted to hard-hitting fast-moving news and features; with the 2nd 30 min saved for in-depth reporting and analysis of news, human interest stories, between-the-headlines reports, etc.; however, after about a month of this rigidity pgm abandoned attempt and returned to more flexibility in setting up the hour.[37]

Today also broadened the scope of the program content and added Charles Van Doren, fresh from his remarkable success on quiz show *Twenty-One*, as a regular new cast member. His responsibilities included conducting daily cultural segments that dealt with such topics as literature, art, travel, book reviews, poetry, and music. In addition, *Today* further expanded its cultural programming by presenting a regular art feature that presented various types of artwork along with biographical background on the artist. A rather unsuccessful new feature was also added. The segment, a weekly talent showcase designed to encourage young professional entertainers, first aired late in 1958 and was dropped by the summer of 1959. *Today* also supplemented its news coverage by adding an editorial cartoon drawn by Norman Moore. The cartoons were added to the regular news segments and expressed a definite point of view on national and international affairs.

From 1958 to 1961, *Today* increased the number of remote location telecasts, which included the first remote abroad, when the show spent the week of April 1959 in Paris. "Availability of mobile video-tape equipment and jet transport allowed *Today* to be recorded in Paris, flown to New York and played the following morning."[38] The success of the Paris trip, particularly such stimulating sights as Brigitte Bardot, the Arc de Triomphe, and pressed duck prepared by a French chef, spawned other weeklong overseas broadcasts, such as the 1960 remote from Rome.

CHALLENGES COME IN THREES

Three devastating programming changes occurred between 1959 and 1961. The first took place when the basic premise of *Today* as a dynamic *live* program was abandoned. Until September 21, 1959, the program had been entirely live except for an occasional videotaped feature insert. Starting on that date, the program began to be completely videotaped except for the live news portions. Under the new format, *Today* taped in the afternoons from approximately 4:00 to 6:00 p.m. and then aired the following morning. The news segments, delivered by Frank Blair, were inserted into the regular news slots that occurred on the hour and half hour. Thus, Blair no longer participated with the rest of the *Today* panel, nor did he attend the afternoon tapings. When the show was live, his other responsibilities had included occasional feature and interview segments. The drastic decision to change from the live format to videotaping the previous afternoon was explained in an NBC Program Analysis memo:

> The use of tape is to provide even greater flexibility, to expand program's area of news coverage and special features . . . to include greater numbers of longer-range projects and more telecasts from other American cities and places outside the US . . . also intervs with more prominent figures in fields of sports, entertainment, art, literature, politics, health, education, etc. . . . because of the better hour at which intervs conducted (late afternoon). Program can be completely flexible—can shelve parts of or all of tape if necessary to cover some major story which breaks in the morning.[39]

But the real reason for taping the show the previous afternoon was much more compelling than a promise of program flexibility. Producer Robert Bendick felt forced into taking drastic action to relieve the severe mental and physical strain of a daily program on host David Garroway. So for nearly two years, *Today* abandoned its original concept of a live informational program, a change that was unpopular with the audience, critics, and even program executives. That new practice lasted until November 28, 1960, when, at first, the Monday programs went back to the live format, while the Tuesday through Friday programs were still videotaped. Then, on June 12, 1961, the Thursday program returned to the live format, and on July 17, 1961, the entire program reverted to its former live broadcast status.

The second major programming misjudgment came in 1959 and involved *Today* in the famous television quiz scandals when congressional investigations into the quiz shows revealed that many of them were rigged and that contestants were often provided the answers to build audience loyalty. Enormously popular and highly successful *Twenty-One* quiz show contestant Charles Van Doren had been hired by *The Today Show* to host regular features on cultural and intellectual topics. Unfortunately, Garroway taped an emotionally emphatic defense of Van Doren that aired the next morning, *after* Van Doren had publicly confessed his own guilt. Not only did that incident point out the inadvisability of taping the show the previous afternoon, but it also put *Today* in the position of jeopardizing its integrity. Van Doren was promptly fired, and the show weathered the event in due time.

The third major detrimental program change came when the show's host of nine years, David Garroway, suddenly resigned on July 19, 1961, after a personal family tragedy. Despite his history of mental health issues, unreasonable demands, and personality conflicts with *Today* producers and writers, his leaving the show was a major shock to the audience.[40] Just about a year earlier, Garroway had demanded and was successful in having the show's title changed to *The Dave Garroway Today Show*.[41] That title was used from September 15, 1960, until the day he resigned. Afterward, it was changed back to *Today*, and never again has the show's title included the host's name.

After Garroway resigned in 1961, NBC removed *Today* from the control of NBC Programming and made it the responsibility of NBC News. In an effort to give *Today* a stronger news orientation, NBC News executives decided that the next *Today* host would not be an entertainer. Instead, they decided that they would audition Edwin Newman, John Chancellor, and Ray Scherer for the position, all three prominent NBC newsmen. John Chancellor was offered the position and served a little more than one year as *Today* host, from June 17, 1961, to September 7, 1962. As for his contributions to the show, one critic said, "Under his aegis, *The Today Show* remained an easy-going conglomeration of news, music, volleyball exhibitions, and light and dark interviews. By doing the show live, instead of taping all feature material the previous afternoon, Chancellor was able to integrate the news broadcasts into the rest of the program."[42]

1962–1967: TAKING NEWS SERIOUSLY

By its tenth anniversary in 1962, *Today* had earned its place as a morning fixture. Although the show had staggered through a number of significant issues and changes between 1958 and 1961, it still retained its basic programming format of news, interviews, and feature segments. *Today* documented its milestone by welcoming back Dave Garroway and former panelist Jack Lescoulie to celebrate its unprecedented accomplishments with current host John Chancellor. They particularly noted the wide range of interviews with an impressive list of guests. *Today* talked with not only politicians but also other people of outstanding achievement. Some of the people who had appeared on *Today* were Dr. Jacques Yves Cousteau, who fathoms the ocean depths; Sir Edmund Hillary, conqueror of Mount Everest, the world's highest peak; two physicians, Dr. William C. Menninger and Dr. Charles H. Mayo, who with their brothers established renowned medical clinics; Dr. Enrico Fermi, discoverer of uranium fission; Mikhail A. Menshikov, former Soviet ambassador to the United States; Charles E. Wilson, former president of General Motors; and Igor Sikorsky, developer of the helicopter.[43] The first of thousands of book/author-related interviews took place with Fleur Cowles, author of *Bloody Precedent*, on January 14, 1952. By the tenth anniversary of *Today*, hundreds of distinguished American and British authors had been interviewed, including Nelson Algren, Catherine Drinker Bowen, Art Buchwald, Pearl S. Buck, Erskine Caldwell, Bruce Catton, John Cheever, Bernard DeVoto, John Dos Passos, James T. Farrell, Aldous Huxley, William Inge, George F. Kennan, John F. Kennedy, Joseph Wood Krutch, Archibald MacLeish, James A. Michener, Ogden Nash, S. J. Perelman, Carl Sandburg, Arthur M. Schlesinger Jr., Irwin Shaw, C. P. Snow, Robert Penn Warren, and Evelyn Waugh.[44]

A few months after that tenth anniversary, NBC News began looking for its third permanent host. By summer, Hugh Downs had accepted the position, and on September 7, 1962, he actively assumed the role of *Today*'s newest host. Outgoing host John Chancellor was moved up to anchor the *NBC Evening News*. *Today* also hired a new producer, Al Morgan, who was to carry the program through its most celebrated years. Jack Lescoulie, who had been off the show for nearly a year, was rehired as a regular panel member. Frank Blair returned to newscasting, and Pat Fontaine assumed the responsibilities of the *Today* girl. *Today* also added new reporters to the panel who would appear occasionally to do special feature pieces:

Martin Agronsky: NBC News Washington, D.C. interviews political figures, domestic and foreign . . . frequently but not daily.

Howard Whitman: Appears once a week, generally on Thursday on medical report "News of Your Life" as on the air reporter.

Cleveland Amory: Social historian, appears on irregular basis to report on social function or society.

Aline Saarinen: Art critic, appears on irregular basis, comments on the world of art, criticizes and evaluates art in the world around us.

Richard Watts: Theatre critic of the *New York Post*, appears on irregular basis reporting on the theatre, Broadway openings, etc. with critiques of same.

John Hills: Physical fitness segment, does exercises in a relaxed manner, appears twice weekly on Tues. and Weds.

Paul Cunningham: Roving reporter appears occasionally in filmed segments or to comment on stories being featured, which he has covered.

Barbara Walters: Writer on staff, appears occasionally on features such as fashions and "Bunny School" which she has covered for *Today*.[45]

It was also in 1962 that *Today* moved the studio origination to the Florida Showcase Studio in Rockefeller Center. *Today* modernized its set, revised the opening sequence of the program, and standardized the news and weather routine. At the top of the 7:00 and 8:00 a.m. hours for one minute, the show opens with a running crawl of *Today* with current date, a voice-over by Lescoulie or Downs, and a camera that pans the window on 49th Street as people gather to watch the show. It switches to inside the studio, where Downs, Lescoulie, and Fontaine are seated behind a desk and in front of a world map and clock. The standard opening was followed by Frank Blair reporting hard news and then weather by Fontaine.

Today became more politically oriented in 1962 and expanded its base of operations to include occasional interviews from Washington, D.C. The aim of the *Today* program was described in an NBC Memo that revealed a greater emphasis on political issues:

The overall aim of the program is to give the American public the opportunity of keeping abreast with the activities of their government in both domestic and foreign affairs by bringing government officials, statesmen, diplomats and personalities who have a major responsibility in a current issue, in to discuss or be interviewed either in New York or as in most cases . . . with Martin Agronsky in Washington, D.C.[46]

Probably the most significant political contribution *Today* made in 1962 was to provide an open discussion of the Cuban missile crisis. Among the people who took advantage of the opportunity to air their views were Senator Kenneth B. Keating and U.S. Representative to the United Nations Adlai E. Stevenson.[47] *Today*, however, was not content merely to respond to significant political issues of the day; the program itself precipitated some issues. Hugh Downs, for example, took a special interest in the Kinzua Dam Project, which violated the Seneca Indian Treaty, which had been signed in the 1700s:

A complete investigation and discussion originally instigated in the fall of 1962 ended with Hugh's going to Washington to meet with the Corps of

Army Engineers, on Feb. 1, 1963. The Dam is going to be built, the Seneca Indian Treaty was broken but declared legal by the Supreme Court, and Hugh
concluded that only public apathy was to blame for a violation of this great
principle; the Dam would provide the most good for the majority—but for
that we broke a sacred trust in breaking the Seneca Indian Treaty which was
signed in good faith during the life of President Washington.[48]

Since the major format revision in 1958, it had been *Today*'s practice to
tape its first hour, which aired at 7:00 a.m. New York time, and replay it to
most Midwest time zones at 9:00 a.m. New York time. The 8:00–9:00 a.m.
hour, New York time, was seen live. Therefore, in Chicago, for example,
the *Today* hours would be transposed. The 8:00–9:00 a.m. portion of *Today*
would be viewed between 7:00 and 8:00 Central Standard Time, and the
normal 7:00–8:00 a.m. portion would be viewed between 8:00 and 9:00
Central Standard Time. This reversing of the hours caused much confusion with the viewing audience. Often, a panel member would refer to a
feature in the "other" hour, which would already have been viewed or
was yet to be seen, depending on the order of the program the audience
was receiving. In 1962, a final attempt was made to correct this situation
when NBC News's special projects director, Carl Lindemann Jr., asked
"whether any good reason exists why *The Today Show*'s first hour can't be
the first hour everywhere to be followed by the second hour in all time
zones. I can give you an awful lot of emotional reasons why the present
pattern is confusing and bad programming."[49] Lindemann suggested that
an investigation begin to determine how best to accomplish the transmission of the correct order of the program. In a later memo, he suggested
that the first hour be fed on a turnaround basis to the Midwest, immediately following the New York broadcast of that hour. He also stated,
"There are so many examples of strange situations created by the inverted
schedule that I won't list them. I find Mr. Read's example of daylight in
the first hour, followed by semi-darkness in the second, one of the more
intriguing."[50] However, the argument was not to be won on the emotional
element. It was simply a matter of finances. After careful analysis of several plans, even the most practical was too costly. In 1963, when the cost
of AT&T charges and Chicago Tape charges were factored in, the total tab
was nearly $200,000 for one year.[51] Apparently, the inverting of the hours
was not considered a major problem in programming after 1963 because
Today continued to broadcast the reversed hours to the Midwest.

From 1959 to 1964, *Today* had a large turnover in female panel members. Their duties were to handle topics of interest to women and provide
the feminine point of view. Among those who served during that time
were Betsy Palmer, Florence Henderson, Robbin Bain, Beryl Pfizer, Anita
Colby, Louise King, Pat Fontaine, Maureen O'Sullivan, and, finally, Bar-

bara Walters.[52] Walters received her first major on-air assignment in 1962 when she followed Jacqueline Kennedy on a goodwill trip to India. Prior to that assignment, she had been a writer at *Today* and delivered occasional on-air features, such as fashion news.[53]

Today added new features during 1963 such as "Exercises," aired on Tuesdays and Wednesdays, which emphasized physical fitness with reporter John Hills. On Thursdays, "News of Your Life" was added as a weekly medical report with Howard Whitman. "*Today* Says" became part of the Friday program, where the cast would give their views on books, movies, plays, or issues. The sports segment "Fearless Football Forecast and Follow Up" featured Jack Lescoulie, who would predict the outcome of college football games on Friday and compare his predictions with the results the following Monday. *Today* also devoted a week to a series on mental retardation and another to baseball spring training. Sports continued to be an important part of *Today* programming. The morning after New York Yankees pitcher Don Larsen pitched the only perfect game in World Series history, he appeared on *Today*. There were also musical tributes to composers such as Jerome Kern, Arthur Schwartz, Victor Herbert, Noel Coward, and Vernon Duke. Two special programs were devoted to the work of silent-screen filmmakers Buster Keaton and Hal Roach, and clips of their films were shown, some of which had never before been screened on television.

In the winter of 1963, *Today* began a series on the presidential cabinet. One cabinet member appeared each week: From January 21 to March 25, Dean Rusk from the State Department, Orville Freeman (Agriculture), Douglas Dillon (Treasury), Stewart Udall (Interior), Anthony J. Celebrezze (Health, Education, and Welfare), W. Willard Wirtz (Labor), Luther Hodges (Commerce), J. Edward Day (postmaster general), and Robert Kennedy (attorney general) were interviewed.

Undeniably, the most significant moments of 1963 were those dedicated to the events surrounding the assassination of President John F. Kennedy. On Saturday morning from 7:00 to 10:00 a.m., November 23, 1963, *Today* aired a special edition on his death and later a remote telecast from Washington, D.C., on the Kennedy funeral. Barbara Walters distinguished herself during this time as a tireless and sympathetic newscaster and mourner.[54]

In 1964, *Today* again covered the Democratic and Republican national conventions. It spent a week in San Francisco covering the Republicans and a week in Atlantic City, New Jersey, with the Democrats. Travel that was unrelated to political activity included many American cities. There were remote telecasts from Chicago; the Shakespeare Festival in Connecticut; a day with the Amish in Lancaster, Pennsylvania; and a week in Arizona.

Today recorded another "first" on March 25, 1964, from 7:32 to 7:40 a.m., when live television from Japan to the United States was transmitted via *Relay II* satellite. Less sensational but still noteworthy was the variety of special programs during 1964 that included fourteen and a half hours of program content on the New York World's Fair, aired between April and October. Other programs included specials on poverty, the primary elections, the aging American, and, in August, an entire program devoted to the Vietnam War.[55]

In 1965, *Today* executives considered another major change in format. Program executives were asked to investigate the feasibility of expanding *Today* to Saturday and Sunday mornings. There were many problems and issues that needed to be considered to make it possible, including the following:

- *Clearance Expectancy:* Children's programs and public-service programming might make clearance difficult.
- *Audience:* There was a presumption that children controlled the television set on weekend mornings, so it would be difficult to attract the desired audience.
- *Host:* The program would have a different host. The extra commercials would overburden one host. Also, they would have another experienced host available to substitute for the other host as required. The tentative recommendation for the weekend host was Mike Douglas.

After further consideration by NBC, the idea was dropped, largely because of the limited potential for significant audience size.[56]

Today incorporated two major technical advancements into its programming format during 1965. The first, on May 3, 1965, featured a historic remote from Europe via satellite relay: "A new television era began as *Today* became the first regularly scheduled program ever transmitted in its entirety by space satellite. Relayed via the Early Bird satellite, this amazingly complex program featured segments from England, Holland, and Italy, controlled from a single source in Belgium."[57] The Dutch cooperated by starting their broadcast day six hours earlier than their normal broadcast operation, but the French were less obliging in the historic moment: "Minor problems were caused by the French Director assigned to the Paris mobile unit. Before the program began, he was requested to rehearse his segment by Coordinating Director Marvin Einhorn from the control room atop the Palace of Justice in Brussels. The Frenchman replied haughtily, 'Rehearse some other country, the French do not need rehearsal.'"[58] The second technological advancement came on September 13, 1965, when *Today* moved from the Florida Showcase Studio in Rockefeller

Center to NBC studio 6B in New York City to regularly transmit the program in color.

Special programs in 1965 included those devoted to the space program and the launching of the *Gemini* spacecraft series. Other features were "A Tribute to Adlai Stevenson," "A Douglas Fairbanks Sr. Film Festival," "Cole Porter: A Remembrance," "The World around the Corner—2,000 A.D.," "Alcoholism," and "Vietnam Protest."[59] But two special events caused NBC to make special provisions for its regular programming. From September 17 to October 8, 1965, NBC allowed its local New York station, WNBC-TV, to drop out of *Today* from 7:10 to 7:30 a.m. to expand their local news coverage so that they could keep their viewers informed during the New York newspaper strike. Then on November 10, after a massive power failure caused a major blackout in the northeastern United States, Jack Lescoulie hosted *Today* from Washington, D.C., where the entire show was devoted to the power failure. Also in 1965, there were two minor personnel developments. Hugh Downs was off the show for extended periods of time when he took one leave of absence to sail the Pacific and another because of a back-related health problem. And Judith Crist was hired as a regular contributor as the new *Today* critic, reviewing movie and theater openings.

The programming in 1966 reflected increasing public concern over social issues. As the U.S. involvement in Vietnam intensified, *Today* added "Vietnam Report" as a regular daily feature immediately following the news, while other segments focused on contemporary issues of the day, including larger amounts of time given over to civil rights issues than had previously been allotted. Special segments included "Testing: A Race for Survival," "The Population Explosion," "Air Safety and Control," "Medicare," "The Gifted Child," "Satellite Communications," "Black Power," "Prisoner Trials in North Vietnam," "Alliance for Progress,"" Public Welfare," "The John Birch Society," "Tyranny of the Teenager," "The Emotionally Disturbed Child," and "Inflation: Economic Effects of the Vietnam War."[60] In addition, two days were spent in the Virgin Islands, five days were devoted to a series on religion, and five days were set aside to cover candidates running for office in the elections of 1966. The year 1966 was summed up in capsule form by *Today* editor John Dunn who placed the following memorandum on the desk of Al Morgan, producer of *Today*:

11 full-scale remotes—originations of the show from other than the studio not including hundreds of remotes in the news segs.
36 specials—one-hour or two-hour shows devoted to one subject; a record for *Today*.
11 series stretching over a period of several days, weeks, or longer.
110 entertainment features, ranging from rock 'n' roll to opera.

91 film features.

1,049 interviews, including 50 with U.S. senators; 19 with Cabinet members; 30 with members of the House; 74 with Government officials; 18 with reps from foreign nations; six with state governors.

The remotes included five two-hour shows from England, a two-hour job from Mystic (New England seaport), a pair of two-hour shows from the Virgin Islands, a show from Williamsburg, Va., and another from Washington, D.C., which was live.

Specials included studies of the Birch Society, black power, book publishing, burlesque, Selective Service, Vietnam, Buster Keaton, Medicare, an hour on President Johnson's operation, and many others.[61]

1967–1972: SOCIAL AND POLITICAL RESPONSIBILITY

By the time *Today* celebrated its fifteenth year on NBC television on Friday, January 13, 1967, it had racked up an impressive coverage of news, human interest, contemporary issues, and cultural events, as indicated by a sampling of programming during that year:[62]

"A Breath of Death"—A two-hour special on air pollution
"Women: The Discriminated Against Majority"
"The Pill"—A two-hour special
"Abortion and Abortion Laws"—A one-hour special
"Joy in Mudville"—A two-hour special on baseball
"EXPO '67"—A two-hour special
"Teenage Marriage: Dream or Disaster?"—A two-hour special
"The Day the World Changed"—Tenth anniversary of *Sputnik*
"Hippies"—A two-hour special
"Marijuana: Is This Trip Necessary?"—A two-hour special
"The Russian Revolution: What It's Meant to the U.S.A."—Two hours on the 50th anniversary of the Russian revolution
"Apollo: Journey to the Moon."[63]

During 1967, *Today* moved out of its traditional weekday morning framework to present two one-hour Sunday evening editions of *Today*. The first was "*Today* in Britain," aired on January 8, 1967, from 6:30 to 7:30 p.m. The other was a special on "The Pill," aired on April 30, 1967, from 6:30 to 7:30 p.m.[64] From March 29, 1967, to April 10, 1967, the American Federation of Television and Radio Artists strike affected the *Today* programming. George Skinner reported the news live at the appropriate news segments, while the rest of the show used repeats of special taped programs that included remotes from Mystic, Connecticut; Colonial Williamsburg, Virginia; the Virgin Islands; Hollywood; and Greece, drawn from 1965 and 1966.[65] *Today* also updated its program format and changed from NBC studio 6B in New York City to studio 3K, and toward the end of the year, Joe Garagiola was added as a regular panel member.

Today continued its remarkable programming record in 1968 as a series of unusual events made some of the programming more significant than others. On April 1, two hours of *Today* covered President Johnson's statement that he would not run for reelection. That event was quickly followed by another, even more important event on April 5, 1968, when *Today* devoted the entire program to cover the assassination of Dr. Martin Luther King Jr. And again, continuous coverage on the assassination of Robert Kennedy resulted in *Today* being expanded on June 5–7 when it was incorporated into NBC News. Other special reports and expanded editions of *Today* covered the *Apollo* space flights and events surrounding the 1968 presidential election, including remote broadcasts from the national conventions.[66] In recognition of *Today*'s remarkable year, *Variety* highlighted the programming totals from the *Today* segments:

17 full-scale remotes (not to include numerous remote pick-ups on both the news and show side).
21 "specials," i.e. shows ranging from one hour to five hours in length on a single subject.
11 series, covering several days, weeks, or longer.
89 entertainment features ranging from rock 'n' roll to classical performers.
113 film features on a variety of subjects.
939 interviews, including 14 with members of the president's cabinet; 64 with senators; 26 with representatives; 41 with other governmental officials; 17 with leaders or diplomats of foreign countries; 14 with state governors.

Included in the remotes were shows from Portugal, San Antonio's Hemisfair, the national conventions and Atlanta, Ga.

Specials included a two-hour salute to the late Woody Guthrie, an hour featuring The Cowsills, "instant" specials on President Johnson's withdrawal from the Presidential race and the assassination of Dr. Martin Luther King, a two-hour show on human transplants, a George Gershwin memorial, hours on student revolt and young film makers and many others.

Series included such regulars and Dr. Haim Ginott's advice to parents and comedians Bob and Ray, fashion shows with Barbara Walters, Judith Crist's movie and theatre criticism and World Series coverage by Joe Garagiola.[67]

There was also a major personnel change that occurred in November, when Stuart Schulberg took over the producing reins from Al Morgan.

Things were quieter in 1969 and 1970 as there were few significant programming format changes. Hugh Downs continued as host of the program, Barbara Walters and Joe Garagiola as panel members, and

Frank Blair as newscaster. Notable special programming in 1969 included the following topics, many that expanded *Today* beyond its normal two hours:

Washington, D.C., for President Nixon's inauguration, Jan. 20
Coverage of Nixon's trip to Europe, Feb. 27
Apollo IX and X space flights, Mar. 3 and May 26
Death and funeral of President Eisenhower, March 31
Remote from Germany, June 2–6
Live satellite coverage of the investiture of Prince Charles as The Prince of Wales, July 21
Three-day coverage from Cape Kennedy of Apollo 11 preparation, launch, and flight to the moon on July 14, 15, and 16
Pre-empted coverage of Apollo 11—man lands and walks on the moon, July 21
Expanded for Apollo 12 moon walk, Nov. 19[68]

Other noteworthy segments covered Vietnam veterans, sex education, and a week from Washington, D.C. One format change was the addition of the "Sky Warn" segment to the weather during the hurricane season. Subjects covered in 1970 included art ("The Andrew Wyeth Exhibit at the White House"), music ("From Ragtime to Rock," black jazz musicians, and the 200th anniversary of Beethoven's birth), politics (five-part series each on the Democratic and Republican parties), ecology, society (focused on aging, women's rights, and the youth rebellion and a five-part series on black leaders), and fashion ("Mini vs. Midi").

Today also added a new regular feature from NBC affiliate WMAQ-TV in Chicago beginning in July. That feature segment was preceded by a weeklong remote from Chicago. Other remotes that year were from California on March 2–6 and Canada on September 14–18. Also, there was live satellite coverage of the funeral of Charles de Gaulle on November 12, 1970.[69] In late June 1970, *Today* once again moved to new studios, from NBC studio 3K to the larger studio 8G.

In 1971, *Today* got a new host and moved the show back to studio 3K to allow *Today* and *NBC Nightly News* to share the same basic set. There were also new features: "Talk of *Today*" debuted on January 29, with Barbara Walters featuring the latest in fashion news; "Business *Today*," with Jeffrey St. John, reported on the progress of American industries on pollution control; and "90-Day Q&A," presented each Thursday with Irving R. Levine, questioned the executive director of the Cost of Living Council on President Nixon's new economic program. Barbara Walters hosted *Today*'s first contest on February 26, 1971, when viewers were asked to guess which day in March would mark *Today*'s 10,000th hour on the air. (March 11, 1971, 8:00–9:00 a.m.)[70] There was a significant amount of special programming broadcast during 1971. Barbara Walters's exclusive interview with President Nixon was aired on March 15 in a two-hour special segment. A five-part series from March 22 to 26 covered "Prison and Prison Reform in the U.S." Two hours were given over to the reaction to Lieutenant William Calley's guilty verdict on the My Lai incident. Remotes included one week in Romania in April and one week in Japan in October.[71] On June 17, 1971, *Today* provided live coverage via satellite of the treaty-signing ceremonies, allowing for the return of Okinawa to Japan. An NBC News Press Department release described the coverage: "Between 8 and 8:30 a.m. NYT, *Today* brought viewers in this country exclusive live color coverage of the signing of the treaty providing for the return of Okinawa and the other islands in the Ryukyu chain to Japan. The event also was telecast in Japan. The signing ceremony was held simultaneously in Tokyo and Washington. Secretary of State William P. Rogers signed the treaty in Washington, and Japan's Foreign Minister Kiichi Aichi signed in Tokyo. Japan's Prime Minister Eisaku Sato spoke from Tokyo, and Mr. Rogers read a message from President Nixon."[72] Probably the biggest change in 1971 came on April 27, when Hugh Downs announced that he was leaving the show. He left voluntarily, saying that he wanted to do things that he could not do while he had the constant responsibility of a daily program. By the time Downs made the announcement public, Frank McGee had already been chosen by NBC to be the fourth permanent host. McGee assumed those duties on October 11, 1971.

1972–1977: A WORLD PRESENCE

On January 14, 1972, *Today* celebrated its twentieth anniversary. The NBC News Press Department promoted the monumental day with the following release:

> NBC Television Network's *Today*—network TV's longest-running weekday program—will celebrate its 20th anniversary Friday, Jan. 14, with a two-hour birthday gala (7–9 a.m. NYT, in color). Stuart Schulberg, the program's executive producer, announced the plans today.
>
> United for the occasion will be the four men who have been program hosts: Dave Garroway (1952–61); John Chancellor (1961–62); Hugh Downs (1962–71); and Frank McGee, the current host, who succeeded Mr. Downs last October. Each will introduce a half-hour segment.
>
> Other *Today* personalities from years past who will be back are Jack Lescoulie (1952–61) and three *Today* girls: Estelle Parsons (1952–54); Helen O'Connell (1956–58); and Betsy Palmer (1958). Barbara Walters, featured on the program since 1964, will lead the *Today* girls—who are expected to be in a reminiscent mood—in a panel discussion.

Frank Blair, who has been with the program from its start reporting the day's news, will report not only the news of Jan. 14, 1972, but also, in one three-minute feature, the news of Jan. 14, 1952. A guest related to an important news story of that day 20 years ago will be interviewed.

Paul Cunningham, who also has been with the program from its start and is now its reporter-at-large, will be on hand with historic film of *Today* in its early days, much of it behind-the-scenes material. He will also conduct a man-in-the-street interview as he did in the early years when the program originated in the RCA Exhibition Hall that looked out on Manhattan's 49th Street.

Joe Garagiola, featured on *Today* since 1962, will talk about the greatest sports events and sports personalities of the past 20 years.

The Modern Jazz Quartet will be back to play the *Today* program's theme song, written by one of its members, John Lewis. On this occasion they will play the song in full—it is regularly heard on the program in part—as viewers see a series of photographs of the famous personalities who have appeared on *Today*: Presidents Truman, Eisenhower, Kennedy, Johnson and Nixon; the chief executives of many other nations; leading representatives of the arts and sciences; and outstanding figures in many other fields.

Highlights of events covered by *Today* during the past two decades will be shown in a feature using both film and tape. *Today* is currently viewed in more households than ever before in its history. Nearly six million people watch the program each morning, according to latest available Nielsen Television Index estimates. Produced by NBC News, *Today* is known for its scope and variety: no other program has greater turnover of new material than this one, with its news and weather reports, topical discussions, interviews, exhibitions, demonstrations, reviews, and other features, including occasionally, entertainment by performers not regularly seen on television.

On the day following its premiere 20 years ago, *Today* was termed by critic John Crosby in the *New York Herald Tribune* as "an incredible two-hour comedy of errors, perpetuated as 'a new kind of television,'" and Janet Kern of the *Chicago American* called it "something without which TV can do very nicely." Recently, a national magazine called it a "TV institution."

Through the years the format and balance of content have changed. Since 1961, when the program came under the wing of NBC News, the emphasis has come to be more on news and serious material. It has been estimated that the program is viewed by 65% of the members of Congress.

"All I can say," says executive producer Schulberg, "is that the first 20 years are the hardest."[73]

President Nixon sent the following telegram to congratulate *Today* on its twenty-year success:

As you and your associates observe the decades of exceptional service to the American people, I am proud to be included among those who applaud the quality, breadth and timeliness of your programs. As an American couple that has enjoyed *Today* as participants, Mrs. Nixon and I have been privileged to experience at first-hand both the caliber of your staff and the value to the public of your stimulating and informative reporting. Congratulations from both of us.[74]

Because 1972 was a presidential election year, most of the *Today* remotes were from states with major primary elections, such as New Hampshire, Florida, Wisconsin, Pennsylvania, Massachusetts, Indiana, Ohio, and Michigan. Election coverage continued with the Democratic and Republican national conventions in Miami, Florida, and ended with an expanded *Today Show* on November 8 for election returns reporting.[75]

Two new features were added to the programming during 1972. Beginning on February 2, Bill Monroe hosted a series called "The View from Washington." In mid-November, *Today* also revived and revised the previously scheduled weekly feature from NBC-owned WMAQ-TV in Chicago, presented by Chicago personality Bob Hale.[76] Programming worth noting in 1972 included special coverage of Richard Nixon's presidential trip to China, which aired from February 21 to 25. Notably, Barbara Walters was asked to accompany the news reporters to China and became the only female network news correspondent to make the trip.

The other programming highlight during 1972 was a seven-part series on American Indians, aired from October 6 to 16 and heavily promoted by the NBC News Press Department:

A *Today* production crew has been filming at various locations throughout the country: the Warm Springs Confederated Tribes in central Oregon; the Navajo and the Hopi reservations in northeastern Arizona; and in Los Angeles, which has the largest Indian population of any city in the United States. Among the issues to be dealt with are land, health, education, the economy, and preservation of Indian culture. The report filmed in Los Angeles will show the efforts of Indians who have moved to the city to find a place for themselves, socially and economically, in a strange and sometimes hostile environment. Stuart Schulberg, executive producer of *Today*, said: "If American blacks have been the victims of 'benign neglect,' then the American Indians have suffered too long from malevolent neglect. Our series shows not so much what we victorious whites have done for the Red Man but what he has somehow managed to do for himself. It's about time we take notice."[77]

In 1973, the majority of the special programming revolved around four major topics: U.S. prisoners of war (POWs) in Vietnam, energy, Watergate, and the Middle East crisis. The first quarter of 1973 was largely devoted largely to POWs: negotiation for their release, their return to the United States, and the readjustment problems they faced once back home. *Today*'s concern for this issue was clearly illustrated in the large amount of time given to this topic. On January 9, an hour of the show focused on American POWs, on January 24 the entire program was devoted to

Nixon's cease-fire announcement, and on February 12 a special three-and-a-half-hour edition was broadcast live via satellite to cover the arrival of released POWs at Clark Air Force Base in the Philippines.

Later that month, a special edition, "While You Were Away," recounted world events that had taken place during the eight years that American POWs had been incarcerated. NBC's Press Department promoted the special program:

> Frank McGee, host of *Today*, will set the stage with a rundown on the headlines and the personalities who made them. During the ensuing two hours, Barbara Walters will discuss the fashion revolution, the cost of living and women's lib, while Gene Shalit will talk about books and magazines, movies and plays. Additional features will be provided by stage and screen star Sammy Davis Jr., and by Joe Garagiola, who returns to the *Today* program for one morning to recapitulate the sports scene. Davis will call attention to the changes in music and entertainment.[78]

In addition, March 5, 15, and 30, 1973, were devoted to the coverage of the returning POWs to the United States.[79]

Today reacted to the increasing American concern over energy by presenting information or clarification on the situation. On March 28 and 29, *Today* presented a two-part report on the energy situation, updating that information on July 9 with a one-hour special, and in August presented "The Automobile: The Love/Hate Machine." There was a renewed interest in energy when winter returned to the United States, and effective October 17, 1973, *Today* weather included a fuel warn feature. In December, as the energy problem became more severe, *Today* produced two five-part series on the energy crisis with energy-saving tips. Then, from December 31, 1973, to April 4, 1974, Irving R. Levine hosted a weekly series of interviews with Energy Chief William Simon.[80]

Because a part of the energy crisis was directly related to the unstable conditions in the Middle East, *Today* incorporated coverage of the area into its programming. On August 23 and 24, Barbara Walters interviewed Israeli Defense Minister Moshe Dayan, and on October 8, the entire program was devoted to coverage of the outbreak of war in the Middle East. Later, on October 26, Frank McGee broadcast live from Washington, D.C., to report on the U.S. military alert due to tension in the Middle East.

The other really significant issue of 1973 was Watergate. *Today* covered the initial Watergate investigations by originating the program from Washington, D.C., on the days (May 1, July 23, and July 24) that major developments took place. Other programs worthy of attention included a three-hour edition to cover the funeral of President Lyndon Johnson on January 23, and October 11 was devoted to the issues surrounding the resignation of Vice President Spiro Agnew after being charged with bribery, conspiracy, and tax fraud. That year, *Today* also originated for a week (June 4–8) from Great Britain and a week (October 1–5) from Ireland. On November 14, *Today* aired a special five-hour edition from England covering the wedding of Princess Anne and on November 22 devoted the show to "The Legacy of JFK" on the tenth anniversary of the assassination of President John F. Kennedy.

There was also a major personnel change that year. In a special farewell program on January 12, Joe Garagiola departed as a regular panel member, and Gene Shalit made his first appearance that day as permanent replacement for Garagiola. Approximately six months later, Shalit developed the successful *Today* feature "Critic's Corner," with reviews of film, theater, and art.[81]

The year 1974 was a period of disillusionment, change, and uncertainty for many Americans. The president of the United States was possibly involved in an impeachable offense, the vice president had resigned in late 1973 after questionable legal conduct, the country was involved in a serious recession and energy crisis, and the recent war in the Middle East left the situation unresolved and tension high. Although there was no direct correlation between these events and the subsequent changes on the *Today* program, there did seem to be the same kind of turbulence and lack of direction on *Today* during 1974 that was evident in the rest of the country.

The first major event disrupting the *Today* format was the sudden death of host Frank McGee on April 17, 1974. NBC did not have a replacement ready who could immediately step in and thereby create an orderly and reassuring succession. Instead, NBC decided to let the *Today* audience share in the selection of the fifth permanent host. It elicited viewer response by having the contenders audition as guest host of the show. Although it was an opportunity for NBC executives to determine how effectively the potential host was in adapting to the format and to sample audience acceptance, it involved a slow selection process that left *Today* without a permanent host for more than three months. The situation was alleviated to some extent when Barbara Walters reminded show executives of the clause in her contract that stated that she would be given cohost status if Frank McGee departed the show. Subsequently, Walters's change from regular cast member to cohost became effective on April 22, 1974. Among the men considered to replace McGee after his death were Garrick Utley, Edwin Newman, John Chancellor, Tom Snyder, Tom Brokaw, and Jim Hartz. Finally, on July 29, 1974, Barbara Walters and Jim Hartz became the permanent cohosts of *Today*.[82]

Most of the programming in 1974 revolved around the Watergate events and the impeachment proceedings, culminating on August 9, 1974, in a special three-and-a-half-hour edition of *Today* that focused on the resignation of President Nixon. Other special programming dealt with taxes, school integration, economy and inflation, religion, the 1974 elections, and the Middle East situation. Special remote broadcasts covered the major news events of the day, such as President Nixon's trips to the Middle East on June 10 and 12, to Brussels for the signing of the NATO pact on June 26, and to Moscow on June 27, 1974. Later, for a week in November, *Today* followed President Gerald R. Ford on his trip to Japan and Korea.[83]

Although ABC and CBS had attempted to counterprogram *The Today Show* on numerous occasions, ABC announced in May 1974 plans for a new two-hour morning news program employing a format similar to *Today*. The premiere date was set for January 6, 1975, giving *Today* sufficient time to react and plan how best to meet its anticipated competition. Therefore, once NBC had decided on Jim Hartz as the permanent cohost, it next decided to modernize the *Today* set in studio 3K. In conjunction with *NBC Nightly News*, NBC designed a set that could be utilized effectively for both programs. The new set, which had interchangeable units and octagonal platforms, was incorporated into its programming by *Today* on December 2, 1974, and included a new logo and the use of a portable minicam for live coverage from outdoor or remote locations.[84]

The year 1975 saw a number of programming additions, changes, and innovations. On March 14, Frank Blair, who had been with *Today* since its premiere in 1952, retired and was replaced by Lew Wood. Blair had been the newsreader for all of those years except for a brief period of time in 1962 when he served as a regular panel member.[85] New features were added to the program. Beginning in March, Dr. Frank Field, science reporter and meteorologist for *News-Center 4* on WNBC-TV in New York, became a regular contributor of health segments. Wood expanded his job as newsreader to include the new segment "Follow-Up," which reflected on major events in the past and examined what had developed since the event. In early spring, Bill White, former member of the TV-radio broadcast team for the New York Yankees, was hired to host sports specials.[86] Also, Gene Shalit became host of a new feature promoted by NBC News: "*Today* will become 'Yesterday' as it looks at the past through the eyes of Fox-Movietone newsreel footage of the years 1918 to 1963."[87]

In 1975, *Today* initiated a more formal relationship with Washington, D.C., where for many years it relied on their D.C. studios to handle news and interviews that were relevant to the nation's capital and government. In March, *Today* added a full-time D.C. producer, Ron Steinman, and enlarged its staff.

During 1975, the National Science Foundation and the Research Foundation of the State University of New York, in cooperation with *Today*, initiated a direct connection between *Today* weather forecasts and earth science classes taught in secondary schools throughout the country. Students would trace the weather map off the screen and take the information to class. It was estimated that between 2 million and 3 million students participated in the project during 1975.[88]

On July 4, 1975, *Today* launched its yearlong observance of America's bicentennial. Each Friday, *Today* "saluted" one of the fifty states following the format for the series explained in an NBC press release:

> Co-hosts Jim Hartz and Barbara Walters and panelist Gene Shalit—one or more—will be on location in the various states. Hugh Downs, who was host of *Today* from 1962 to 1971, will return as guest host for the salute to Arizona, his adopted state, September 19. Since there will be 53 weeks in the commemorative year, the series will offer three additional Friday telecasts: a salute to Washington, D.C., which will open the series; a salute to Philadelphia, which will wrap up the year July 2, 1976; and an extra observance to be announced later. Each state salute will contain five basic features: a capsule historical survey, a visit to tourist attractions, entertainment indigenous to the state, a segment devoted to its political leaders, and, on occasion, a brief essay on the state by a prominent native son.[89]

In conjunction with the launching of the weekly state salute, NBC presented a special evening edition of *Today*: "*Today* at Night: America the Humorous." The program, which was aired on Saturday, July 5, 1975, examined humor in America, ranging from colonial jest books to contemporary humor.[90]

At the close of 1975, the NBC News Press Department summed up the accomplishments of *Today*. In that year, it had done the following:

> Interviewed 800 persons, including 65 U.S. Senators, 50 members of the House, 20 Cabinet members, 20 state governors and 200 authors.
> Telecast 100 satellite feeds—75 from Europe, 25 from Asia—for a total of 4,500,000 satellite miles.
> Required 50,000 hours of work by studio technicians for operations in New York and Washington alone.
> Sent co-host Jim Hartz on 130 air flights to 26 states.
> Sent Hartz traveling faster than sound in an F-15, the Air Force's new interceptor fighter.
> Sent Hartz 200 miles north of the Arctic Circle to Prudhoe Bay. To the top of the Haleakala Crater, 10,023 feet high, on the Hawaiian Island of Maui. And then 1,900 feet under Lake Erie to a salt mine near Cleveland.
> Ordered transportation for its various staffers; hydrofoil, horses, mule, kayak, jeep, hay-cutter, pick-up trucks, farm tractor, motorcycle, helicopters, rental cars and assorted types of aircraft, both jet and prop.
> Used 3,500,000 feet of videotape to record programs for delayed broadcast.
> Dispatched its Bicentennial Unit, starting in July, on 130,000 miles of travel to 26 states.
> Invited Barbara Walters, an 11-year-old beekeeper from Long Valley, N.J., as a surprise for co-host Barbara Walters.

Sent co-host Walters to the People's Republic of China and to Cuba. Also to
a pig farm in Iowa.
Reimbursed co-host Walters $3.25 for losses playing Las Vegas slot machines
in the line of duty for *Today*.[91]

In 1976, *Today* began its twenty-fifth year on the air. It had survived in
spite of the early predictions of certain failure. However, 1976 was the
second year of the 1970s when *Today* was to endure major cast and format
changes. *Today*'s executive producer described the second quarter of 1976
as "an unhappy time, a time of great trauma":

> Never before in its quarter century on the air has there been such a coming
> and a going, such a shifting of personnel and of format, such an unsettled—
> and unsettling—mood about the show. Within the past three months, *Today*
> has lost its supervising vice president, its executive producer, its female host,
> its male host, its newsreader, its Washington editor and its reporter-at-large.
> Indeed, the only on-air performer filling the same role he did three months
> ago is the show's resident wit, Gene Shalit. "It's as if three-quarters of a base-
> ball team had been killed in a plane crash," says a worried NBC executive,
> "and you had to put together a squad with new talent who had never played
> together before."[92]

Today's ratings had begun to slip in 1975, reaching a low point in July
1976. Several factors contributed to the low ratings, which were only
slightly higher than ABC's. Although ABC's *A.M. America* had failed
within a few months of its debut, in November 1975, ABC revised,
restructured, retitled, and rereleased their morning show as *Good Morning America*. Within a short time, it became evident to the *Today* staff
that *Good Morning America* was going to be a serious threat in luring
away the *Today* audience.[93] *Good Morning America* may have lured away
the 1976 audience, but *Today*'s ratings had been slipping steadily in the
past year. According to NBC, there was a direct correlation between
the arrival of *Today* cohost Jim Hartz in late 1974 and subsequent falling ratings in 1975. As a result, program executives began to criticize
his low-key hosting style and his singular lack of assertiveness in his
interviewing style.

But the most devastating blow to *The Today Show* occurred in April
1976, when ABC lured Barbara Walters away to coanchor *The ABC Evening News* with Harry Reasoner. Shortly thereafter, NBC began a clean
sweep and reorganization of *The Today Show*. There was panic at the network over the falling ratings of both *Today* and *NBC Nightly News*, whose
evening news program had been steadily declining, falling substantially
behind the very strong CBS network news. NBC made changes by first
replacing Jim Hartz as host and offering him a position as the "traveling

cohost." Tom Brokaw was the unanimous choice as *Today* host number six:

> There was no real search for Hartz's replacement. By May, Wald and the other responsible executives knew they wanted Brokaw, the network's bright, aggressive White House correspondent. Indeed, Brokaw had been many people's top choice to replace McGee in 1974. According to one widely heard scenario, the network's executives had been divided between a "California faction" which preferred Tom Snyder, the host of NBC's *Tomorrow* show, and a "New York faction" which wanted Brokaw. In this deadlock, they turned to "everybody's second choice" Jim Hartz.[94]

Another reason that Tom Brokaw was not the unanimous choice in 1974 was his refusal to compromise his journalistic principles by "pitching" commercials, as other *Today* hosts had been required to do.[95] But now, to accommodate its new host, *Today* executives implemented a new policy whereby "the major on-air performers—the male host, the new woman, Gene Shalit and chief news reader—were exempted from reading commercials, the show would hire two new performers—a man and a woman—to do commercials as well as light features."[96] Under those more professional journalistic conditions, Tom Brokaw began hosting *The Today Show* on August 30, 1976.

The next major decision was for NBC to select a female replacement for Barbara Walters. The new *Today* woman was to be given "regular panel member" status because, according to NBC, she would not be filling Barbara Walters's cohost position. "Brokaw will be the central figure around whom everything revolves, including the new woman." To help in the selection, NBC ran auditions similar to those held in 1974 during the search for the male host replacement for the late Frank McGee. The most promising positive feedback was secured by Jane Pauley from WMAQ-TV in Chicago. Other contenders for the position were Catherine (Cassie) Mackin, Betty Furness, Candice Bergen, and Linda Ellerbee. At the time, Betty Furness had been filling in for Barbara Walters until a permanent female panel regular could be chosen. Jane Pauley was hired and began her long, successful career on *Today* on October 17, 1976.

Still another talent change, minor by comparison, completed the upheaval of familiar faces on *Today* when Lew Wood was replaced by Floyd Kalber, anchorman for NBC's WMAQ-TV in Chicago. Wood was reassigned to weather, sports, and commercials. In addition, two major staff changes also took place. The vice president and news supervisor of *Today*, Richard Hannah, was replaced by Richard Fisher. And very significantly, Stuart Schulberg, executive producer of *Today* for eight years, was replaced by Paul Friedman.

With those changes, *Today* took on a new appearance that NBC executives hoped would exhibit a new attractiveness. The most apparent change was the youthfulness of the new panel and staff. Tom Brokaw was thirty-three years old when he joined *Today*. Jane Pauley was twenty-five when she joined, and Paul Friedman, the new executive producer, was just thirty-one.

To facilitate *Today*'s recovery from poor ratings, Friedman initiated broad changes in the programming format, but in a *New York Times* interview, he explained the dilemma involved in making those changes: "We have to keep enough of the old to reassure our traditional audience while changing enough to attract new viewers."[97] Some of the changes he did make in 1976 included shortening most of the segments, adding health and consumer features, and drastically reducing the number of books reviewed on the show. He hired Frank Field for the health and medical segments, Betty Furness on consumer issues, and Dick Schaap to host sports features. But even minor changes in format brought heavy criticism and reaction from *Today*'s audience. During that period, some viewers voiced their concerns by mail, while others simply turned to the competition, particularly ABC's *Good Morning America*. The remainder of 1976 saw the ratings stabilize and begin to grow very slowly as the new team members became more accustomed to their positions.

TWENTY-FIVE YEARS: AN AMERICAN INSTITUTION

On January 14, 1977, *Today* celebrated its twenty-fifth anniversary on the air. The program reunited old *Today* panel members who reminisced about the best and worst of *Today*. Joining those invited to celebrate the silver anniversary was *Today*'s originator, Sylvester "Pat" Weaver. Much of the credit for *Today*'s longevity had to be given to Weaver for creating and developing the basic concept of *The Today Show*, which appealed to viewers in 1952 and still appealed to viewers in 1977. Probably the most important factor built into that programming concept was flexibility. The show was designed to easily accommodate programming changes that might be necessary to keep it current with a rapidly changing society.

Back in 1952, when television was still a novelty, *Today* fascinated its viewers with rows of television monitors and electronic gadgets, claiming them to be the most sophisticated communications equipment available. When it became apparent that communication "bulletins" from around the country or Europe were not very interesting if the news was not important, *Today* revised its flashy technology image but not the basic programming concept. It retained the hard-news element but became more selective in choosing information and reorganizing it into regular segments or features.

In the first years of *Today*, those features were repeated in approximately twenty-minute intervals. In keeping with the original *Today* concept, this made it possible for viewers to tune in to *Today* for short periods of time. It was not expected that all viewers would watch the show for the entire two hours. Indeed, it was not expected that all viewers would "watch" the show. Although the set was visually stimulating for those who would watch, it was assumed that many people would simply listen to the program while they completed their morning tasks, with only an occasional glance at the television set.

Although the first year of *Today* was somewhat unstable, it survived in part due to the persistence of Weaver but also because of a brilliant talent acquisition. It is generally conceded that the "adorable" chimpanzee, J. Fred Muggs, helped *Today* become successful by attracting a large and regular audience. Over the next few years, Weaver and the *Today* producers spent their time making the actual *Today Show* more closely resemble its original philosophical concept. The major programming changes in the 1950s and 1960s came about because of improved technology that made it possible to add West Coast stations to the *Today* lineup because of improved broadcast transmission over long distances. Later, the invention of videotape made it possible to tape delay the show and feed it to different time zones. This in turn made the feature segments more flexible since many could be pretaped. Each *Today* hour was then programmed separately rather than in repeated segments. At last, the content was aided by technology, not overshadowed by it. Videotape made it possible for another major format change in 1959, when *Today* was taped the afternoon before it was to air the next morning. However, the newscast segments were inserted live during what were formerly the normal morning hours of the program. This change in format was unpopular, and *Today* reverted to its "live" format in 1961. In 1965, *Today* began to transmit regularly in color.

After *Today* began to be produced by the NBC News Department in 1961, the show became more news-information oriented. This was reflected in the host they selected to replace David Garroway (NBC newsman John Chancellor) and the subsequent programming. Although John Chancellor was ultimately unsuitable for the position, the change in programming brought a new integrity to *Today*, which became a major national forum for social and political issues. Because *Today* was not subjected to the same time constraints as the network evening news, it was possible to present a topic in depth. In the early and mid-1960s, many topics were treated in terms of a featured series that was broadcast over a number of days. Although this approach remained popular and was frequently used, later in the 1960s, *Today* began devoting first one hour and eventually the entire two-hour program to a single subject. Often, the program was expanded beyond its normal two hours if there was a significant or compelling event or issue needing to be covered in depth.

Certainly, the change in focus to news occurred because of the change in production responsibility from the Programming Department to NBC News. There were other contributing factors, too, and by the mid-1960s, *Today* was securely established as a morning television viewing habit. With the combination of strong ratings and virtually no significant competition, *Today* was in the enviable position of being able to experiment with its programming. It was possible for the producers to boldly program social and political issues, many of which were controversial in nature. During that time, *Today* more than accomplished one of its primary goals set back in 1952, which was to present information to the American public so that they would start each day socially and politically aware.

In the early 1960s, *Today* broadened its programming by increasing the number of remote telecasts. At first, overseas remotes were possible by recording on videotape and then flying the tapes to New York for broadcast the next morning. However, in 1965, *Today* transmitted its first overseas remote via satellite. In the 1970s, the development of high-quality, truly portable equipment made remote broadcasting much easier and more prolific. In addition, minicam scenes were incorporated into the regular *Today* opening sequence.

Over twenty-five years, the integrity of the original programming concept was maintained. *Today*'s features or segments were devoted to art, music, sports, entertainment, interviews, and contemporary social and political issues. One category may have overshadowed another at different periods, but the overall programming remained essentially balanced. The specific information contained within the feature and the method of presentation, however, had developed in response to the requirements of its current audience. *Today* had always been contemporary in its programming and loyal to its original goal of providing whatever was necessary to have every American well informed and enlightened at least five days a week.

3

Producing *Today*

Behind the Camera

A ll programs have two sides: one in front of the camera, familiar to viewers of the program, and one behind the camera, familiar to the producer and production crew. It is debatable whether the right talent is more important to a program than the right producer. In the case of *The Today Show*, it was the combination of good talent and good producing that made the program successful for those first twenty-five years. It was important for *The Today Show* to have producers who were capable of developing and implementing a workable format and also to hire talent able to effectively communicate the material in a way that was attractive to an audience.

To find talent who were well received by the audience and who would remain manageable for the sake of the show was a challenging task and one that is rarely carried out successfully. Conflicts on a program often come between the producer and its "stars." It is the producer's responsibility to determine and supervise all aspects of production. But stars generally are granted most demands if they are in a successful show where any replacement could affect audience loyalty and thereby the all-important program ratings. Frequently, however, and in many instances on *Today*, allowing the talent to make programming decisions or granting excessive demands interfered with or altered the format. Very often, the talent became indispensable to the program, and when that occurred, the star rather than the producer was in a position to make programming and personnel decisions. It was not unusual for the talent to acquire enough power to fire the producer. That was the case with David Garroway, who fired several *Today* producers, and with Hugh Downs, who fired producer Al Morgan.

EARLY PRODUCERS: PLOWING THE FIELD, 1952–1962

Although it in no way proves conclusively that the talent is more important to a show than the producer, *Today* has had more than twice as many producers as hosts. In the very early years, the show had both an executive producer and a producer, but from 1955 to 1971, there was just a producer. Then after 1971, *Today* once again had both a producer and an executive producer.[1]

Although Pat Weaver, vice president in charge of programming at NBC, was the originator of *The Today Show*, his efforts were needed in the management and development of all of NBC's programming, so he could not devote himself exclusively to *Today*. Therefore, it became the responsibility of *Today* producers to translate the Weaver program concept into a working on-air format. Within a few months of the show's debut, John Kingsley Herbert was given the general responsibility for managing *Today*, and Abe Schechter filled the role as its first executive producer, hired by Weaver to help develop the program. Although he was in charge of the production during its first few months on the air, Schechter did not fully accept the concept of *The Today Show* and frequently argued with Weaver about its "hodge-podge" nature.[2] Despite Schechter's background in news, he failed as the *Today* producer to secure the necessary cooperation from NBC News for the *Today* news segments. So it wasn't surprising that within a few months, Weaver replaced Abe Schechter with Richard Pinkham, who had already been working with Weaver as the manager of television planning.

Weaver then selected *Today* staff member Mort Werner, who was an associate of his during the war, to function as the line producer. It was Werner who had first suggested that Dave Garroway might make a good host for the program.[3] Werner was a dedicated producer who developed an excellent rapport with David Garroway so that when Pinkham left in 1954, Werner was moved up to the executive producer slot.

Because they were responsible for implementing the directives issued by Weaver, Werner and Pinkham had the most difficult jobs as *Today* producers. The show was not an immediately popular or critical success, according to Pinkham. "People said, '7 A.M. No one will watch.' And no one did, during that first year."[4] In fact, *Today* had been built up in so pretentious a manner that it was difficult for the show to meet the standards set by Sylvester Weaver. It took both producers several months to alleviate the basic problems on the show, simplify the format by dropping some of the "gadgetry," and concentrate on the "message."

By the end of the first year, the quality of the program had been steadily improving, but the show had failed in the one critical area: attracting advertisers. It was Pinkham's responsibility to get higher ratings for the show to attract advertisers, and in January 1953, Pinkham found the answer when he came across chimpanzee J. Fred Muggs and his owners, Carmine Mennella and Roy Waldron, in the NBC casting room. Charmed by the antics and appeal of the chimp, Pinkham decided to put Muggs on the next day. He described the decision: "A production assistant who was sort of a gopher for us showed me a man with a chimp in the casting room. I said, 'Sure put him on tomorrow.' The assistant said, 'No, every day,' and we did. We put J. Fred Muggs on every day. That monkey saved the show."[5] On February 3, 1953, Muggs became a regular cast member:[6]

> As Pinkham sees it, J. Fred Muggs served the same purpose for *Today* as a comic strip serves for a newspaper. Just as the children would grab for the comics when the daily newspaper landed on the doorstep, they began monopolizing the television set from the moment Muggs made his appearance. . . . Young viewers guarded the TV dial like goalies protecting the nets at Madison Square Garden, threatening tears or mayhem if a parent tried to change channels. Consequently, parents who had shunned *Today* the whole first year suddenly became involuntary regulars. Though captive at first, many became fans, discovering that *Today* was a good news show.[7]

It was probably the most important casting Pinkham did as executive producer. Pinkham himself said, "That 'wretched little ape' did more to put *Today* over the top than *Today*'s news coverage."[8]

But critically, *Today* was essentially a news program, and in those early years one of the most difficult problems faced by Schechter, Pinkham, and Werner was getting cooperation from NBC News. Having failed to establish a workable relationship with the News Department, *Today* was forced to develop its own news staff and techniques. Gerald Green, who was hired away from International News Service to become *Today*'s news editor, described the situation with the news department: "The NBC news department hated *Today*, [and] tried to discredit and sabotage it. They really wanted it to die. We'd have been better off if we had been a part of the news department instead of a rival, separate entity."[9] The problem wasn't solved until many years later, in 1961, when *Today* was placed under the control and budget of the NBC News Department.

During the summer of 1954, Mort Werner was promoted to executive producer, and the job of producer was taken over by Robert Bendick, who lasted only a few months. Then from 1955 to 1958, there was a rapid turnover in the *Today* producers.[10] During that same time, as *Today* gathered strength in ratings and advertising, David Garroway's position as program host became extremely important to the show. He gradually assumed power over the program as a succession of weak producers were hired and fired. "Garroway had the authority to dismiss anyone on the show, including producers whom he fired with increasing frequency in his final years."[11] One producer that had established a good relationship with Garroway was Gerald Green, former news editor of *Today*. "Green developed a genuine affection for Garroway and confidently programmed the show thinking about what 'the big fellow' could handle best. Even when Garroway did not like all the material, Green could usually persuade him that it was best for the show and best for Garroway."[12] A little more than a year later, in September 1956, Green voluntarily resigned as producer of *Today* to write the novel *The Last Angry Man*. Green was replaced by Jac Hein, who stayed with the show for nearly two years. When Garroway fired Hein, he did not replace him with another producer. Two associate producers, Mary Kelly and Jack Otter, produced the show under the supervision of *Today*'s general manager, John Lynch.[13]

In October 1958, Robert Bendick was rehired by Garroway to once again produce the show. Bendick, however, was not a strong producer, and Garroway continued to make all major programming and personnel decisions. Unfortunately, Garroway assumed the greatest power when he was least capable of exercising it, and the pressure of hosting a two-hour daily program began to affect his mental health. Because of that, producer Bendick made what he considered to be a major production error—the decision to videotape the show in the previous afternoon—to give Garroway desperately needed relief. "He arranged to tape *The Today Show* late in the afternoon for telecasting at the usual hours the next day. The primary motivation, according to Bendick, was to give Garroway a chance to recover his physical stamina and perhaps give him a little brighter mental attitude."[14] The show was taped in this manner from September 21, 1959, to July 17, 1961. In 1960, Bendick made another serious programming error as a result of his close relationship with David Garroway.

During the 1950s, quiz shows and giveaway programs were immensely popular. To attract even more viewers, television producers capitalized on the quiz show popularity by increasing the prize money and creating dramatic tension between the contestants. "There was only one catch: the contests were rigged. Contestants often knew in advance what to expect, they won or lost in accordance with carefully laid plans to maximize suspense, producers coached them how to act out agonized brain-racking for the best effect."[15] The scandals affected the integrity and credibility of the entire television industry. Although *Today* had no connection with the quiz shows, it became involved through Charles Van Doren, favored opponent of Herbert Stempel on the quiz show *Twenty One*. Week after

Jack Lescoulie, Charles Van Doren, Betsy Palmer, Frank Blair, and David Garroway.

week, America watched as they battled for the prize money. Van Doren won both the admiration of the American public and $129,000. Capitalizing on his popularity, *Today* hired him to do daily segments on intellectual and cultural topics. Although there was speculation that the quiz shows had been fixed, as yet there had been no investigations or public accusations. *Today* had no reason to suspect Van Doren of misconduct. Then, in the summer of 1958, Stempel divulged that *Twenty One* had been fixed.[16] Van Doren, substituting for vacationing host David Garroway, took the opportunity to use *The Today Show* as a forum to publicly proclaim his innocence. Over the next few months, Van Doren received thousands of letters of viewer support. Then a special House of Representatives committee began an investigation. In the meantime, Garroway decided to make a public show of support of Van Doren by doing a teary-eyed defense of him during one afternoon taping of *The Today Show*. But before it aired the next morning, Van Doren startlingly confessed that the allegations were all true. Until the moment of his confession, Garroway and producer Robert Bendick had no way of knowing that Van Doren was guilty of the charges. The confession had been untimely, but for whatever reason (Bendick did not explain), they decided to air the tape the next morning as it was, unedited. *Today*, by defending and supporting Van Doren, received heavy criticism for allegedly deceiving the public. However, *The Today Show*'s reputation was not permanently damaged. Van Doren was immediately dismissed from the show, and *Today* turned its efforts to reestablishing its credibility.

In the last year that Garroway hosted *Today*, there were quick changes in producers. In August 1960, Bendick was fired and replaced by Robert (Shad) Northshield, who held the position for only six months. During that short time, Garroway asked him to produce a one-hour evening special called *Dave's Place*. There were many conflicts between Garroway and Northshield over the evening production. It was "all about Rockefeller Center and not a particularly good show."[17]

Norman Kahn was selected as acting producer but was soon replaced by Fred Freed, who became the regular producer in March 1961. Freed held the distinction of being *Today*'s shortest-reigning producer.[18] However, under the direction of David Garroway, he made his presence felt by firing most of the *Today* production staff. During that same period, Garroway was nearing a mental breakdown, and the condition had intensified after the recent suicide of his wife, Pamela. As a result and under pressure from NBC executives, Garroway resigned as host of the show.

Then in that same year, in a move that significantly changed the focus of *Today* from entertainment to news, *Today* was placed under the control of the NBC News Department, a long-overdue move that neatly solved the problem of cooperation between *Today* and NBC News.[19] It was the News Department that searched for Garroway's replacement, and it was only natural that they found someone with a strong news background. The new host, John Chancellor, chose his own producer, rehiring Shad Northshield, who had been the *Today* producer only six months earlier. In the year that John Chancellor was host of the program, the *Today* panel was revised, disastrously affecting the programming and resulting in a drop in audience viewing and a loss of advertisers.[20] Frank Blair was moved to light features and replaced with Edwin Newman as the newsreader. Jack Lescoulie was retired from the program. Unfortunately, the new uncharismatic combination of personalities launched *Today* into one of its lowest rating periods. To compensate for that lack and to add a bit of lightness and humor to the program, the panel was persuaded to do comedy skits. The result was so ludicrous that it drove viewers away by the thousands. To compound matters, sales began to drop drastically. And because Chancellor came out of the News Department at NBC, he was not forced to do commercials, which had disastrous financial consequences. Producer Northshield, dismayed by the escalating series of financial problems, said, "We began to lose sponsors like nothing you ever saw." Less than a year after the new cast took over, he said, "We were certainly not making any money."[21]

But better days were ahead, and when *Today* celebrated its tenth anniversary on air, it included an interesting segment on the many contributions of the various producers of *Today*:

> *Producers segment*—seated at a roundtable were Chancellor with the eight men who at different times through these ten years produced *Today*: Abe Schechter now heading his own public relations firm of A.A. Schechter Associates; and *Today*'s first producer. . . and following in order . . . Richard Pinkham, new Senior V.P. of Ted Bates Advertising Agency; Mort Werner, V.P. Programs, NBC-TV Network; Robert Bendick, now a producer-director of NBC News TV producer & screenwriter . . . Jack Hein, Pres. of Cine-Dyne, a motion picture and television production company . . . Fred Freed, NBC producer . . . and Robert Northshield, *Today*'s current producer. Each gave his opinion as to what he thinks kept this show on the air for ten years; then each told of most difficult decision he had to make while producer of show; and finally, as to what purpose could and should be served by such a TV show as this one.[22]

Northshield tried several format changes with no success, and when viewers turned to other programming in the morning, NBC was forced to take drastic action. It hired a new host and a new producer.

AL MORGAN, 1961–1968

The new producer was Al Morgan, who arrived before new host Hugh Downs. Al Morgan produced *Today* during what were considered to be the "golden years" of the show. He was an exceptionally talented producer who exercised authority, demonstrated strong leadership, and developed innovative programming. Unfortunately, he did not get along well with host Downs. NBC executives had made it clear that *The Today Show* was not to be dominated by the host as it had been by David Garroway. Consequently, Morgan exercised whatever power he had to keep Downs from wresting control of the program, causing the two to assume an adversarial relationship. When Morgan first came to *Today*, "viewers had been abandoning ship, with the advertisers following them into the life rafts."[23] It was Morgan's job to rebuild the show, a task made easier by choosing the right host. Downs, familiar to viewers because of his association with talk show personality Jack Paar, had essentially the same likable, low-key qualities as Garroway. He was also clever enough to handle the intellectual side of the show with ease, although many claimed that he relied heavily on the writers and rarely prepared for an interview. In addition, he was popular with housewives because he hosted NBC's game show *Concentration*. Producer Morgan correctly surmised that the most important aspect of Downs was that he was well received by viewers. Downs also provided stability for the program by hosting *Today* for nine years. It is to Morgan's credit that he was able to meet the demands of the host (which were considerable) and still retain control of the program.

Morgan initiated many successful production practices. He was responsible for making *Today* truly a "window to the world" by having the show travel frequently to remote locations. New technological developments made it possible to do the show remotely and Morgan took advantage of the opportunity. He also moved the *Today* studio back to the street. Today had originated in 1952 from the RCA Exhibition Hall, which allowed passersby to view the actual production. It had been moved into NBC studios in 1958 and remained inside until 1962. It was Morgan's idea that the show should capture the excitement of the New York street scene, so he moved *Today* into the Florida Showcase area, which had windows overlooking Rockefeller Center. But three years later, in 1965, Morgan was forced to move back to NBC studios when NBC decided to broadcast in color.[24] NBC could not afford to have four expensive color cameras out of the main studios where they were unavailable for other NBC programs.

In addition to many other excellent decisions made as producer of *Today*, it was Al Morgan who decided to launch the career of Barbara Walters. Early in 1964, "*Today* girl" regular Maureen O'Sullivan was fired. She could not cope with the early morning hours or the pressures of the live camera. Nor was she comfortable with interviewing. But most important, she and Hugh Downs were constantly feuding. Although Downs had not wanted O'Sullivan to replace Pat Fontaine when she left the show, producer Morgan had been adamant that O'Sullivan would fill the position. Consequently, she and Downs made little effort to work successfully together. With O'Sullivan's frequent absences from the show, *Today* writer Barbara Walters often substituted as hostess. David Garroway had originally hired Walters as a *Today* writer in 1961. She handled her job well and was soon given occasional on-air reporting assignments. Walters filled in frequently and competently enough to be hired on a thirteen-week provisional basis when O'Sullivan left the show. "Morgan was tired of the glamorous light-weights who had occupied the hostess chair for twelve long years, and he considered that Barbara had paid her dues."[25]

When Barbara Walters became a regular on the show, her title was changed to the more dignified *"Today* reporter." As a writer, she had been given occasional on-air reporting assignments, but "her big break came in a most tragic manner when, on November 22, 1963, President John Kennedy was assassinated in Dallas. It was certainly the biggest story of the decade and one of the biggest of the twentieth century. Barbara was sent to Washington to cover the funeral."[26] She did an excellent job and was given high praise by the viewers, other journalists, and the *Today* staff. Eventually, under the approval of Al Morgan, she became more aggressive in her role and began to assume some of the serious interviewing responsibilities that were gladly relinquished by Hugh Downs. In defense of Walters and in criticism of Downs, Morgan said that Walters filled "the vacuum created by Hugh Downs who was the laziest man in television. Barbara sat there morning after morning," he recalled, "while interviews went down the drain. One day she finally stepped in and did his job."[27]

Undoubtedly, Al Morgan's biggest flaw as a producer was his inability to get along with Hugh Downs. Morgan was outspoken in his scorn for Downs, referring to him as "the idiot."[28] The running feud between Downs and Morgan came to a head in 1965 when, as a condition to signing a new three-year contract, Downs insisted that Morgan be fired. Morgan, however, had just recently signed his own three-year contract with NBC:

> Al Morgan had reveled in the power of the job, though he did become bored with it in the last two years of his six-year command. He regards the position as the "last monarchy," conferring the power of a great newspaper publisher, a power to shape events as well as chronicle them. Morgan says that producing the show was, in a paraphrase of Orson Welles, "like owning the biggest and most expensive set of electric trains in the world."[29]

Therefore, to appease Hugh Downs, NBC met the exorbitant monetary demands in his new contract, and Downs accepted. But the next three years were worse than the first three as far as the Morgan–Downs relationship was concerned:

> Morgan was confident that he would outlast Downs in their fight to the finish. Like some other producers in network television, Morgan sometimes felt like a ventriloquist. He believes it is the producer's talent that makes a show succeed, not the on-camera personality, despite his superior pay. If Morgan provided quality grist for Downs, the star looked good. A strong star would do better, but even a weak star could survive if he got strong backing from the production staff. Some say that Morgan was guilty of a classic blunder in failing to recognize the enormous power of the on-camera personality. You just didn't win against a star.[30]

Three years later, in 1968, the star won. Al Morgan was fired as producer of *Today*. However, NBC had renewed his contract with the network and was obligated to retain his services in some capacity. Later, Morgan and NBC agreed on a contract settlement that released him from the network. Prior to becoming the producer of *Today*, Morgan had been a writer for several radio programs, including *The Thin Man* and *The Lone Ranger*. He wrote a Broadway musical and then worked for CBS for ten years before joining NBC to help produce *The Home Show*. He has also written a novel, *The Great Man*, about a broadcast personality. Morgan produced *The Today Show* for six successful years, and many of his innovations and practices were carried on by subsequent *Today* producers. *Today* movie critic Judith Crist reflected on his singular accomplishment: "Al Morgan invented the *Today* show. Instead of featuring so many beauty contest winners, *Today* concentrated more on the great events of the year—civil rights demonstrations, the radicalization of American society by the war in Vietnam, the assassinations of the Kennedy brothers and Martin Luther King, Jr."[31]

STUART SCHULBERG, 1968–1976

In a year that saw so many staggeringly significant news events, there was one personnel change that was destined to impact the future of *Today*. On November 1, 1968, Stuart Schulberg was named as *Today*'s new producer, taking over the reins from visionary Al Morgan, who produced the show from 1962 to 1968. Although Schulberg joined the show after host Hugh Downs had been entrenched in power for the last six years, he had no difficulty in assuming control over the program. He once described himself as a "benevolent dictator" who made "all the final programming decisions for *Today*." Schulberg was a man used to power, and he was able to wield it successfully on the *Today* program:

> Power means sitting down with his "books coordinator" once a month to pick the fifteen authors (more or less) who will get the priceless *Today* interview treatment over the next four weeks. It means saying no to twenty-four out of twenty-five politicians who propose themselves for interviews. Power also means constantly weighing a variety of considerations in order to produce something known as "good television.". . . Schulberg's special problems, and his special power, grow out of the daily process of programming interview and feature segments. They are at the heart of the show, and because of their impact, the principles behind their selection are of substantial public import.[32]

Many of the successful production procedures implemented by *The To-day Show* were developed by Stuart Schulberg. In July 1971, in recognition of all his many contributions, Schulberg was made executive producer, a title that had not been used since 1955, and Douglas Sinsel took over as producer.[33] Among the more significant and representative contributions made by Schulberg were those that involved the writing of the show, producing the news segments, selecting book/author-related interviews, and producing the entertainment segments.

PRODUCING *TODAY*

Producing *The Today Show*, a daily two-hour live production, was an enormous task that in 1976 required a staff of nearly one hundred people. That figure included only those involved in some capacity with the production aspects of the program. It did not include secretarial or managerial staff or personnel from other NBC departments, such as sales, ratings, research, and affiliate relations, whose services were also vital to the program. At various times throughout its history, *Today* had either a producer or an executive producer (or both) who had the overall responsibility for producing the program and supervising the production staff. It was impossible to personally arrange and coordinate all aspects of the program. Therefore, the producers were forced to delegate the responsibility of producing the various segments of the program to assistant producers and feature coordinators.

News Segments

Producing the news and news-feature segments on *Today* became the most important production element of the program, particularly when *Today* began to be produced under NBC News. Although hard-news segments had always been a regular part of the *Today* format, in the early years of *Today*, internal friction between programming and news caused a serious lack of cooperation between the two areas. NBC News was reluctant to share its sources, film footage, and news copy with *The Today Show*. *Today*'s first news editor, Gerald Green, described the acrimonious early days: "We couldn't get the NBC films. . . . There were always convenient ways of keeping exciting news footage off the *Today* Show. Often they would be 'reserved' for John Cameron Swayze and the *Camel News Caravan*—at 7:45pm."[34] Despite those real obstacles, Green initiated a news routine that enabled *The Today Show* to compete with the very convenient early morning radio by dividing the news into A and B segments. The A segment was aired at the top of the hour and consisted of lead stories based on their importance. The B segments were aired on the half hour and briefly outlined the lead stories of the day followed by less significant news items.

Despite the importance, only a few men served as news editors in charge of the news segments in the early days, including Dick Graf (1962–1966), Leonard Leddington (1966–1972), Jack Smith (1972–1974), and Tom Furey (1974–1977). In 1972, an actual news "producer" position was finally created and was filled by Gene Farinet, who served from 1972 to 1976.[35] Originally an NBC news writer and editor, Farinet had been with NBC for sixteen years when he joined *Today*. It was Stuart Schulberg, however, who reorganized the news-gathering operation. Because the *NBC Nightly News* and the *Today* units were still competing for the best coverage of the same stories, Schulberg devised "NBC News Gathering" in response to the increasing cost resulting from a duplication of effort. Lee Hanna, vice president for NBC News, became the supervisor of NBC News Gathering, which centralized the staff and funding for news events. NBC News Gathering directed the news information either to *Today* or to *NBC Nightly News*, depending on which was the next scheduled telecast.

Schulberg and Farinet also created "mini-unit" news teams to cover news events with a limited budget. "Farinet took one or two writers, a production assistant and a crew to cover such events as a presidential trip or a political convention." Major or continuing events that required extended coverage were budgeted through NBC News Gathering.[36]

In addition to the regular network news source, Schulberg received news pieces from the *Today* news bureaus in Chicago, Los Angeles, Cleveland, Atlanta, and Houston. In March 1975 the Washington Bureau was given a more significant role in providing national and political news to the nation. Schulberg explained his decision to expand the Washington, D.C., staff and to add full-time producer Ron Steinman to the bureau:

"A full-time producer in Washington fills a long standing need for *Today*," Schulberg said, "not only in beefing up our daily news coverage from there, but in improving our almost-daily features visually and technically." Most important, he noted, the program's new minicam capability in Washington gives the program "the chance to break out of the studio for live remote interviews, stories and general coverage which will finally take advantage of an enormous range of material in and around the capital—material which has been ignored far too long. With an expanded staff, Steinman will give us the kind of across-the-board Washington coverage which goes beyond politics and into social, cultural and sports stories which promise to add up to an important new contribution to *Today*."[37]

The *Today* Washington studio also produced regular reports and interview segments each week. The number of reports depended on how important the events were or the volume of the news in Washington.[38] Bill Monroe became the Washington editor and host of "Washington Report." He was responsible for scheduling three or four interviews per week with Washington individuals who were associated with a particular event.[39]

Frequently, an entire scheduled program would be dropped to cover a major news event. Even though the *Today* production was complex, because it was always "live," producing the show could become routine. But often it was necessary to have an expert, skilled production staff for those times when a major news event or crisis occurred. That meant that *Today* had to be ready to go on remote with an instant's notice, requiring the crew to work extra hours under the pressure of a limited amount of time. Never was that commitment more important to *Today* than under executive producer Stuart Schulberg, who often said, "We are truly 'today,' and not 'yesterday' or 'the day before that.'" The strain caused by special event programming was vividly illustrated during the week of January 22–26, 1973:

> The dedication of the *Today* staff to the Schulberg philosophy of timeliness never was more exemplified than during last week when the program originated in Washington. Guests for the entire post-inaugural week in the capital had been scheduled, and staff members felt they could relax temporarily, when two major news events within a 24-hour period, the death of former President Lyndon B. Johnson and President Nixon's announcement of the cease-fire in Vietnam, virtually erased the week's programming.[40]

The *Today* staff was staying at the Sheraton Park Hotel in Washington because of the weeklong origination from the capital when they received word of President Johnson's death in the early evening of Monday, January 22, 1973. Molly Sharpe, Washington writer and assistant to Washington editor Bill Monroe, contacted colleagues of the late president. The *Today* unit managers arranged for lines to receive remote pickups from Bill Moyers, President Johnson's former press secretary, and from Ray Scherer, former NBC White House correspondent during Johnson's administration. Producer Douglas Sinsel and news producer Gene Farinet edited videotape until 3:00 a.m. for broadcast later that morning. By the time *Today* went on the air Tuesday morning, a distinguished group of guests had gathered in the NBC Washington studio, WRC:

> Present for interviews by *Today*'s Frank McGee and Barbara Walters during the 7 to 9 a.m. colorcast were former Ambassador Averell Harriman; former Supreme Court Justice Abe Fortas; Senator Hubert Humphrey; Jack Valenti, a Johnson aide and longtime friend, now head of the Motion Picture Association; Mrs. Elizabeth Carpenter, who was Mrs. Johnson's press

secretary; Representative Andrew Young (D-Ga.), onetime aide to the Reverend Martin Luther King; and William "Fishbait" Miller, doorkeeper of the House of Representatives, who knew President Johnson before he was elected to Congress.[41]

That was how just one of the incidents of that week was handled. There was also the monumental cease-fire in Vietnam to be adequately covered. For this event, arrangements had to be made for satellite feeds from Saigon and Paris. "'We've never had a week like this,' declared Schulberg as he and the sleepless, exhausted staff added a third hour to the Thursday, January 25 program, to encompass coverage of the Johnson funeral, and reshuffled the schedule for the final day in Washington, Friday, January 26th."[42]

Although news is the most important programming element of the show, it is also an important part of the *Today* format to have regular features and segments. Feature segments were assigned to various coordinators, but all major decisions concerning *Today* were made by executive producer Schulberg. The goal of the show was to achieve a balance of news, information, and entertainment in its programming. No matter what the subject, it was tested by the criteria that it must be current and of national interest.

Book / Author Interview Segments

One regularly recurring feature on *Today* was the book-related interview. Since at that time there were approximately three thousand books published each month, individuals or publishers who were looking for a spot to promote their books inundated the show. To keep track of new and interesting books, *The Today Show* book coordinator, Betsy Osha, reported to Stuart Schulberg and contacted the major publishing houses for books that would be appropriate for the program. She then met with Schulberg to select books to fill three or four interview slots per week. Because there were more good books than there were time slots available on *Today*, the final selections were carefully considered. Generally, *The Today Show* preferred nonfiction material that supplied new or important information to the audience. "Novels are rarely selected unless the author has something to say beyond his plot and prose style to talk about. Peter Benchley (*Jaws*) was ideal. 'He had three things going for him,' Osha explains, 'sharks, three generations of writers in his family, and his phenomenal sales story.'"[43] Schulberg also considered the appeal of the book to a mass audience. "A book on the cell by a leading cancer researcher is rejected as 'too complicated,' and a journalistic novel about the black recording industry is dismissed as 'too specialized for our audience.'"[44] Books that were well received on *Today* were those that sparked debate or were controversial, such as *All the President's Men* by Carl Bernstein and Bob Woodward. *Today* was particularly interested in presenting a public forum for the issues involved and maintained "its own house experts who were paid to lead panels in their fields or to represent a special point of view." These experts included Lewis Young of *Business Week*; Brian O'Doherty, the art critic; Roger Caras, the naturalist; and George Will of *National Review*.[45] Osha sent a memorandum to each of the publishers outlining the program philosophy in regard to the suitability of potential book reviews and authors:

> More than any other quality a publicity person should have—for us—is honesty, good taste and programming sense. Please know the program before you send us your ideas. By doing so you will realize that certain ideas just won't go. It is a news oriented program. When you offer suggestions, remember we need visual ideas—and we need variety of presentation. The book doesn't have to be political in nature—good new books having general human interest are always good. Remember the program is aired from 7:00–9:00 AM every morning and most of the audience is made up of middle-America. In an average minute over 5 million people watch the *Today* program. They are mostly college-educated, professional and managerial types who make upper level incomes. The largest percent of the audience is women. In Washington, the audience of Senators and Congressmen has doubled over the last four years. Books are used on the program as a source of information. They are used in lieu of reporters. Authors are talking to their strengths. We are using their research. In a sense they become consulting experts to the program.[46]

Ultimately, the final selection was made by Schulberg, who programmed three or four reviews into the show each week and then selected the panel member who would host the segment. It was generally agreed by publishers that *The Today Show* was tremendously beneficial to book sales:

> "*Today* is probably the single most important show for an author to do," says Richard Barber, director of publicity at Viking Press. He points to the size and literacy of the audience, the news format, and particularly the "way they treat the writer" as the basic causes behind the impact of a *Today* appearance. "An author gets a short but courteous moment of his own on *Today*. He doesn't have to compete with Don Rickles or James Coco."[47]

After a book was selected, the information was turned over to a *Today* writer. The writer's responsibility was to contact the author, procure copies of the book for the *Today* panel, make all the arrangements for the appearance, and, finally, write the segment.

Entertainment Segments

In the early 1970s, *Today* frequently offered entertainment features. Those segments were tightly controlled and selected by the talent coordinator, who would work within a small entertainment budget of approximately $1,500 per segment. NBC was reluctant to increase the entertainment budget because the program was produced under the News Department, and it was NBC's opinion that *Today*'s primary emphasis should remain on news and information. Since performers were paid union scale, it was necessary for the executive producer to monitor carefully the final entertainment selections. After the performers were selected, the information was turned over to a *Today* writer who gathered appropriate material and wrote whatever was necessary for the segment.

After Stuart Schulberg eliminated the Judith Crist drama reviews from *Today*, he decided to add more dramatic segments. Because of the expense, they did not usually bring on large casts or do more than one entertainment segment per week. Most of the entertainment segments selected by Schulberg consisted of either theatrical or musical pieces. "Herbert Breslin, a prominent publicity agent for classical musicians, complains: 'They use music for relief. They're not really interested in music. I wish that they would try to make music controversial.'"[48]

Writing *The Today Show*

Writing is and was an important element of the *Today* production. In the early years of *Today*, aspiring writers began working for the program in lesser staff positions, such as "gofer," or in a production assistant capacity. Eventually, if they wanted to write, many were given the opportunity. One such person, Alan Smith, worked his way up from production assistant to writer and then became the managing editor of *Today*. Barbara Walters is another example. Although she began her career as a *Today* writer, she progressed to reporter and then to regular panel member and finally became cohost of the program.

Writers were extremely important to the early *Today Show*. They wrote all the introductory and continuity material for the show, but the extent of their writing was somewhat determined by the host or panel member for whom they were writing. Some preferred that everything be scripted, as in the case of Hugh Downs; others, such as Tom Brokaw, preferred to work with an outline that could be adapted to an extemporaneous style that appeared to be ad-libbed.[49]

There have been many approaches to the writing on *Today*. The responsibilities of the writers have been as diverse as the writers themselves.

Originally, writers were assigned to write specific segments or features rather than all the material for an entire program. Shortly after Al Morgan became producer of *Today*, he initiated a new approach to writing by meeting with the writers and assigning each one to write a specific program, which included everything from opening credits to closing remarks. The writer would also contact the guests, read the book if there was a book interview, write interview questions, and prepare all feature material. This approach, which in a sense made producers out of the writers, was successful in creating a cohesive program. It also helped to give the program a better balance because of the long-range planning. Writers were given sole credit for the entire two-hour program rather than shared credit. This "producer-writer" practice continued under Stuart Schulberg but was changed in 1976. According to then-producer Doug Sinsel, writers were assigned features or other material according to their strength or interest in a particular area. For example, one writer would write only political features, another fashion, another cultural segments, and still another special material for the host. Usually, the writing responsibilities were determined by the producer in conjunction with the needs of the panelists. Under this approach, a number of different writers would contribute to the two-hour production.

Occasionally, a show needed to be rewritten because of a late-breaking news event. This required all writers to be on twenty-four-hour call to come in and alter the script if necessary. Each day, the final script was delivered to the NBC Broadcast Standards Department, where the script was checked for objectivity. Copies of the script were given to the producers and delivered to the homes of the talent during the evening prior to the morning telecast. It was the responsibility of the writers to meet with the *Today* unit managers, producer, and director to discuss the production aspects of the program. This would have included securing props and other visual materials such as graphics, film, and videotape; the precise timing of the program; and the blocking of possible camera shots. In addition, the writer had to clear the program budget with the unit manager "who arranges for all equipment rentals, fees for talent, and other costs of operation."[50]

Unit Managers

In the mid-1970s, to keep *Today* within the assigned budget of approximately $6 million per year, unit managers controlled and approved expenses. The unit managers themselves were rotated to other units by NBC every two years. This practice helped to avoid attachments to any particular unit and helped the managers to keep their objectivity in evaluating the production against the budget. Even so, the producers of the show felt confined by the small budget, particularly since *The Today Show* had been extremely profitable under Al Morgan and Stuart Schulberg. Justifying this small budget, former NBC president Julian Goodman said that "the success of highly profitable shows like *Today* allows the network to cover special news events like the presidential press conferences and news stories which are very expensive both in terms of production costs and preemption of prime time and local programming, and which bring in little or no revenue."[51]

PAUL FRIEDMAN, 1976

In 1976, Paul Friedman became the new *Today* executive producer, and Douglas Sinsel became the producer. When Stuart Schulberg stepped down, he commented on his feelings about leaving: "Eight years of sunrise to sunset, Monday through Friday, with weekend emergencies thrown in just to maintain the adrenalin count—that's enough for any mortal producer."[52] Schulberg was transferred to the NBC News Documentary Division. Richard Wald, the president of NBC News who initiated the producer change, said that Schulberg, who "is an old hand at producing news specials ('The New Voices of Watts,' 'The Angry Voice of Watts: An NBC News Inquiry'), will be right at home in the documentary division."[53] Schulberg died just three short years later in 1979, still producing special programs for NBC.

Paul Friedman's appointment to executive producer was an excellent example of the "in-house" promotion policy at NBC. He began as a news writer for NBC's Washington station, WRC-TV, in 1967. From there, he was promoted to field producer of *NBC Nightly News*, then to executive producer of *NewsCenter 4* at NBC's owned and operated New York station, WNBC-TV, after which he joined *NBC Nightly News* as the producer.

When Friedman was hired to produce *Today*, the ratings had been steadily declining. This was in part because Barbara Walters had left the show and because of the growing competition from ABC's *Good Morning America*. NBC hoped that Friedman would be able to restructure the show and attract a larger audience. Among the immediate programming decisions Friedman made were to reduce the number of book-related interviews, shorten the segments, and add consumer information and health features. It was not possible at that early date to determine the overall effect of the programming changes, but the ratings slide leveled off, and the ratings were steadily rising by December 1976. Friedman recognized the need to proceed cautiously, as he said in an interview shortly after assuming the position of executive producer: "It's scary to tamper with an American institution."[54]

THE PRODUCTION OF *THE TODAY SHOW*

The actual production of *Today* was a very complex operation and one that continually evolved over those first twenty-five years. *The Today Show* producers found it was possible to change personnel, the method of presentation, and the content of the information whenever necessary and still retain the original concept and framework of the show developed by Sylvester Weaver in 1952. The production itself encompassed everything that was necessary to put the program on the air, including writers, producers, directors, crew, talent, and staff. In 1952, *Today* was live for three hours from 7:00 to 10:00 a.m. The technical format, which called for a "communications center," was extremely complex. At a time when the technological development of television was still in its infancy, *The Today Show* required a fully developed and operational system. Added to this demand was the immediate pressure of being "live." In many instances, the *Today* crew and technicians were pioneering the production techniques used on the program. Years of experience developed the production into a smooth routine.

The development of technology that resulted in better equipment helped to keep *The Today Show* current over the years. Better cameras, improved long-distance transmission, more sensitive microphones, videotape, the miniaturization and portability of equipment, the development of color, jet transportation, and satellite communication are just a few examples of the technology that directly affected the *Today* production and format.

Because of the mutable nature of production, it is difficult to identify a typical production that would fully represent all 6,500 mornings that *The Today Show* had been on the air by 1976. But there are some generalizations that can be made from a description of the production techniques used when *Today* was under the control of executive producer Stuart Schulberg. During those years, he employed a highly successful and much-imitated production routine.

Typical Production Routine, June 30, 1977

Today was produced in NBC's New York City studio 3K at the RCA Building in Rockefeller Center, where the crew reported for work at 1:00 a.m. Director Marvin Einhorn or Jim Gaines would first check the NBC newsroom to obtain updated scripts and the studio production routine sheets that were prepared by the *Today* overnight staff. In the meantime, the crews gathered to block and light the set. The studio and many of the *Today* set pieces were the same ones used by *NBC Nightly News* each evening. The *Nightly News* set would be struck and the *Today* set assembled. The regular set and the talent were placed in the same positions for each program, but each night, interview sets, commercial sets, and entertainment areas needed to be lighted and blocked for camera shots according to the needs of the show in the morning.

Most of the production involved readying the "software," such as videotape, film, slides, theme, scripts, and teleprompter material. Both the news film and the film used in feature segments had to be checked, cued, timed, and readied for air. A rear-screen projection unit provided visuals for the *Today* logo, news, commercials, and chroma-keyed information. The scripted material was typed and readied for the teleprompter devices. Although the content of *Today* was fully scripted, each of the panel members adapted his or her performance to a combination of ad-lib comments and straight teleprompter reading. Panel members were encouraged to exchange remarks with each other, particularly during introductions and segues to other segments.

The producer usually arrived by 6:00 a.m. to make any last-minute changes in the show. If there was important or late-breaking news that morning, the producer could cut back on the other portions of the show in order to give the news segment more time. If an interview or another segment was important, the producer could adjust the news time, deleting lesser stories to give extra time elsewhere in the program. All last-minute changes were cleared with the director and talent. If the Washington studios were being used, a phone line was put on hold to ensure communication between the New York studios and Washington studios until the segment was finished.

The *Today* host, other members of the panel, and the newscaster would arrive by about 5:30 a.m. From 1952 to 1976, when the panel members were responsible for the commercial segments on the show, they would arrive earlier to rehearse the commercials with the crew and director. The talent reported to makeup, familiarized themselves with any last-minute changes in the script, and met their guests in the green room.

Minutes before airtime, the crew, director, and talent would take their places. Microphones were placed on the panel members and newscaster by the sound technicians. The stage manager announced the time to air, supervised the crew movements, and ushered guests and panel members to their proper positions on the set at various times during the show. He would count down the seconds to air with his fingers, and the *Today* logo was faded in by the director. At the exact moment indicated by the director, he would cue the host by firmly pointing to the camera lens. The host would then say, "Good morning, this is *Today* on NBC," the same words that had welcomed viewers for the first twenty-five years. During the show, the director watched fourteen monitors, twelve of which were for the program. The other two were tuned to the competition: ABC and CBS.

Off-camera activity continued during the show. While one person was live on camera or during the commercial breaks, the other panel members relaxed, read the newspaper, walked off set for a cup of coffee, or smoked cigarettes. The producer would often go into the studio to reassure the talent and crew that all was going well or to make a last-minute adjustment. The studio lights were brought up in the one area of the studio that was live and were dimmed in all other areas. This served as a visual cue to the talent to quickly take their places and also saved money for NBC by not having the entire studio lighted for two hours. The crew worked from both a "live routine sheet," a detailed account of the exact segments and timing of the show, and a "studio worksheet," a short outline form of the live routine sheet. In table 3.1, the live routine sheet from the first hour of *Today*'s June 30, 1977, broadcast illustrates the varied production segments and precise timing for the show.[55]

To analyze the live routine sheet, some general observations about the sheet and structure of the program are necessary. The routine sheet broke down the program into various numbered segments. The running clock time was listed under the segment number, which indicated when the segment was expected to begin. The time in parentheses indicated the anticipated duration of each segment. The "Audio" column listed all sound sources, an abbreviated description of the segment, and any other pertinent information, such as guest names or set area. The "Video" column listed all video sources and, when necessary, further broke down the segment time.

The production routine breakdown revealed the precision and complexity of the timing involved in a two-hour live production. The running clock time under "Segment" was an approximate time, as was the segment time indicated in parentheses. Live production made it difficult to begin and end each segment precisely on time. Therefore, the local stations had to watch and listen for the video and audio break cues, which occurred as close to the listed times as possible. The only times that are exact are the times indicated for the duration of the commercial breaks, co-op time, and station breaks. Although NBC could cue the breaks late or early, the duration of the break would run exactly for the length of time indicated in parentheses. For example, segment 3 was the first local commercial break. Assuming that segment 2 ran a few seconds late, NBC would not cue the break until a few seconds after the indicated time of 7:06:00. However, the break time itself would run exactly two minutes and ten seconds from whenever the cue was given. The local station was

Table 3.1. *Today* **Live Routine Sheet, June 30, 1977**

Segment	Audio	Video
1)		
7:00:00	ANNOUNCE SCRIPTED	VC: TODAY OPENING #5
(2:00)		
	WITH VC OPENING	MINI: BATTERY PARK
		CHR: DAY/HEADS
		CHR: TODAY/NEW YORK
	WTH WASH TEASE	WASH INSERT VIDEO ONLY
2)		
7:02:00	KALBER: A NEWS	
(4:00)	THIS IS TODAY ON NBC	NET CUE
3)		
7:06:00	LOCAL COMMERCIAL #1	NET CUE
	ELOISE	SLIDE: COLOR LOGO :10
	CHUCK RAINEY	TEMP CRAWL 1:50
	CART 33 BAND 1	SLIDE: COLOR LOGO :10
4)		
7:08:10	KALBER: A NEWS CONT.	
(4:00)		
5)		
7:12:10	WOOD: WEATHER	
(:45)		
6)		
7:12:55	TEASE	
(:10)	THIS IS TODAY ON NBC	NET CUE
7)		
7:13:05	LOCAL COMMERCIAL #2	MINI/LOGO :10
	HOW LONG WILL IT LAST	TEMP CRAWL 1:50
(2:10)	CHUCK RAINEY	MINI/LOGO :10
	CART 133 BAND 2	
8)		
7:15:15	AUDIO CART STING (3)	MINI/3K LOGO
(9:00)	BROKAW INTROS, INTVUS	
	PAUL ALTMEYER RE:	
	NBC SPECIAL "PASSPORT	
	TO THE UNIVERSE"	GRAPHICS: 5 VIZMOS
	SET: DESK	CHR: ALTMEYER
	BROKAW INTROS WASH:	WASH INSERT WITH TWO
	REP. DANTE FASCELL	WAY AUDIO
	& BARBARA WATSON,	CHR: FASCELL
	STATE DEPT.	CHR: WATSON
9)		
7:24:15	STATION BREAK	MINI/LOGO
(:45)		BLACK
10)		
7:25:00	CO OP: CAST PAD	
(4:15)		

Segment	Audio	Video
11) 7:29:16 (:45)	STATION BREAK	MINI/LOGO BLACK
12) 7:30:00 (1:00)	AUDIO CART STING (6) ANNOUNCE SCRIPTED	MINI/LOGO
13) 7:31:00 (3:00)	KALBER: B NEWS	NET CUE
14) 7:34:00 (1:30)	KALBER LEADS COCA COLA/WISHBONE	MINI/LOGO VC: COCA COLA #KOMT7309 :30VC VC: WISHBONE #TLID7203 :30VC
15) 7:35:30 (1:45)	KALBER INTROS WOOD: WEATHER NOTE CUT	 NET CUE
16) 7:37:15 (1:30)	WOOD LEADS DENTU CRÈME/POLIDENT (SCRIPTED LEAD)	MINI/LOGO VC: DENTU CRÈME #BDDC6033 :30 VC VC: POLIDENT #BDPT6063 :30 VC
17) 7:38:45 (2:15)	WOOD: SPORTS	
18) 7:41:00 (:10)	TEASE	MINI/LOGO BLACK
19) 7:41:10 (:45)	STATION BREAK	
20) 7:41:55 (7:15)	AUDIO CART STING (3) SHALIT DOES CRITICS CORNER RE: MOVIES VTR (FROM FILM): THE OTHER SIDE OF MIDNIGHT SET: CRITICS CORNER AUDIOTAPE: RUNAWAY	MINI/LOGO VTR RUNS 1:15 NET CUE

(continued)

Table 3.1.   (continued)

Segment	Audio	Video
21) 7:49:10 (1:30)	SHALIT LEADS KODAK/ ORE IDA	MINI/LOGO VC: KODAK #EKCP6873 :30 VC VC: ORE IDA #HZOT6033 :30 VC
22) 7:50:40	PAULEY INTROS VTR: NOW PAULEY TAG	GRAPHIC VIZMO VTR RUNS 4:30 SOT NY 77003B NET CUE
23) 7:55:40 (1:30)	PAULEY LEADS ORKIN/ FASTEETH	MINI/LOGO VC: ORKIN #ORKN 7033 :30 VC VC: FASTEETH 3RXFP0183 :30 VC
24) 7:57:10 (:30)	CLOSE. NOTE CUT	
25) 7:57:40	CART THEME	MINI INSERT CHR: TOMORROW BW SLIDE
26) 7:58:24	STATION BREAK	BLACK
27) 8:00:00 (2:00)	ANNOUNCE SCRIPTED WITH VC OPENING	VC: TODAY OPENING #5 MINI: BATTERY PARK CHR: DAY/HEADS CHR: TODAY/NEW YORK

expected to rejoin the network within the last ten seconds. Adjustments in time frequently occurred even though every effort was made to keep the clock time and segment time as close to planned as possible. Although this helped to keep the production running smoothly, audience research indicated that the timing on the program was so strict that the audience was keenly aware of the limited amount of time for each segment, particularly for interviews. Very often, an interview was abruptly ended in order to "break away." As a result, the research executives suggested that the talent try to close interviews as though they were naturally concluded and to avoid phrases such as "This has been a very interesting discussion but I must interrupt because we're out of time" or "We only have twenty seconds left, could you tell us . . ."[56] Those reminders of time seemed to frustrate the viewing audience.

A major contributing factor to that frustration was the number of interruptions caused by the commercial breaks, station breaks, and local co-op time. To somewhat alleviate the frequency of the breaks, *Today* grouped its commercial time into slots of approximately two minutes to avoid the more frequent interruptions that occurred when the breaks were only one minute in duration. Long breaks, however, tended to disrupt the continuity of a segment, so *Today* rarely continued with the same feature or segment after a break.

The amount of feature time was very limited during the first and third half hours because of the long "A news" at the top of each hour, the commercial breaks, and the co-op time that began at 7:24:15 and 8:24:15 a.m. Therefore, only about ten minutes were available for other programming during those half hours. In contrast, the second and fourth half hours of the program each had nearly fifteen minutes available for other programming.

The commercial breaks and timing were an integral part of the production and require still further explanation. The first and third half hours of the *Today* program were available to local stations to sell local advertising. The second and fourth half hours were sold by the NBC network. NBC broadcast the New York–area local commercials originating from its New York station, WNBC, during the local break time, while the NBC network continued to feed video (temperature crawl) and audio (background music) to all its stations. The crawl and theme were bookended by the *Today* logo. If the local stations did not sell the time slot or did not wish to use the time for local announcements, they were not required to break away during the local half hours. They could stay with the network feed rather than cut away. After two minutes and ten seconds, stations that did cut away rejoined the network.

Production Routine

As indicated on the production routine sheet, the program began with a standard opening on videocassette, a minicam scene, the morning headlines, and a scripted announcement. On that particular morning, there was a Washington "tease," which was a video insert of the Washington studios. Tom Brokaw outlined the segments and introduced himself and the members of the panel who would verbally highlight the segments in which they would be participating later in the program. Tom Brokaw then introduced Floyd Kalber, who read four minutes of the A news, after which he gave the network break cue: "This is *Today* on NBC." The cue was a verbal signal that warned the stations to insert their local commercials. The visual cue, a color slide of the *Today* logo, was broadcast and held for ten seconds. It acted as a bridge that allowed the local stations time to cleanly insert the local spots and then rejoin the network within the last ten seconds.

The program continued with Kalber finishing the A news and then introducing Lew Wood, who did the weather report. At approximately 7:12:55, NBC again provided exactly two minutes and ten seconds for local breaks. The video cue bridge for the second commercial break was the *Today* logo keyed over a minicam scene. The show continued after the break with Brokaw conducting an interview with Paul Altmeyer about an NBC special program, *Passport to the Universe.* The set was indicated as the desk area, and the supporting visuals consisted of five graphics without sound accompaniment. One camera was assigned to get the camera shots of Altmeyer.

No exact time was indicated on the routine sheet, but the nine minutes that were allowed for this segment were divided between the Altmeyer interview and the live interview insert from the Washington studio. In order for the two studios to communicate with each other, the NBC *Today* studio in New York and the NBC *Today* studio in Washington each had two-way audio and on-set monitors. That allowed either studio to participate in an interview that originated from the other studio.

The station break that followed the Washington segment allowed the local station to cut away to identify themselves as required by the Federal Communications Commission. The network break also provided a chunk of co-op time for local stations that was generally filled by local news and weather. However, the local stations could decide to stay with the network feed after their break for the local station identification. During the co-op time, the network continued to feed the *Today* show with nonessential programming, such as an extended interview or cast ad-lib conversation. The NBC network "bookended" the entire break period with ten seconds of the *Today* logo to allow stations to smoothly break and return to the network feed.

After the station break, *Today* began its "network" half hour, which meant that the commercial time was for network inserts only. All NBC stations were required to carry the network advertising spots during the times indicated, thereby providing local outlets for network advertising. Stations were not allowed to "cut away" or insert local material during that time. The second half hour would start with a brief theme ("sting") and the *Today* logo. Tom Brokaw would read a scripted announcement and then introduce Floyd Kalber, who read the B news. Just prior to the network commercial, Kalber would do a lead-in to the network sponsor that would simply act as a verbal cue for the network commercial insert. Commercials on videocassettes were carefully logged on the routine sheet along with the exact time.

After the first commercial slot, Kalber introduced Lew Wood, who delivered a longer version of the weather report. He was given a cut cue so that he could end the report on time and announce a scripted lead-in to the network commercials. On that particular program, the commercials were on videocassette, but often the commercials were announced and performed live by Wood or other announcers. After the commercial, Wood continued with the sports followed by a station break. All stations "break" to identify themselves and rejoin the program within forty-five seconds.

There were approximately eighteen minutes remaining in the second half hour after the station break. During the break, the crew would quickly set up for the next feature segment, Gene Shalit's "Critic's Corner." That morning, Shalit reviewed current films and showed videotaped excerpts from those films. The segment ran approximately seven minutes, and then Shalit introduced the network commercial for Kodak. After the commercial, Jane Pauley introduced a videotaped feature on the National Organization for Women (NOW). Then there was a short cast ad-lib time before the station break, which concluded the first hour of *Today*.

The second hour began nearly identically to the first hour and was similar in breakdown of news, weather, sports, commercial breaks, and co-op time. Major differences occurred only in terms of the feature content. The second hour of that particular program had only two major feature segments. One segment was Jane Pauley conducting an interview with three corporate women directors, and the other segment was Gene Shalit interviewing Gregory Peck about his latest film, *MacArthur*. The Peck interview segment was longer than the usual *Today* segments, lasting approximately thirteen minutes and thirty seconds. As indicated, it was the producer who decided which segments, if any, would be extended, and that would generally occur if the content were important or unusually interesting. In that case, the appearance of movie star Gregory Peck was attractive enough to warrant the extended time.

Immediately after the show, which ended precisely at 9:00 a.m., the videotaped first hour of *Today* was broadcast to the Midwest, and any segment or features that required pretaping for future programs were taped. If no further production was necessary that morning, the talent and production staff began work on future *Today* shows. By 9:00 a.m., the production crew has already put in a long day, and most of them would leave within a short time.

REMOTE BROADCASTING OF *TODAY*

A major commitment of the original programming concept was to cover significant news and cultural events from all over the world. This commitment placed a heavy burden on the *Today* production staff since remote telecasting required a great deal of skill and coordination. However, as technology developed and improved, it became physically easier to have *The Today Show* originate from a remote location. In the early years of the show, remote audio content was brought in by telephone line, and a facsimile machine transmitted the video feed. It was also possible at that time to use kinescope reports, but that involved a time delay to record and process the film. Later, videotape and jet transportation made remote reports more timely, but most remotes could not be carried live over long distances. It was satellite transmission that finally made it possible to transmit instantly from almost anywhere in the world. *Today* took advantage of the new satellite transmission capability by frequently broadcasting live remotes in the 1960s and 1970s.

By the 1970s, the development of the minicam allowed much greater flexibility and portability in live transmission from remote locations. Its use at that time was limited generally to the continental United States where program inserts were usually fed through regional facilities. Even though technology had improved and remote telecasts became more feasible, originating *The Today Show* from a remote location was indisputably a major effort. An example of a remote trip to Portugal in February 1968 explained the typical coordination and organization necessary for *Today* to originate from overseas:

> Prior to a remote, Morgan sends a reconnaissance troupe to the designated location in advance of his staff. In this case, the producer said, he and a basic group, including a unit manager, made a trip in December to Europe. "We spent 12 to 15 hours a day traveling within a radius of 150 miles of Lisbon scouting locations. Every site, on and off the tourist's list, was surveyed. After six days, we returned to New York with a basic format for five shows." Two months later, the full-scale invasion began. While most of the New York staff is used on the actual taping of the shows, cameramen and other members of the production crew, plus equipment are obtained from Intertel in England. This, of course, creates a logistics problem for the producer. The crew, which has been used on *Today* show remotes before, had to cross the English Channel, then drive down the coast across the Spanish border to Portugal. The whole trip takes five days, which includes a good seven-hour delay, which we understand, is par for cutting through red tape there. There are 25 people in the Intertel group and another 30 in the Today staff sent to Portugal. These people arrive in waves, depending upon their responsibilities. The last to join the group prior to the taping are the talent—Barbara Wal-

ters and Hugh Downs. Their not-so-easy job is to assimilate all the material quickly, then work from 6:30 a.m. until 5 in the evening on location, rain or shine. Still, the basic responsibility for each show, according to the producer, falls on the shoulders of the writers. "One writer is assigned a two-hour program and he in turn is assigned a guide and interpreter. It's his responsibility to keep his eyes and ears open to soak up as much material as possible and to work on his assigned location before putting a script together."[57]

Although each remote, like each program, was unique in some aspects, the basic production techniques were similar. The most ambitious series of *Today* remotes were those done between July 1975 and July 1976, when *Today* honored the nation's bicentennial by devoting every Friday to a salute to one of the fifty states. A special bicentennial production unit was formed to devote its efforts entirely to the remote telecasts.

ORIGINATION

An important part of the *Today* production has been the studio origination of the program, along with set designs and the *Today* theme music. *Today* began telecasting from the RCA Exhibition Hall in 1952, and for nine of its twenty-five years on the air, *The Today Show* was produced in ground-floor studios with windows accessible to the street. That made it possible for observers to watch the *Today* production and for NBC cameras to observe the people on the street. The window view created a feeling of immediacy with the outside world that home viewers throughout the country responded to very positively. The same effect was later re-created by the use of the minicam, which showed early morning scenes of New York. Later, *Today* affiliates would sometimes feed local scenes for the opening of each hour of the program. Most adjustments in the *Today* origination at NBC studios were made to accommodate changes in technology, set design, and a greater commitment to news.

TODAY'S THEME

When *Today* premiered on January 14, 1952, the theme music was "Sentimental Journey" by Bud Green, Les Brown, and Ben Homer. That theme remained until July 17, 1961, when John Chancellor took over as host of the show and "Melodie au Crepuscule," written by Django Reinhardt and recorded by the Hat Club of France, became the regular theme music. Although Chancellor soon departed, "Crepuscule" remained until 1968. During those seven years, "Misty" by Erroll Garner was used occasionally as a second theme. In 1968, producer Stuart Schulberg changed the theme to "*Today*," arranged by the Modern Jazz Quartet, and in 1972, "This Is *Today*," arranged by Ray Ellis, became the new *Today* theme.[58]

TODAY'S SET

The *Today* set changed many times over those first twenty-five years. The earliest was in 1952, when much of the overwhelming electronic gadgetry was moved behind the scenes to give the set a less cluttered appearance. But most set changes occurred simply because of the need to update or modernize the set or to accommodate changes in technology, such as the switch to color. Very often, the set was revised when the show was relocated to another studio or because a new producer or host desired a different arrangement. When *The Today Show* shared studios with *NBC Nightly News*, the two sets were made compatible. At the time, producer Doug Sinsel explained that having interchangeable units drastically reduced the amount of time necessary to strike and set for either of the shows. Occasionally, the *Today* set was criticized for being "cold" in design. In 1974, after Frank McGee died, the set was designed to represent an ultramodern news set with very sparse furnishings and bright ceiling lighting. But in 1976, when Tom Brokaw became host, the colors were made warmer, although the set retained its basic ultramodern appearance. On the other hand, *Today*'s main competitor, ABC's *Good Morning America*, capitalized on the *Today* set criticism by designing its set in exactly the opposite motif. *Good Morning America* used a comfortable living room style with thickly cushioned chairs and sofas, plush rugs, and warm colors. Set design needed to be functional as well as aesthetically pleasing. The positions of the host and panel, newscaster, interview areas, and entertainment areas had to be functional if the talent were to operate effectively in the studio. Monitors, rear-screen projection, microphones, and other technical facilities were required to be integrated attractively into the set. In addition, the design had to accommodate regular camera patterns and movement.

PRODUCTION CREDITS

During the course of the first twenty-five-year history of *Today*, many people were responsible for the everyday production of the program. The production credits, as compiled by the NBC Program Analysis Department on a yearly basis, reveal the changes in positions, the number of people required to produce the show, and who was responsible for each production function.[59] The early *Today* credits seem to have been given only to the major positions, listing the positions of executive producer, producer, directors, and associate producers. By 1955, a managing editor position had been added and the title of executive director created. By 1958, the credits were expanded to include a general manager, assistant managing editor, news producer, writers, and editorial cartoonist. In 1960, the credits became even more diversified, including a manager of administration, a publicity director, a person responsible for talent booking, a talent coordinator, and a commercial producer. In addition to the positions already mentioned, in 1962 the production assistants received name credit along with the talent production assistant, the research assistant, and the film editors. In 1963, the writing credits were divided according to specialty: program writers and news writers. Other positions that were credited that year included the unit managers, stage managers, book editor, and graphic artists.

In 1967, after *Today* expanded its news operation by creating a Chicago news bureau, the newly created position of news coordinator was listed in the credits. Other specialized position credits that year included the makeup and hairstylists. In 1968, *Today* continued its news expansion by creating the Washington, D.C., editor. The positions of feature editor, Chicago film editors, news assistant, and feature assistant were added in 1970. More specialized news positions were credited in 1971: reporter at large, assignment editor, Washington writer, and meteorologist.

By 1972, many technical positions were also credited: scenic designer, technical director, technical director in Washington, lighting director, audio director, and video director. The property manager and book coordinators also received credit in 1972. A Los Angeles news coordinator was added in the 1974 credits along with a supervising unit manager, a set designer, a person responsible for projection effects, and a Chicago director. In 1975, a special bicentennial unit was created for the bicentennial state series, and the positions of producer, associate producer, and writer of the unit were listed in the credits. The credits for 1976 listed even more specialized positions, including production coordinator, electronic graphics, studio technical staff, videotape editors, news set design, and *Today* theme.

The credits also revealed that although more people became involved with the production, it was not that more people were being added to do the same job that previously required fewer people. Rather, sophisticated technology, more remote broadcasts, and an increased number of feature segments required a larger staff with specialized skills to handle increasingly complex and diverse technology and expanded production. In part, too, the growing staff could be explained at that time by the increasing strength of specialized unions, which caused positions and responsibilities to be more narrowly defined.

Producing *The Today Show* is and was even then an extremely complex task. It involved the coordination of all production elements and the supervision of staff, crew, and talent. For the producer or executive producer, it meant making all programming decisions that affected the program format and required the ability to handle the complex relationships between the talent and program executives.

The producing of *The Today Show* can be evaluated in three phases. The early *Today* producers, Richard Pinkham and Mort Werner, faced the problems of developing a program that would attract morning viewers. Although they sometimes experimented with the format, the composition of the panel, the types of programming, and the introduction of new technologies, they were for the most part able to maintain the original concept of the program that was created by Sylvester Weaver. During the second phase, from 1957 to 1962, *Today* experienced a period of continual disruption in terms of major format changes, production responsibility, programming changes, and the loss of host David Garroway. In addition, there was a quick turnover of *Today* producers that left the show with a lack of stability and direction for several years.

But *Today* emerged from those rough times into its most distinguished and profitable phase at the time, from 1962 to 1976. A number of factors contributed to that success, and the most important contributions were made by producers Al Morgan and Stuart Schulberg. Morgan was responsible for the initial rebuilding of the program that began in 1962. In a remarkable and far-reaching decision, he added the very competent Barbara Walters to the *Today* panel, revised the program's writing responsibilities, and implemented a serious commitment for *Today* to originate frequently from remote locations. By the time Schulberg took over the producing reins in 1968, the program was experiencing strong ratings, solid advertising, substantial profits, and high regard as a news-information program.

With that legacy as a strong starting point, *Today* became even more successful under Stuart Schulberg. He strengthened the commitment to news by developing the Chicago and Los Angeles news bureaus, added a Washington editor, reorganized the news-gathering process, and increased the news staff. He also reorganized the program by developing the two-hour production methods and routines that were used for many years.

The actual production of *Today* was complex for many reasons. It was produced two hours per day, five days a week, without repeats. In addition, the fragmentation of the show into short segments meant the development of more features per day, more long-range planning to ensure balanced programming, and increased difficulty in studio coordination in terms of camera blocking and set design for each of the segments. The increased sophistication of the technology made the "live" production more complicated and required a specialized studio crew. The production was further complicated by the technical coordination of the various NBC news bureaus; the Washington, D.C., studio connection; and the frequent remote origination of the program. The strong commitment to news meant that an entire program or parts of the program were often expanded or eliminated to accommodate an important or late-breaking news event.

With few exceptions, the *Today* producers had certain characteristics. They were able to maintain good relationships with the talent while retaining control over the programming, and they were able to delegate responsibility to their staff. *Today* producers were dedicated to the original design of the program and resisted attempts to alter the format significantly. Although some alterations were made by several of the *Today* producers, particularly in the mid-1950s and early 1960s, when the change involved major deviation from the original format it was generally not successful. For example, the attempt by producer Robert Bendick to have *Today* pretaped lasted approximately two years, and the program reverted to its live format concept.

Today producers were responsive to the demands and expectations of their audience, particularly in regard to format changes. Most decisions were carefully made by the producers to determine what the effect would be on the viewing audience, who had found a sense of trust and security in watching *Today*. Viewers had come to rely on the familiarity and stability of the program and generally responded negatively to changes in format and talent.

In the 1970s, with the threat of strong competition from ABC's *Good Morning America*, the *Today* producers were under constant pressure to produce a high-quality news-information program that would continue to attract a large audience. *Good Morning America* was already seriously threatening the *Today* audience, particularly in the prime advertising target area of women eighteen to forty-nine years old. As the early producers of *Today*—Richard Pinkham and Mort Werner—realized, a high-quality program does not guarantee advertisers. It is the size of the audience (i.e., ratings) that attracts advertisers to a program. Executive producer Paul Friedman was forced to respond with programming designed to compete with *Good Morning America* and tailored changes to attract a more youthful audience.

Although each *Today* producer faced a different set of problems, for the most part, they successfully met their responsibilities. They were responsive to daily production demands, incorporated significant changes in technology, programmed to the needs of a changing society, and met the challenges of competition from other networks. And they managed to do all that while maintaining the original concept and integrity of the program for twenty-five years.

4

✛

The Faces of *Today*

On-Air Talent from
Dave Garroway to Jane Pauley

It has been said that a good producer can make good talent look good and mediocre talent look good. That observation proved itself on *Today*, which had the good fortune to be blessed with good talent *and* good producers. In the beginning, especially during those formative months and years, it was important to the success of the show to have talent that was appealing to an audience. It is a tribute, however, to the exceptional program concept that *Today* was able during those first twenty-five years to withstand several changes of talent, including six hosts.

DAVID GARROWAY

More than any other host, the first one would make or break the show. So when Pat Weaver, at the urging of Mort Werner, made an inspired decision to hire David Garroway to be the "master communicator" (as the host was called), it turned out that Garroway was definitely an asset. In 1939, Garroway had gone to the NBC School of Announcing in New York and was said to have finished twenty-third out of a class of twenty-four. But despite that inauspicious beginning, Garroway moved through a series of good reporting jobs for NBC and finally settled in Chicago, joining NBC's owned and operated station WMAQ-TV. It was there in 1948 that he hosted *Garroway at Large*, a show that NBC fed to the network live on Sundays from 9:00 to 9:30 p.m. Eastern Standard Time. After a successful run, the show was canceled by NBC when sponsor Procter & Gamble bought the prime-time half hour for another show.[1] According to Weaver,

Garroway was looking for another format when he heard about NBC's search for the *Today* host. He called Mort Werner, who was impressed enough to suggest that Garroway be scheduled for an NBC audition. Weaver liked his easy and casual style, sincerity, and competence.[2] Even though Weaver was looking for a strong comedian type to host the show such as Fred Allen, Bob Hope, or Milton Berle, he eventually decided to hire Garroway.[3] Garroway had the responsibility of creating the image of the host and setting the precedent for all succeeding hosts. One particular Garroway asset was his sense of humor. "*Today* was basically a news program, Garroway's informality and willingness to improvise allowed humor to creep in. Everyone knew this was a big plus for the show. Besides, humor was a Pat Weaver dictate."[4]

Garroway was very successful in handling the live commercials that Weaver had initiated in order to attract sponsorship. He was so successful that many advertisers refused to buy time unless he personally performed the commercial. Since it was also Garroway's responsibility to sell the program to advertisers, he actively went out with the sales representatives and talked to the advertisers themselves.

Producing *Today* was a team effort, and the early years of *Today* were a special challenge because of the large degree of experimentation with creative ideas and format. Garroway worked with the producers to develop those ideas and significantly contributed to the format. Although initially there were doubts that *The Today Show* would succeed after critics panned it, Garroway was so confident that the program would succeed that when he moved to New York to serve as host, he took out a four-year lease on a Park Avenue apartment. Ultimately, his easy demeanor and casual style proved to be perfectly suited to the *Today* host position:

> Most television professionals agreed that Garroway was the perfect host for the *Today* show and its unique requirements. . . . In contrast to radio's frenetic disc jockeys and talk show hosts with whom he competed in the morning, Garroway spoke quietly, in a mellifluous baritone. He was informality in a formal age, intelligent, casual and, at all times, sincere, even with the commercials. . . . As he shifted from set to set, Garroway moved with a grace that belied the 240 pounds his 6-foot-2-inch frame sometimes carried. While he often walked at a brisk pace, such was his on-camera style that he appeared not to rush. Rather he moved in kind of a vague manner that matched the mood of those in his audience who tarried before the set on the way to breakfast.[5]

Although Garroway was very effective as an on-screen personality, his personal relationships and private life were filled with uncertainty and tension. He was described as an "essentially decent man who tries to get through to people and just doesn't know how." Another friend said, "He

David Garroway, master communicator.

was not a conversationalist, not a party guy. He was at his best in front of a mike."[6]

Garroway was a very nervous and insecure person off-screen. The demanding daily responsibility of hosting the show at times seemed to overwhelm him. To help cope with stress, he took doses of a "pep-up" vitamin tonic that he referred to as "the Doctor." When pressures on *The Today Show* increased and his personal problems became more intense, he resorted to the Doctor with increasing frequency.

During his years as host, Garroway had many confrontations with the producers. He began to feel persecuted and thought that the production people were taking advantage of him. He became ill-tempered, confused at times, increasingly insecure, erratic in his behavior, and inconsistent in his hosting performance. At a time when he was least able to handle power, Garroway was given nearly complete control over the show. All major decisions were cleared with him, and by 1960, Garroway had become irrational and frequently undependable. But he demanded—and NBC agreed—that the show's title be changed to *The Dave Garroway Today Show*. Then, on April 28, 1961, Garroway's life took a stunningly tragic turn. His second wife, Pamela, committed suicide by taking an overdose of sleeping pills, leaving behind their three young children. It was that tragedy that prompted Garroway to leave *The Today Show*, although he did not resign immediately: "After a brief leave from *Today*, Garroway returned so edgy that once he lost his temper on-camera over a technical snafu, and NBC president Robert Kintner had to make a public apology. Then Garroway asked out of *Today* to put his life back in order."[7]

Garroway's departure from *Today* was greeted with relief by the network. The network was also relieved that Garroway made his exit with his characteristic grace and eloquent style: "Of all the TV departures the most moving was Dave Garroway's. . . . Bowing off, Garroway vowed to be 'father and a half to his three children' and also 'to make what contributions I can' to a pet cause that he had used as his sign-off for 10 years: 'Peace.'"[8]

After Garroway left the show, he semiretired to straighten out his private life. He became moderately active again in 1963 by hosting a series for National Educational Television called *Exploring the Universe*.[9] Over the years, Garroway returned to *The Today Show* as a guest on the anniversary programs. He was said to have emotionally and mentally recovered, remarried, and reengaged in life. But on July 21, 1982, after having undergone heart surgery and experiencing complications, he committed suicide by a self-inflicted gunshot. The next day, July 22, *Today* honored its first host with a program largely dedicated to his remembrance.

JOHN CHANCELLOR

After Garroway left *The Today Show*, NBC moved the responsibility of producing the program from NBC Programming to the NBC News Department. NBC abolished the producing unit of *Today-Tonight*, which had been under the control of David Levy's Entertainment Program Department. From that point, *Today* was produced by the NBC News staff headed by Bill McAndrew and under the direct supervision of Carl Lindemann Jr. Although Robert Northshield was the actual producer of *Today*, it was the News Department that decided that the next host should have a strong background in news. Auditions were planned for Edwin Newman, John Chancellor, and John Daly. Daly, popular host of *What's My Line?*, was in consideration for the position for only a short time. According to *Variety*, "The Daly-NBC dickers never came off because, as was reported, the performer wanted virtually complete control of the morning network video strip."[10] Arlene Francis was also said to have negotiated with NBC for the host position. Like Daly, she "wanted more control of the format than the news department was willing to allow."[11]

Thus, John Chancellor was offered the permanent position before the auditions were even completed. His early career as a journalist began in Chicago where he worked for a short time at the *Chicago Sun-Times* and then took a position as an NBC Chicago radio reporter. Later, as an NBC correspondent, according to an NBC advertisement in *Variety*, he

> covered just about every type of assignment for [NBC] both here and abroad. Political conventions in Chicago and San Francisco. Racial trouble in Little Rock. Civil War in Lebanon. Uprising in Algeria. The Francis Gary Powers trial in Moscow. Castro's anti-Batista campaign in Cuba.[12]

Chancellor's last assignment before accepting the *Today* offer was as chief of the NBC News Moscow Bureau, earning approximately $25,000 a year. The *Today* host position paid an attractive yearly salary of $125,000.

After auditioning for the host position, Edwin Newman was hired as the *Today* newscaster, moving Frank Blair to handle interviews and feature segments as a regular panel member. Changes to the show itself included a return to its live format. According to NBC, that change was "strongly endorsed by the show's new producer, Shad Northshield, who believes it will permit the program to react much more quickly in a world of continuing crisis."[13]

Although NBC expected Chancellor to successfully fulfill the position as *Today* host, they soon realized that his personality was unsuitable to the role. There has been great criticism of the year that he was the host of *Today*, which ranged from June 17, 1961, to September 7, 1962, and that criticism was most often directed specifically to Chancellor himself, but it was actually a combination of factors that made that short period of time so unsuccessful. Some of the responsibility can be placed on the NBC News executives and *Today* producer Northshield, who were responsible for the disastrous decision to revise the *Today* panel. Those decisions resulted in certain personalities being asked to perform in roles for which they were not particularly well suited. For example, in order to bolster their falling ratings, Chancellor and Newman were often asked to compromise their professional integrity by performing in *Today* comedy skits.

As *Today Show* host, Chancellor tried to bridge the gap between newsman and entertainer but never felt comfortable with the position. During an interview, he explained his feelings: "This job required someone whose satisfaction is in the art of performing . . . but I come from the disciplines of the news business, where the whole craft is concerned with getting through with facts and ideas."[14] He was even uncomfortable with NBC's press releases about him: "Good natured embarrassment hits NBC's John Chancellor whenever he reads a press report describing him as a newsman interested in everything from Mozart to baseball. He doesn't deny it, but what he resents is the implication that he's some sort of latter-day Leonardo. 'That baseball-to-Mozart combination makes me sound like a guy who's really too much,' he protests. 'Hell, first thing you know, they'll have me collecting stamps.'"[15] Chancellor also liked to rely more on himself than on the *Today Show* staff: "The *Today* show doesn't let you control your own environment. It requires a hundred-odd people to get three of us on the air ten hours a week. A lot of people, in a sense are shaping my style. Before the *Today* show, I wrote everything myself. It was months before I could deliver a funny line that someone else had written and not say, 'One of our writers has written.'"[16]

When NBC News hired Chancellor, he was not required to do commercials, which resulted in a serious loss of advertising. That became one of the critical reasons NBC and Chancellor mutually agreed that he should leave *The Today Show*, although he remained with NBC News as anchorman for political specials. He also frequently served as substitute host on *The Today Show* for many years. Eventually, he was hired to anchor *NBC Nightly News*, the position for which he was best suited and was anxious to occupy. He occupied that chair for twelve years, from 1970 to 1982. Chancellor died of stomach cancer in 1996.

HUGH DOWNS

NBC News looked for qualities similar to those of David Garroway when they hired the third *Today* host, returning to the entertainment field to find him. Hugh Downs was already well known to the public because of his supporting role as announcer on the *Jack Paar Tonight Show* and as host of the popular game show *Concentration*. The Hugh Downs years (1962–1971) are considered to be among the best years in *Today's* history. It was Carl Lindemann Jr., NBC executive in charge of *Today*, who hired both Downs and producer Al Morgan. All three had previously worked together on Pat Weaver's *Home* show. Downs started his early career as a radio announcer in Lima, Ohio, and in 1943 began work for NBC in Chicago. In 1954, he appeared with Arlene Francis on the *Home* show and later he became Jack Paar's announcer on *The Tonight Show*. Weaver must have considered Downs the ideal television personality since Downs appeared on three of Weaver's creations: *Home*, *Tonight*, and *Today*.

Barbara Walters and Hugh Downs.

Downs had gone to college in Bluffton, Ohio, and Wayne State University in Michigan. He was considered to be an intelligent man, although some of his critics maintained that his intelligence was exaggerated. Producer Al Morgan, who did not like Downs, was the most uncharitable in his comments. "Not long after Downs joined *Today* someone remarked that Downs had been the intellectual of the *Jack Paar Show* and Al Morgan quipped, 'J. Fred Muggs could be that.'" Another critic said, "Downs is a mile wide and an inch deep."[17]

Generally, he was criticized by an envious staff but loved by the *Today* audience:

To the nation's mothers, Hugh was the ideal young man, a marvelous, well-informed peach of a guy who would make daughter a perfect husband. To some associates—including Al Morgan—Downs was an advertiser's dream, supersalesman viewers trusted implicitly. At best, though, he was a barely adequate interviewer. He was a "six foot toe in the sand," a "race track in Ohio," or a "mashed potato sandwich" to *Today* writers who envied his $500,000 network salary and his easy schedule.[18]

Al Morgan resented that Downs rarely prepared for an interview or for anything else on the show. It was on this particular lack that Barbara Walters capitalized when she became a regular panel member. On a typical day, after serving as host for *Today*, Downs would rush to another studio to host NBC's game show *Concentration*, and then he would go home. It was not necessary for him to prepare for *The Today Show* since the program was completely scripted for Downs, including the interview questions.

Downs made many demands on NBC while he was host, and nearly every demand was granted. He wanted a bathroom in his office. "Success on *Today* goes to the bladder as well as the head," said Al Morgan.[19] He also demanded that his wife, Ruth, be allowed to accompany him on re-motes despite rules that did not allow spouses to go on remote locations. In addition, he was consulted on personnel decisions and demanded an unprecedented salary. Finally, he managed to remove Morgan, the most valuable *Today* producer the show ever had. But Downs was worth it. By his consistent presence, he created stability for the program that made it possible for viewers and advertisers to rely on the show. He was well liked by his audience, and during his nine years as host, *The Today Show* consistently received the highest ratings in its history. The station lineup also increased during his reign. When Downs took over as host in 1962, *Today* was broadcast to 160 stations. When he left the show in 1971, it was seen on 211 stations.[20]

Downs left the show voluntarily in 1971:

"I wish now to become actively involved in several other pursuits and in-terests," Mr. Downs said. He added that his parting with the program is an entirely amicable one and that he expects his long relationship with the NBC family will "continue happily and successfully for a long time to come." The official NBC press release was equally gracious to Hugh Downs: "We are sorry to lose Hugh Downs, whose contributions to the increasing popularity of the *Today* program have been beyond measure," Donald Meaney, Vice-President, NBC News, said. "During Mr. Downs' nine-year tenure as host, *Today* has become not merely a tremendously successful television program but a well-spring of daily information to millions of Americans."[21]

Downs stayed with NBC television after he left *The Today Show*. He nar-rated a series of NBC ecology specials during the 1972–1973 season, and for a brief time he hosted *Not for Women Only*. He then moved to ABC, where he coanchored *20/20* from 1978 to 1999 and where he also reunited with his former cohost Barbara Walters. He is currently retired and living in Arizona.

FRANK MCGEE

Hugh Downs's notification to network executives that he planned to retire from *Today* came early enough to give NBC sufficient time to select Frank McGee as the next and fourth host of *Today*. In order to ease that transition, NBC devoted the entire week of October 11–15, 1971, to the introduction of its new *Today* host and a prolonged farewell to retiring host Downs. McGee was originally from Monroe, Louisiana, but started his broadcasting career working part-time in a radio station while attending the University of Oklahoma. In 1955, he worked for the NBC-TV affiliate station in Montgomery, Alabama, earning nationwide recognition for his coverage of the Martin Luther King Jr. civil rights movement. Then in 1957, NBC News hired him as a Washington correspondent. After moving to New York in 1959, he covered such events as the *Apollo* space flights, political conventions and elections, and the assassination of Robert F. Kennedy.

Although NBC had been disappointed with Chancellor, they decided to give another chance to a host with a solid background in news. Producer Stuart Schulberg wanted to strengthen the news orientation of the program and felt that this time they had made a good choice. "We feel we are fortunate that in Frank McGee we have found a worthy successor. Mr. McGee is not only a journalist of great stature but a man with a warm personality and lively interest in many fields. His talents are eminently suited to a lively program which spans a wide range of topics. We believe that in his capable hands, *Today* will continue to be television's most influential weekday program."[22]

The most obvious contrast between Hugh Downs and Frank McGee was that McGee was a strong interviewer. He also prepared thoroughly for interviews and faithfully kept abreast of current events. He described his position as host of *Today*: "I am sometimes called the host of the *Today* show but I don't like the word. One of the first things I did when I arrived here was to persuade everybody to stop using the word 'guest' to describe interviewees. There's a suggestion that you must be nice to people because they are guests. While we are not rude to anybody, we do ask the questions we have a right to ask . . . even if they are sometimes uncomfortable."[23]

When Frank McGee took over as host, Barbara Walters was forced into a less prominent position. She had earned the reputation of being

Joe Garagiola, Barbara Walters, Frank McGee, and Frank Blair.

an aggressive interviewer when she worked with Hugh Downs, but then Downs was not a good interviewer. McGee, on the other hand, considered himself to be the only true journalist on the program and was reluctant to relinquish the interviewing responsibility to Walters:

> I think Barbara has areas of competence that I can't approach, based upon her own background, her natural fields of interest. I have areas, too, in which I have special competence. I do my areas and she does hers and I don't see any apparent conflict. I don't think I could handle show business the way Barbara does. But, by the same token, I don't think she can handle the kind of material in which I have had my experience the same way that I can. She's not being relegated to certain areas because she's a woman but because she does them well.[24]

Although their on-air relationship seemed to be effective with viewers, they were not close friends off camera, and Walters herself has said that McGee insisted that he ask the first three questions if both were doing an interview:

> When McGee became host of Today it quickly appeared that he either was jealous of Barbara Walters' skills and accomplishments or, purely and simply, was a male chauvinist. He was so uncivil to Barbara that, she has said, he wouldn't speak to her when the TV lights went out. On the rare occasions when he did speak to her, he was condescending—speaking as journalist to non-journalist. When Barbara was especially good, the best Frank could summon up was, "We'll make a reporter out of you yet." Never mind that Barbara had interviewed President Nixon, Henry Kissinger, Egypt's Anwar Sadat, and Israel's Moshe Dayan and Golda Meir by the time McGee arrived at Today. McGee saw himself as the only heavyweight on the show.[25]

When Frank McGee accepted the Today position, he knew he had cancer, although he did not know how seriously ill he really was. But by the spring of 1974, his condition deteriorated rapidly, forcing him to take several minutes to rise from his chair after the sign-off. Then unexpectedly, on April 17, 1974, he died. The end was quite sudden, and although Today had sensed the inevitable, it had not acted earlier to select a new host. The Today ratings had dropped only slightly when McGee took over as host, but after his death, it began a steady period of decline. Since viewers of the program were not given any warning about McGee's condition, they were shocked at news of his death. There was also a lack of direction and leadership to guide it out of its period of mourning. It was Barbara Walters who then went to producer Stuart Schulberg and reminded him of the clause in her last contract, stating that when McGee left the show, she would be elevated to host status. The clause was honored, and she was promoted to cohost, effective April 22, 1974.[26] NBC News, however, continued to look for a male cohost to balance the program.

BARBARA WALTERS

When Barbara Walters began her career as a writer for The Today Show in 1961, she was often referred to as "their best writer," which is not surprising since she had quite a lot of writing experience before joining Today. After attending Sarah Lawrence College, she embarked on her broadcasting career in the mid-1950s. She held a series of writing jobs with WRCA, WPIX, and CBS, where she worked for a short time with Walter Cronkite. During the mid-1950s, she was asked to write for The Morning Show, which was at the time in direct competition to *The Today Show*. When CBS fired her in 1957 during a budget cutback, she worked for a while as a theatrical publicist for Tex McCrary, Inc. Then, in 1961, Walters was offered a job by David Garroway to write for *The Today Show* and research features geared toward women.

She performed her job so conscientiously and competently that she was often given other opportunities, including occasional on-air reporting assignments. Within a short period of time, she became the regular "substitute hostess." She wrote on-air material for the "*Today* girls" and often substituted for them if they were unable to perform.

When *Today* executives decided to relieve Maureen O'Sullivan of her "hostess" duties, Al Morgan considered Barbara Walters for the permanent *Today* girl position. Morgan was tired of the typical show-business *Today* girl and gave Walters a thirteen-week trial period. She proved to be so competent that the thirteen weeks turned into twelve years. The term "*Today* girl" was dropped when Walters joined the show; she was given the more dignified official title of "*Today* reporter."

Barbara Walters's background had prepared her for the job she performed. She was comfortable with celebrities because her father, Lou Walters, owned the Latin Quarter nightclubs, which were frequented by show-business personalities, politicians, and such notables as Howard Hughes and Joseph Kennedy. She was often criticized for her lack of journalism background and particularly for her lack of "on-the-beat" reporting experience. However, she did learn the "tools" of her specialty through her early broadcasting experience. Not only did she have basic writing experience before taking the *Today* position, but she also learned the jobs of producer, scriptwriter, film editor, and researcher. What set Walters apart from other *Today* girls who appeared before her was that she was able to write, as well as read what was on the teleprompter. Further, her show-business and political connections were highly valuable to her since she took an active role in securing her own guests and was often able to get interviews that other reporters were denied.

When Barbara Walters signed her contract with NBC in 1973, Richard Wald, then the president of NBC News, issued a press release praising their morning star. "We are happy to be able to maintain the continuity of the longest running television program. . . . With Barbara, with Frank Mc-Gee as host, with Gene Shalit and Frank Blair, the *Today* program has been increasingly successful. During the first six months of 1973 it reached an all-time high in number of viewers."[27]

During her years on *The Today Show*, Barbara Walters had accumulated a long list of noteworthy accomplishments:

Barbara Walters and Frank McGee.

In addition to her role on *Today* Miss Walters has accepted many challenging assignments, including one with the NBC News team that accompanied President Nixon to China; a trip to Persepolis, Iran, to report on that country's 2500th anniversary; and a report on the investiture of the Prince of Wales.

In keeping with the diversified programming of *Today*, Miss Walters has filmed special reports ranging from a day in the life of a Playboy bunny to a sensitive account of the problems of the mentally retarded adult. She has taken television viewers into the cloistered quarters of Maryknoll nuns and the enclosed world of a female reform school.

Miss Walters has conducted news making interviews on *Today* with H. R. Haldeman, when he was assistant to President Nixon, and with Mrs. Nixon, after her return from a goodwill tour of West Africa. Her exclusive interview with Henry Kissinger, following Dr. Kissinger's conclusion of peace negotiations with the North Vietnamese, was telecast in prime time on the NBC Television Network Feb. 25, 1973.

Earlier, she arranged and conducted exclusive interviews with President Nixon, England's Prince Philip, former Secretary of State Dean Rusk and painter Andrew Wyeth. Her "First Lady" interview credits include, in addition to Mrs. Nixon, Mrs. Lyndon B. Johnson and Mrs. Dwight Eisenhower, as well as Israel's Prime Minister Golda Meir and Princess Grace of Monaco.[28]

It was a combination of aggressiveness and competence that made it possible for Walters to attract good interviewees and to handle the interview successfully. Because she earned a well-deserved reputation for interviewing, she wrote the book *How to Talk with Practically Anybody about Practically Anything* detailing the technique. In the book are "tips on how to have face-to-face conversations with celebrities, tycoons, royalty, politicians, diplomats, clergymen and military men among others. There is also a marvelous chapter on how to talk with difficult people, including bores and belligerent types."[29] During her years with Hugh Downs as host of the show, Walters was able to practice and perfect her techniques. She did not have quite the same freedom or opportunity when Frank McGee took over the show. She explained the sometimes acrimonious situations during an interview:

> Frank had never worked with a woman before. It was very difficult for him. In all his time on the air, he never really learned to accept a woman, and he found it particularly hard to accept me as an equal. Although I have not discussed this before, what I'm telling you is known by NBC. During the time that I was on the air with Frank, it was part of his agreement that he could choose whichever interviews he wanted to do and keep me out of them. That is, on serious or important interviews, I would be excluded. Furthermore, on interviews with political people that originated in Washington, Frank could decide whether or not I could participate. When I was allowed to participate, I could participate only after Frank had asked the first question. If he decided not to ask the first question, then I could not ask any at all. This procedure never showed on the air; I never complained about it, and as far as the public knew, Frank and I had a very compatible relationship. NBC never doubted that I would accept this role—which was not only secondary but submissive; and yet, even at this time I was considered by many to be too aggressive. One of the reasons that I used to go out and arrange for the very hard-to-get interviews was this: if I got them myself, I would be allowed to participate; but if the program arranged for them, they would be done exclusively by Frank McGee and I would be excluded.[30]

Barbara Walters was extremely successful during the twelve years she was with *The Today Show*. In 1975, she won an Emmy Award as "Outstanding Host or Hostess in a Talk, Service or Variety Series, *Today*," for the 1974–1975 season. For a guest-host appearance on *The Tonight Show*, she received the highest "one-shot" ratings of any guest host. She was also chosen broadcasting "Woman of the Year" by the *Ladies Home Journal* magazine.[31] Even with all the success, which was well earned and duly appreciated, Walters was never able to adjust to the "murderous" early morning hours. "There are times I'm so bone-tired I'm ready to cry if someone touches me."[32] It was one of the reasons Walters was ready to leave *The Today Show* in 1976. However, it was not the only reason.

In 1974, when Barbara Walters was elevated to cohost of the program, she exercised her new power by voicing her preference over the selection of the new host. Although stronger personalities were in contention for the position, Walters chose, in conjunction with NBC, "pliable, unassertive Jim Hartz." It gave Walters the opportunity to assert herself once again, but it was disastrous for the show. *Today* became dull, and viewers deserted in droves. "Many stayed with the show while the hard-nosed McGee was alive to watch the two strike sparks against each other. The veteran newsman had little affection for this somewhat abrasive junior, and he showed it. By contrast the airwaves marriage between Barbara and Jim Hartz was decidedly uninteresting. Hartz was amiable and pleasant—a great favorite with the mercurial *Today* staff and almost no one else. Before long the ratings had dropped by 25 percent."[33]

The time was right for Barbara Walters to make a change. She approached NBC executives in 1975 to discuss the possibility of leaving or to renegotiate her contract. She was represented by the William Morris talent agency, who presented her formal demands to NBC's senior vice president of television, Al Rush. "Barbara, they said, wanted a seven-year contract—$7 million for a package to include veto power over major changes in the *Today* format, reimbursement for extensive home entertainment expense—NBC executives were frequently among her guests—and NBC to pick up the tab for Barbara's long-employed personal press agent. Barbara also wanted to do product endorsement without prior network approval. The latter was a perk no other NBC personality enjoyed."[34] NBC was concerned with the money and with the demands, which would give her great control over the program. When NBC did not meet those demands, the talent agency asked ABC if they were interested in Walters. They were, and on April 19, 1976, ABC made her an offer to coanchor the *ABC Evening News* with Harry Reasoner. While she considered the offer, NBC asked that they be given the opportunity to make a counteroffer. "But Barbara let it be known that 'a new way of life' was what she was really turning over in her mind. The evening job at ABC would mean a more normal existence and, presumably, a richer social life for America's most prominent woman broadcaster."[35]

The only possible way that Barbara Walters might have remained with NBC was if they offered her a coanchorship on *NBC Nightly News*. They did not make her that offer. On April 22, 1976, Walters accepted the ABC contract, which consisted of $1 million per year for five years. The nature of the salary has generally been misconstrued. "Walters is being paid about $500,000 a year for her work on the *ABC Evening News*, now roughly comparable to the current salaries of Walter Cronkite, David Brinkley, John Chancellor and Reasoner; the rest of her salary is for work on four prime-time specials, to be paid from the budget of ABC's programming department."[36] However, it was not the money, Walters claimed, that made her decide to accept ABC's offer. "When ABC made me the offer to be the first evening news anchorwoman, it was a very great challenge. The challenge was so exciting and so demanding that I felt I simply couldn't turn it down."[37]

ABC had much to gain by acquiring Barbara Walters. First, if she were able to attract enough viewers to raise the *ABC Evening News* by two rating points, it would be profitable for ABC. And even if the coanchor experiment were unsuccessful, they would have lured Walters off *The Today Show*, and they hoped that the loss would sufficiently weaken the show to give the edge to ABC's morning show, *Good Morning America*. After leaving *Today*, Walters continued on with her impressive career in prime time, cohosting ABC's *20/20*, which took advantage of her interviewing skills. Later, she created the highly successful daytime talk show *The View*, and, though currently semiretired, she still serves as a special correspondent for ABC News and occasionally hosts ABC special programming.

JIM HARTZ

When Frank McGee died, NBC gave Barbara Walters cohost status, although they continued to search for a male cohost to replace McGee. The search was lengthy because NBC wanted to consider carefully who would fill the position. In early July 1974, because of the large number of press inquiries, NBC News president Richard Wald issued a statement concerning the search:

> Since Frank McGee died in April, NBC News has enlisted a number of its most experienced newsmen to serve as co-hosts of *Today*. They are: Edwin Newman, Garrick Utley, Bill Monroe, Tom Snyder, Tom Brokaw, and—last week—Jess Marlow. In subsequent weeks, other co-hosts will be used. NBC News hopes to select the new *Today* co-host by the end of July or in early August.[38]

Another NBC executive explained, "They're trying to make up their mind whether to go with somebody controversial, somebody offbeat, or Mr. Nice Guy."[39] An article in *Time* magazine speculated as to how the job ad for the position might read:

> Wanted: young journalist (under 40), bright, personable, quick thinking, with warmth, charm and humor. Must be wide-awake at 7 a.m. Top pay (around $350,000 a year), plus travel, fame and social status. Women need not apply.[40]

As NBC narrowed the search, the preference seemed to be for candidates with a news background. All eight of the finalists were from the NBC News Department:

Los Angeles Reporter Jess Marlow, 44; Washington Correspondent Douglas Kiker, 44; *Today*'s Washington Editor, Bill Monroe, 53; and that perennial *Today* substitute and network newsman, Edwin Newman, 55; London Correspondent Garrick Utley, 34; New York Anchor Man Jim Hartz, 34; *Tomorrow* Host Tom Snyder, 38; and White House Correspondent Tom Brokaw, 34.[41]

Because *Today* wanted to attract a younger audience (the more desirable demographic for attracting advertisers), it leaned toward candidates under forty. Complicating the search was the *Today* requirement in 1974 that the new host would perform commercial copy. Several of the serious host contenders were publicly adamant that they would not accept the position if they were required to do commercials. In spite of that attitude, NBC executives were even more adamant about their position, declaring that there was "absolutely no chance that the network would exempt a *Today* host from reading commercials at this time, because the company was determined to preserve all that had made the program successful over the years."[42]

After the initial guest-host auditions, NBC narrowed its search to four men: Tom Brokaw, Tom Snyder, Jim Hartz, and Garrick Utley. Each was given another one-week audition as guest host. NBC was anxious to get the new host firmly established before rival ABC debuted its new morning program, *A.M. America*, in January 1975. In order to predetermine which candidate was most likely to be accepted by the *Today* audience, NBC set up a viewer response survey:

The decision on who gets the *Today* job will be based partially on audience reaction tests now being conducted. Viewers are telephoned in key markets around the country and asked about their reaction to substitute co-hosts they have seen on *Today*. The sampling is done under the supervision of William Rubens, vice-president of research and corporate planning for NBC.[43]

Ultimately, Jim Hartz was chosen as the new cohost, and his regular appearances on the show began on July 29, 1974. He was under forty (thirty-four), had a solid news background, and agreed to do commercials. He also received a very favorable response from the audience polls. At the time, Hartz was the anchorman of NBC-owned local WNBC *NewsCenter 4*, and his selection was an opportunity for him to join the network. Richard Wald and Barbara Walters explained some of the reasons that led to their decision:

"Like Frank, Jim has a low-key delivery which can turn chaos into order and calamity into calm. . . . He also has the gift of being able to deal with complicated, often highly technical issues in a simple and clear way." Other major assets are Hartz's boyish smile and soothing friendliness, which nicely complement Walters' occasional tartness of tongue. "He has intelligence, humor, charm and sex appeal. . . . Jim is very easy to take in the morning."[44]

Jim Hartz and Frank McGee had been close friends. McGee was god-father to one of his children, and at McGee's funeral, Hartz delivered the eulogy. Like McGee, Hartz was from Oklahoma, where he was a medical student at the University of Tulsa. Hartz began his broadcasting career at KOTV in Tulsa and joined NBC News in 1964. When he accepted the job at *Today*, NBC was reported to have paid him a salary in the range of $250,000. As for the commercials, Hartz said, "Doing commercials has not affected Barbara's reputation. . . . If *Today* can make extra money by having us do them, then that's going to help other news shows that don't

Jim Hartz.

make money, like space and election coverage. The only thing is—I don't know if I'll be any good doing commercials."[45]

Even with the careful search, NBC made a poor choice when they hired Jim Hartz. Although he was well qualified and was well liked by the *Today* staff and NBC executives, Hartz was not well accepted by the audience. He did not have the ability to attract viewers, and it was possibly simply a matter of "bad chemistry." Barbara Walters and producer Stuart Schulberg explained the challenge of being the new *Today* host: "'The man for *Today* is expected to be more than just a good newsman. . . . The person must be able to do interviews and ad-lib those awful 30 seconds at the end of the show.' He must also supply what Schulberg calls 'chemical balance' to the stand-up comic pace of *Today* reviewer Gene Shalit and the alternately sweet-and-strident Walters."[46]

Whatever the reason, at the time Hartz joined the show, the ratings had already begun to decline. By the time he completed two years with *Today*, the ratings had plummeted. It was estimated that nearly 2 million viewers had deserted the program. Of course, it was not all directly attributable to Hartz since any number of factors may have contributed to the decline. However, NBC decided to take drastic action to rebuild the show. Barbara Walters had already left *Today* and NBC was searching for a new female panelist. They decided to do what amounted to a clean sweep and replace the host and people in other key staff positions as well. Hartz went on to anchor the news at WRC-TV in Washington, D.C., until 1979, and later hosted several PBS programs before retiring to Virginia.

TOM BROKAW

Having been in strong contention for the cohost position in 1974, Tom Brokaw was the unanimous choice in 1976. The first time, he was the NBC News White House correspondent and was not offered the *Today* host position because he refused to do commercials. In 1976, NBC was ready to accept Brokaw's conditions. Brokaw was born in Yankton, South Dakota, and graduated from the University of South Dakota. He began his broadcasting career at his hometown radio station when he was fifteen years old. In 1965, he worked for WSB-TV, the NBC affiliate station in Atlanta, Georgia, covering the civil rights movement. He then joined KNBC-TV in Los Angeles as anchorman for the 11:00 p.m. local news. After five years with KNBC-TV, he became the NBC White House correspondent during the final Nixon days. He also anchored the Saturday edition of *NBC Nightly News*.[47]

When Brokaw considered accepting the position as *Today* host, he was able to negotiate with considerably more power than he had had in 1974.

Tom Brokaw.

He also had the advantage of knowing that NBC wanted him for the program. That made it possible for him to ask for an increase in the original salary offer and demand that he not be required to do commercials with some hope that his demands would be met:

> "Negotiations with Mr. Brokaw had been going on for several weeks, and earlier reports had noted that the difficulties were over the salary demands by his lawyer. These demands were said by the network to have been inspired by the $1 million-a-year salary that ABC News offered Barbara Walters to hire her away from *Today* last April." NBC met the demands and Tom Brokaw accepted the position starting as the official host on August 30, 1976. "Neither the network nor Mr. Brokaw's lawyers, E. G. Hookstratter, in California, would discuss their terms of the agreement, but according to unofficial NBC sources, Mr. Brokaw is to be paid close to $400,000 a year initially under a five-year contract that carried increases to nearly $500,000."[48]

Brokaw's first day on the job was not as impressive as expected, considering the trouble NBC went through to get him the position. His opening remarks suggested a livelier format than was evident in the remainder of the program: "Good morning. I'm Tom Brokaw on *Today,* with Gene Shalit and Betty Furness—and so far so good, I gather. . . . It's no real surprise that I will be here each morning at this time with my friends and my associates on this program, and I am looking forward to it. We expect to have some fun and we expect, as well, to keep you abreast of what has happened and what is likely to happen in the days to come."[49] The *New York Daily News* reviewed that first morning:

> The two-hour morning eye-opener is so sterile that we had visions of Brokaw, weatherman Lew Wood, newscaster Floyd Kalber, Betty Furness and Gene Shalit washing up with masks on, powdering and putting on rubber, gloves before starting to work. . . . Someone should tell the young *Today* crew that a little laughter; an occasional smile and even a fluff now and then will not rock the boat . . . it looked like the word was out to clear the way yesterday for Brokaw. No interrupting. No upstaging. Even the usually irrepressible resident humorist Gene Shalit was subdued and the representatives of *Mad* magazine that he and Brokaw interviewed looked like editors of the *Christian Science Monitor.*[50]

The *Daily News* went on to criticize the format:

> So far, *Today* seems to have fallen victim to the old business about change for change sake. We saw nothing new under NBC's sun yesterday that we haven't seen many times before. If anything, the show is too self-conscious and needs a little morning warmth.[51]

Of course, the first day is always the most difficult, and soon the *Today* panel was interacting more freely. Under Brokaw, *The Today Show* was less formally scripted, particularly at the beginning of the show and in the statements introducing program segments. This gave the show a more ad-lib style that tended to relax the talent and created a friendlier atmosphere that was more acceptable to the early morning audience than a stiff, scripted show. Those early critics were wrong. Brokaw anchored *Today* with style and warmth until 1982, when he left to anchor *NBC Nightly News with Roger Mudd*. In 1983, he became the sole anchor of *NBC Nightly News with Tom Brokaw* until he retired in December 2004. He remained at NBC as a special correspondent. He is also the author of many critically acclaimed books, including the highly regarded *The Greatest Generation*.

TODAY PANEL MEMBERS

Jack Lescoulie

There were other on-air positions on *Today* that were important to the overall concept of the show. It was Sylvester Weaver's original idea that there should be at least three key people on the program to establish the necessary interaction within the panel. They would also be responsible for doing light feature segments. Jack Lescoulie was the first person chosen to fill that position. Prior to joining *Today*, Lescoulie had hosted a radio show called *The Grouch Club*. Richard Pinkham, then executive producer of *Today*, said that Lescoulie was "one of the nicest men alive, whose single talent is a nice smile." He was hired to be the comic relief for the program, and his main duties in the early years of *Today* included creating light features and comedy skits, which became a regular part of *Today*'s format. Lescoulie stayed with *Today* for fifteen years. Then, in 1961, he was taken off the show for about a year when NBC News took over *Today* and John Chancellor became the host. When Hugh Downs took over as host in 1962, Lescoulie was rehired. Although he remained with the program for several more years, his return brought conflict to the show, causing an unsatisfactory relationship between Lescoulie, Downs, and *Today Show* executives:

> When Lescoulie returned to the *Today* show in July 1961, he had somehow gotten the idea that *he* was the star of the show, not Downs. His manager encouraged him in that dangerous belief, and Lescoulie became dissatisfied as Downs' importance proved to be paramount to the show. He continually complained about his second-banana role and about not getting enough airtime.[52]

The resentment penetrated to the on-air relationship between Downs and Lescoulie:

Lescoulie was hired to help Downs keep the ball rolling, but, according to an associate, Downs would "pass some pleasantry" and Lescoulie would "cold-cock him." For example, Downs might say, "Well, Jack, it certainly is warm for March, isn't it," and Lescoulie would "just sit there and stare at him."[53]

The situation deteriorated until a series of events resulted in NBC's refusing to renew Lescoulie's $100,000-a-year contract in August 1966. But producer Al Morgan said that Lescoulie was not fired from *Today*: "'Everybody on the *Today* show is under contract including me,' he contended. 'Some contracts, are not renewed.' Lescoulie . . . insists he was fired and says he doesn't know why." Morgan gave credit to Lescoulie for his many years of contribution to the show. "'I have tremendous respect for Jack,' Morgan said. 'He had as much to do with the initial success of *Today* as Dave Garroway, the original host.'"[54]

Joe Garagiola

The new "second banana" at *Today*, Joe Garagiola, began his career at *Today* as early as 1962 with intermittent appearances as a guest panelist and conducted sports-related interviews. On December 5, 1967, NBC announced that he had been added to the show as a regular panel member. He was very well liked by the *Today* audience and competent in his work and soon became an integral part of the program. Garagiola was also given assignments other than light features and sports reports. He was an excellent interviewer, although he was not considered to be an intellectual. Al Smith, managing editor of *Today*, said that Garagiola asked the straightforward types of questions that everyone in the viewing audience wanted asked. For example, once "as Downs finished asking a stuffy and famous lawyer some 'convoluted' questions about torts, Garagiola popped up with 'It always seemed to me that lawyers do little and charge a lot. How come?'"[55]

Joe Garagiola's first career was as a professional baseball player. He was born in St. Louis, Missouri, where he eventually played catcher for the St. Louis Cardinals. He also played for the Pittsburgh Pirates, the Chicago Cubs, and the New York Giants. "I thought I was modeling uniforms for the National League," he once said.[56] Although he played in two World Series, he joked about his competence as a ballplayer and seemed to enjoy his second career as television broadcaster much more. He was a perfect addition to *Today*'s panel:

When Joe became a regular on the show in 1967, those bull's eye questions— the ones a cab driver might ask—became his trademark. The gentlemanly

Hugh Downs, the astringent Barbara Walters, and the happy-go-lucky Joe Garagiola proved to be a very successful mix for the show.[57]

Friday, January 12, 1973, was Joe Garagiola's last morning on *Today*. He resigned voluntarily from the program to pursue other broadcasting ventures, which included hosting NBC's game show *Sale of the Century* and hosting the sports programming on the NBC radio network. He also wanted to spend more time with his family. The *Today* staff and audience were genuinely sorry to see Garagiola leave. He was "everybody's favorite taxicab driver type, the regular guy with no side, comfortable as an old shoe. . . . Everybody loved him, even the advertisers, but the studio crew most of all."[58] In honor of his retirement, *Today* devoted the entire two hours of Friday, January 12, 1973, to a "Farewell to Joe Garagiola." After a seventeen-year absence and subsequent strong and varied broadcasting career, Garagiola was sought out by NBC to return to *Today* as a cohost with Bryant Gumbel and Deborah Norville. Hired in 1990 in an attempt to revive slumping ratings, he stayed until 1992, when he returned to his active career. He retired in February 2013 and died on March 23, 2016, at the age of ninety.

Gene Shalit

On January 15, 1973, Gene Shalit took over the vacancy left by Joe Garagiola. It was not an easy transition since the *Today* staff was mourning the loss of Garagiola. However, Shalit did bring to the show a great deal of experience and wit. He had been the book editor of *Today* since 1969; movie critic on WNBC-TV, New York; KNBC, Los Angeles; and NBC Radio Network's *Monitor*. He wrote the "What's Happening" column in the *Ladies Home Journal* magazine and "Gene Shalit's New York" for the *Long Island* newspaper. He was the movie critic for *Look* magazine before it folded, and he wrote the "Sports Talk" column for *Sport* magazine. His duties on *The Today Show* included "everything from books to sports and the light side of world events." He was also responsible for book, movie, and theatrical reviews on *Today*. Shalit was "the only movie critic whose views are read or heard regularly in every major medium—television, radio, newspapers and national magazines."[59]

Shalit was born in New York City; grew up in Morristown, New Jersey; and graduated from the University of Illinois with a major in journalism. He did not have the same style as Lescoulie or Garagiola, and his contributions to *The Today Show* were unique. He brought a combination of wit and sophistication to the panel. *Newsweek* described him saying that "no one has ever accused Gene of being just another pretty face. His lumpy visage is crowned by an aureole of bushy black hair and slashed quizzical eyebrows and a 5-inch-wide mustache, conjuring up a cross between Jerry Colonna and a startled bullfrog."[60] After forty years, Shalit retired from *Today* in 2010 at the age of eighty-four.

Jane Pauley

When Barbara Walters left *Today* in 1976 to coanchor the *ABC Evening News*, NBC launched an extensive search for a new female panelist. There was great speculation as to who "the next Barbara Walters" would be, but NBC set the ground rules early. First, they decided that the new panelist would not be given the same status that Walters had enjoyed. According to *Today* producer Stuart Schulberg, *Today* was returning to the "single"-host format, and the new female was definitely going to be in a secondary position. Because NBC executives were not necessarily looking for a "mature" panelist like Walters, it opened up an opportunity to give *Today* a younger image that would, they hoped, attract younger viewers to the show. NBC searched for its new female panel member using many of the techniques used in 1974 when they searched for Frank McGee's replacement. In the meantime, Betty Furness served as the substitute hostess. She was also one of the people considered for the permanent position, along with trial auditions for actress Candice Bergen, writer Shana Alexander, and former New York City consumer affairs chief Bess Myerson.[61] Catherine Mackin and Linda Ellerbee, NBC Washington correspondents, were other possibilities. Jane Pauley, coanchor of the local news on Chicago's NBC affiliate, WMAQ-TV, was also considered a leading candidate.

Pauley was given two audition days, July 30 and August 2, and then joined Tom Brokaw for the week of September 6–10, 1976, after which she was offered the position and joined *The Today Show* on Monday, October 11, 1976. President of NBC News Richard Wald announced her appointment in an NBC press release:

> "This talented and personable young woman is very well qualified for *Today*," Wald said. "For the past year she has co-anchored the nightly news at WMAQ-TV, the NBC television station in Chicago—the first woman to co-anchor a regularly scheduled weeknight news program in that city. She was one among several eminently capable women who appeared on *Today* this summer and, measured in terms of viewer response, emerged as the clear favorite of the *Today* audience for the assignment."[62]

Jane Pauley was not given the same status or salary as Barbara Walters had been given. She reportedly was offered a contract of approximately $125,000 per year. Some of her critics felt that the twenty-five-year-old Pauley did not have the journalistic experience that the job required. Although she may not have had much experience in terms of years, she did

Gene Shalit, Jane Pauley, and Tom Brokaw.

have an impressive career, considering her youth. In 1972, she graduated from Indiana University with a degree in political science. Shortly after graduation, she was hired as a reporter for WISH-TV in Indianapolis, Indiana. She moved rapidly from reporter to midday news coanchor and then began anchoring the weekend news reports. In 1975, she joined WMAQ-TV in Chicago to coanchor the NBC local news *NewsCenter 5* with Floyd Kalber. Her initial contact with *Today* was in 1975, when she hosted *The Today Show*'s salute to Illinois as part of *Today*'s bicentennial series.

Jane Pauley's debut was highly approved of by most critics, including *Newsweek*, which said she looked and sounded "eerily like her predecessor" Barbara Walters. She continued to be compared with Walters, particularly in terms of her contribution to the program. Paul Friedman, then executive producer of *Today*, thought she did a good job for the show, although her early interviewing techniques were weak compared to those of Walters. In response to her critics, Pauley said that although she felt "too young" at twenty-five, she did not find the comparisons to Walters to be quite fair. "When Barbara Walters started 10 or 12 years ago, she didn't start out interviewing Henry Kissinger. She grew into it. I hope to."[63] Pauley was an incredibly competent and popular cohost from 1976 to 1989, working alongside Tom Brokaw and later Bryant Gumbel. In 1989, it is thought that NBC began to groom Deborah Norville to assume more of Pauley's on-air responsibilities. As a result, Pauley left *Today* in 1989 and occasionally served as substitute anchor for *NBC Nightly News* and then hosted her own show, *Real Time with Jane Pauley*. From 1992 to 2003, she cohosted NBC's *Dateline*. In 2001, she was diagnosed with bipolar disorder and actively engaged in public mental health issues.

TODAY GIRLS

When Barbara Walters became a regular *Today* panelist in 1964, her title was "*Today* reporter." Prior to that time, all female panelists were referred to as "*Today* girls." Some of the women were regular members of the panel and others appeared occasionally to do light feature pieces. For a short period of time, *Today* changed girls on a weekly basis, so they came to be known as the "*Today* girl of the week." A few weeks after the program's debut, a reviewer for *New Republic* magazine wrote, "I hear through the grapevine that one of the producers has lined-up a gorgeous dame (he describes her as 'highly visible') to act as a reporter on the air because her presence will infuse some sex appeal."[64] Actually, when the remarks appeared in print, *Today* had been using Estelle Parsons for several weeks as a weather reporter. She excelled at her job and was soon given other responsibilities, such as handling feature segments and interviews. Parsons stayed with the program for about two years. Although attractive, she was hardly "gorgeous," and she certainly contributed more to the program than to function as a set decoration. The *New Republic* critic's comments could more accurately have been applied to the second regular *Today* girl, Lee Ann Meriwether, Miss America of 1954. She was "highly visible," and she was hired primarily to "infuse some sex appeal." All the *Today* girls were hired for their physical appearance, but the ones following Meriwether portrayed a more wholesome "girl next door" image to appeal to both the men and the women in the audience. Even though Helen O'Connell, Betsy Palmer, Florence Henderson, Beryl Pfizer, Anita Colby, Robbin Bain, Louise King, and Pat Fontaine were considered to be regular panel members, they did not appear on *Today* on a daily basis. Their feature responsibilities were confined to topics of interest to women, such as fashion, child care, and homemaking.

From about 1960 to 1962, *Today* tried the "Girl of the Week" approach. Those women were used to compensate for the lack of a regular female panel member when *Today* was "between" girls. This approach was abandoned because of the difficulties in coordinating the various girls with the programming. Producers felt, too, that regular female panelists were more effective, particularly those who developed an audience following. Host Hugh Downs opposed the hiring of Maureen O'Sullivan as a regular panel member, but Al Morgan had grown tired of the constant parade of pretty but shallow women and adamantly defended his choice. O'Sullivan was attractive and middle-aged, and Morgan felt that her experience and age would enable her to relate to the older women in *Today*'s audience. At the time, it was a small step toward making the female panelist position less decorative and more relevant, but Morgan chose the wrong female and the wrong criteria. Age was far less important than background, intelligence, and experience. Morgan must have come to realize just that because his second selection, Barbara Walters, turned out to be a superb choice. As Morgan soon noted, she was capable of handling material other than that reserved for the special interests of women, and she was far more capable of conducting interviews than host Hugh Downs. Prior to 1964, there had been twelve regular female panelists. Then, Walters served solely in that position for twelve years, from 1964 to 1976. When relative youngster Jane Pauley was selected in 1976, it was primarily for her impressive broadcast journalism qualifications, though her legendary attractiveness was certainly a bonus. Although her initial range of responsibilities on the program was not as broad as that of Walters, Pauley's duties were determined by her ability to handle them, not by the content of the segment.

NBC's Program Analysis Department kept records of all the *Today* women, and the listing reflects the change from occasional decorative presenter to regular contributions by female journalists. The roles of women on *Today* reflected the changes in social and professional status for women in society. *Today* kept records of the on-air appearances and titles of the girls:[65]

TODAY GIRLS

Estelle Parsons
January 14, 1952, to January 26, 1954, with occasional appearances thereafter

Lee Ann Meriwether
Miss America of 1954
October 11, 13, 14, 1955
Permanent *Today* panelist: effective October 17, 1955, to November 30, 1956

Phoebe B. Beebe
Chimpanzee-sister of J. Fred Muggs
Debut December 2, 1954, with numerous appearances until late 1956

Helen O'Connell
August 29, 30, 31, 1956—subs for Lee Ann Meriwether
Permanent panelist: December 7, 1956, to August 15, 1958
Off 3/17/58–6/6/58 to have a baby

Betsy Palmer
March 31 to April 4, 1958—subs for Helen O'Connell
April 28 to May 2, 1958
May 26 to 30, 1958
June 2–6, 1958—subs for Helen O'Connell
Regular panelist: effective August 18, 1958, to October 31, 1958
Girl of the Day—June 29, 1959

Florence Henderson
September 21 to 25, 1959, Girl of the Week
Permanent panelist: effective October 19, 1959, to May 20, 1960

Beryl Pfizer
September 12, 1960, to April 28, 1961

Anita Colby
April 13, 1961, to August 25, 1961

Robbin Bain
Miss Rheingold 1959
August 28, 1961, to September 15, 1961, Girl of the Week
September 18, 1961, to December 29, 1961, permanent panelist

Louise King
January 1, 1962, to June 29, 1962

Pat Fontaine
July 16, 1962, to July 27, 1962, Girl of the Week
August 13, 1962, Girl of the Day
Permanent panelist: effective August 14, 1962, to February 6, 1964

Maureen O'Sullivan
March 2, 9, 16, 30, 1964
April 6, 13, 20, 23, 27, 1964, appears as Girl of the Day
Permanent panelist: effective May 4, 1964, to September 18, 1964

Barbara Walters
Filmed reports from 1961
Approximately September 1964 named *Today* reporter
Effective September 1966: regular member of panel
Effective April 22, 1974: named permanent cohost

Jane Pauley
October 11, 1976: regular member of the panel
(cohost 1976 to 1989)

TODAY'S NEWSCASTERS

Perhaps the most stable on-air position on *Today* was the job of news-reader, originated by NBC news editor Jim Fleming, a broadcast journalist and former foreign correspondent for NBC. He was with *Today* until March 20, 1953, and was replaced for a short time by Merrill Mueller. On August 3, 1954, Frank Blair assumed the position and retained it for more than twenty years until he retired on March 14, 1975. Lew Wood replaced Blair in March 1975, and then Floyd Kalber replaced Wood in July 1976.

Frank Blair, Lew Wood, and Floyd Kalber

Frank Blair began his broadcasting career in 1935 in South Carolina and later became the general manager of station WSCR in Scranton, Pennsylvania. In 1950, he was hired by NBC in Washington, D.C., and in 1952 became the Washington correspondent for *The Today Show*. "Blair was unique compared to his predecessors. For one thing, he read the news slowly. It was almost as if he intuitively sensed that people listened as slowly as he talked." He has often been criticized for his lack of vitality in his performance. "Compared to his colleagues at NBC, everybody agrees, Blair was the one man who seemed to have paralysis of the face. He was so stiff and spare of his expression, it was rumored that he was born in the shadow of Mt. Rushmore."[66] Nevertheless, Blair was well liked by the audience, and *Today* received heavy mail if he was off even for a few days. Television critic Marvin Kitman wrote shortly after Blair left the show that his "quality of semi stupor often seemed to be the secret of his wide popularity with average American early morning TV viewers. After all, they aren't very alert in the mornings either." Another reason for his success seemed to be that because he was so expressionless in reading the news, he read it in a completely objective manner. "One could never tell where he stood on what he was reading. In all of his 22 years on the air, nobody can remember hearing him express a single viewpoint." It was rumored that "after Jim Hartz replaced Frank McGee as host, consideration was given to writing the word 'Jim' into Blair's script, lest he say one morning, 'Now back to you, Frank (or Hugh or Dave).'"[67]

When Frank Blair left the show, *Today* devoted the entire two hours of March 14, 1975, to honoring his retirement. He was replaced by Lew Wood, who held the position for slightly more than a year. In 1976, when the new executive producer Paul Friedman took over the show, he brought in Floyd Kalber to read the news, and Wood was reassigned to a lesser position, handling sports, weather, and some commercials. Kalber was originally from Omaha, Nebraska, where he was the news director for eleven years for KMTV in Omaha. He left to join WMAQ-TV, the NBC affiliate in Chicago, where he served as anchorman for WMAQ's evening news from 1960 to 1976 when he began his role at *Today*. Interestingly, for a short time in 1975, Jane Pauley was Kalber's coanchor on Chicago's *NewsCenter 5*. They began their careers with *Today* at approximately the same time in 1976. When Tom Brokaw left *Today* for *NBC Nightly News*, Kalber returned to Chicago to anchor the news for WLS-TV until his retirement in 1998. Kalber died in 2004.

Host: Newscaster or Entertainer?

Every *Today* host has had a background either in entertainment, as with David Garroway and Hugh Downs, or in news, as with John Chancellor, Frank McGee, Jim Hartz, and Tom Brokaw. All the hosts have been recruited from within NBC. Garroway and Downs came from the Entertainment Department, and Chancellor, McGee, Hartz, and Brokaw all worked in some capacity for NBC News. It was NBC policy that talent be developed "in-house" rather than recruited from other networks. The original host, Garroway, came from the entertainment field primarily because Pat Weaver felt that the host should be an entertainer. Garroway convinced Weaver of his suitability for the position, although Weaver considered having a comedian host the program. Garroway's charm and long-term success at hosting *Today* set up certain expectations from the audience, who wanted his successor to have a personality similar to Garroway's.

They were disappointed with starchy journalist Chancellor. It was a logical choice, though, that when *Today* began to be produced under NBC News, they would choose a host with a news background. There was an increased emphasis on news, and a journalist would strengthen that commitment and lend integrity to the program. NBC executives were also afraid of relinquishing control of the program to a "personality"; they felt Garroway had overpowered the program and consequently were reluctant to work with an entertainer. As it turned out, NBC News did a better job of producing the news, but their choice of host, a personality that NBC News found "manageable," was too weak to come across effectively with the audience. NBC News failed to recognize that it was a combination of format and host that had made *Today* successful. The audience clearly rejected the "anchorman" personality of Chancellor.

The third *Today* host, Hugh Downs, had a "homey, folksy," slow-moving, soft-spoken personality similar to David Garroway's. A description of Downs's personality in a *Variety* review could have applied to either Downs or Garroway. "Downs is a pleasant man, quick to communicate at a distinctly—almost instinctively—honest level to the people around him. So long as he keeps that one quality, along with his gentleness, he has nothing to fear about being out of work in TV." Those qualities made the audience highly receptive to both Garroway and Downs, but they watched the program because they also liked the format and content. When Downs assumed the host position, he was well known and brought an audience with him to *Today*. But as his popularity increased on *Today*, so did his personal demands in terms of content, personnel, and monetary compensation. What NBC News did not recognize with Chancellor but did realize with Downs was the importance of a good host. The host serves as the connecting link to the audience, and program identification usually takes on the personality of the host. In the case of Garroway, his personality overwhelmed the show until even the title carried his name. Although the off-camera personality problems and demands of the host are troublesome for the producers, the audience remains unaware of it. In fact, negative images of the talent are protected from the audience. As long as the personality successfully performs the hosting duties and ratings remain high, it is in the interest of the program to preserve and protect the public image of the host and meet his or her demands. NBC News also failed to realize that the host, in combination with the other *Today* talent, creates what Stuart Schulberg referred to as a "chemistry" in which certain personalities would mix well together or not. Unfortunately, the chemistry of the Chancellor panel did not.

NBC News tried again in 1971 to place a journalist into the host position and was successful with the choice of Frank McGee as the fourth host of *Today*. Although his personality and that of Hugh Downs were entirely dissimilar, there were many reasons why McGee was a success. Although not "folksy" in his approach, McGee was comfortable with the host position, skillful in his interviewing techniques, and well known and well respected for his journalism background. Schulberg described McGee as having a warm personality (although this was more evident on-screen than off-screen) and said that he managed to appear friendly while conducting tough interviews. Further, when McGee was hired, the program was in a very stable period, and the transition from Downs to McGee went quite smoothly. There were few revisions accompanying the change, and the remainder of the *Today* panel consisted of the familiar faces of Barbara Walters, Joe Garagiola, and newscaster Frank Blair, all of whom had been with the show for many years. Also, as the years mounted, *Today* became more of a viewing habit with its audience. Without major disrupting or disorienting changes, there was little reason for the transition to McGee to have much of an effect on audience viewing.

It was a different effort entirely when it came time to select Frank McGee's successor. It was an enormously complex and scientific process that took approximately three months. Although the contenders were subjected to popularity auditions designed to objectively secure the best personality possible, when the actual decision was made, it involved some fairly subjective human input. There were certain preferences made in terms of qualifications, and despite the objective data, Barbara Walters had considerable input into the selection of her cohost. After playing a submissive role to McGee, she was not anxious to endorse a candidate with a strong, dominating personality. All the finalists were from the NBC News Department. NBC preferred the younger candidates, and a few of the contenders refused to do commercials, further narrowing the field. The decision finally came down to Jim Hartz and Tom Brokaw. Although Brokaw refused to do commercials, he was still considered a strong contender based on his other strong assets. NBC executives preferred Brokaw, but they were reluctant to meet his terms and so offered the position to Hartz.

That long selection process was a failure. It was only slightly more successful than when NBC News hurriedly decided to hire John Chancellor. The process itself contributed to the failure by dragging new faces before the audience for several months, thereby adding to the overall instability of the program. Hartz was simply a poor choice as the host, but in comparison to the other candidates, he may have been the best of what was offered. NBC News rejected from the beginning the possibility of a personality other than a newsman. Since *Today* had been so indisputably successful under Garroway and Downs, it appeared rather stubborn of NBC News not to have given an "entertainer" the same auditioning opportunity. The fact that Hartz possessed the most "gentle-mannered" personality suggested that the audience chose against the "anchorman" personality.

The failure to isolate a potential strong host indicated that the audition process itself probably created an artificial situation and was too short a time in which to make a long-term judgment. One of the problems with Hartz was that his gentle manner came across as a "weak" personality (particularly in contrast to the overpowering Barbara Walters) when he assumed the daily duties as host.

Probably the decision should have gone to Tom Brokaw in 1974, but because he and NBC could not come to terms, Hartz was hired instead. In 1976, NBC was willing to renegotiate in order to secure Brokaw for the position. NBC was looking to change the orientation of the program in order to attract a younger audience, and the youthful and popular Brokaw was ideally suited. His background was in news, and he possessed a "boyish," warm personality. Brokaw's roots, like panelist Jane Pauley and newscaster Floyd Kalber, were midwestern. At the time, there had been a trend for *The Today Show* to avoid programming to the New York area and specifically to the "New York sophisticate" and instead to aim the program at middle America. This trend was *Today*'s answer to the "folksy" programming that was so popular for *Today*'s chief competitor, *Good Morning America*, in the mid-1970s.

Pat Weaver's original vision of a morning show was characterized by a combination of news and entertainment. Therefore, the perfect host would have both credibility and charisma. Hard news would be presented along with entertaining segments. Weaver also felt that it was desirable to have a third person on the *Today* panel who would share some of the hosting responsibilities, such as interviewing and handling features. Ideally, that person would serve in a supporting capacity off which the host could bounce ideas, comments, and witty exchanges. That panel member served to handle the "light" features and provided comic relief while the dignity of the host remained intact. That "sidekick" or "second banana" position was held for many years by Jack Lescoulie and later by Joe Garagiola. The nature of the panel and the definition of that role changed somewhat in 1973, when Gene Shalit assumed the position. The "clown" role was exchanged for more sophisticated humor and wit and was displayed in a more controlled format, as in "Gene Shalit's Critic's Corner," where humor was combined with professional criticism of film, literature, art, music, and theater.

The other panel member was the newscaster who originally interacted more freely with the other talent and segments of the program. That position later became more narrowly defined when the newscaster duties were relegated to only those segments that involved the news. But undoubtedly, the position that evolved most dramatically was that of the female panelist. The original *Today* girl, Estelle Parsons, carved a viable presence for a woman on the program, but the producers soon opted for a more visible woman who would presumably attract men to the program. Later, to attract both men and women to the audience, *Today* developed programming features geared toward women and delivered by attractive but not overtly sexy women.

Beginning in 1964, a substantial new role for *Today* women was developed by Barbara Walters. Although producer Al Morgan provided her with the opportunity to display her talents, it was Walters who determined her own success. By setting a superior example, she created opportunities that allowed other women to assume similar responsibilities in news. She submerged her femininity and established her credibility as a newswoman by handling "tough" assignments to break down the assignment barrier whereby women were systematically relegated only to "soft" news. More important, she served as a successful female role model for young women who could identify with and pattern themselves after her. When Walters moved on to even greater success, new female panelist Jane Pauley was hired primarily for her qualifications as a newswoman. Her youth and wholesome attractiveness were just a serendipitous bonus.

5

✢

Selling *Today*

Advertising and Station Relations

Before cable or satellite ramped up programming choices into hundreds of stations and specialized networks, there were really only the three major networks (NBC, CBS, and ABC) that distributed their programming over the air or via special landline connections to local stations. When *Today* originated in the early 1950s and throughout much of the history of broadcasting, the relationship between a network and its stations was established as a mutual arrangement involving programming and advertising. At the time, Federal Communications Commission (FCC) rules allowed the networks to own only seven TV stations, which they tended to do in the largest markets, such as New York, Chicago, Los Angeles, and Philadelphia. In order to reach a broader national audience, the networks sought out local stations in other cities. Those local stations could enter into contracts, becoming "affiliated" with the network for the purpose of obtaining high-quality programming. If the local affiliated station agreed to carry a network program, it also agreed to carry the network advertising or commercials. The networks also gave the local stations further incentive by giving them a small share of the advertising revenues and/or making available commercial minutes that could be sold locally. During the years from 1952 to 1976, broadcasting looked very different from today. Generally, there were few broadcast stations in the major cities, but those that did exist tended to "affiliate" or contract with either NBC, CBS, or ABC to carry the network programming and advertising. Stations that carried the programming were said to "clear" or air the shows produced and offered by the network. The networks provided high-quality programming that was prohibitively expensive for a local station to produce or purchase. In return, the local station agreed to air the program as broadcast, along with the presold network advertising. That would give the networks and advertisers access to a large aggregate audience distributed among individual cities across the nation. The relationship between the network and its stations required a great deal of coordination. The NBC Sales Department set the sales policies for network programming, while the stations' relations departments communicated to the NBC-affiliated and -owned stations information about advertising policies, time changes in both network and local breaks, special sales packages, and changes in program feed. That also included any communication that was necessary for smooth operation between the network and its stations.

EARLY DAYS AND FINANCING

The Today Show began as an innovative program with a unique advertising concept. Over its first twenty-five years, the sales policy was constantly reviewed and often revised by network and sales executives who would have suggested changes in order to make the most profits, attract advertisers, and satisfy the stations that carried and participated in the advertising of *The Today Show*. From the outset, Pat Weaver recognized that the unique concept of *Today* would require significant financing to cover the costs of such lengthy, frequent, and ambitious programming. But he also recognized that although it was just getting up and running, he expected the audience to grow substantially as the program delivered on its myriad promises. In a memo to Harry Bannister, vice president for station relations, he explained the program concept in relation to the problem of financing:

> It is important for us to remember that *Today* is a program service which has a tremendous future. Everything that happens in terms of network coverage of the real world in color and throughout the planet, by transcontinental and overseas interconnections, by live pick-ups, by vidicon-placed observer posts, and a thousand other plans which we have announced and still have on the drawing board—all of this extensive and dramatic, incredibly expensive coverage—is essentially first usable on *Today*. It is, therefore, an absolute certainty, that as the years go on, this program will become a fixture which will, more and more, reach peak circulations when anything important in the real world is happening for the special event coverage that will take place on *Today*. It will always be used by the people who missed something the day before. It will inevitably increase its coverage in depth of the news. Interesting devices and new program ideas will bring more genuine entertainment and informative substance to *Today*. Its audience will ever broaden. Further-

more, the slave television sets, the TV audio sets individually manufactured as a second "Blind" television set, plus the use of the TV audio bands on radio sets to be manufactured later, plus the purchase of a new set without selling the second set, and all the other reasons why television coverage is going to expand in the home, means that the *Today* audience will go ever higher. This program, of course, is simply not possible within the range of any client's purse. It is, indeed, with extreme difficulty that the R. J. Reynolds Company is able to pay for the *Camel Newsreel* today, and, of course, their costs do not even attempt to cover the basic expense of running even part of the NBC coverage operation.[1]

As Weaver indicated, the most difficult problem for the *Today* staff was to attract sufficient advertising to offset the heavy production expenses accrued by the program in its early years and to conceive a sales plan that would expand along with the program. Thus, a special advertising plan was set up for the *Today* program. It was not sold on the same basis that other network programming was sold; instead, Weaver, who had initiated the idea of "participating advertising" for NBC network "specials," implemented the idea for *The Today Show*. Instead of being sponsored by a single advertiser, the program was sold to multiple advertisers who purchased time on a participating basis. Participating advertising has been described as a type of advertising in which "no one advertiser would dominate, and many small advertisers, previously excluded from television network advertising, were able to participate in the sponsorship of big network shows that gave their advertising messages a national circulation previously obtained only by a small number of advertisers."[2] At the time, only certain programs had been available on a participating basis. In the early years, NBC specials and *Today* were offered for sale on a participating basis, and later *Home* and *Tonight* were added. Subsequently, NBC Participating Program Sales sold such programs as *Saturday/Sunday Tonight*, *Tomorrow*, *Weekend*, *Saturday Night*, and *Midnight Special* on that same basis. Ultimately, it became the standard advertising practice that nearly all programming was sold on a participating basis, and only rarely would programs be "sponsored" as in the early sense of that practice.

During that first year when NBC tried to sell *Today*, they sought two objectives. The first was to improve the ratings so that it would be reasonably attractive to potential advertisers, and the second was that *Today* would have its own sales staff of devoted salesmen who were specifically interested in selling *Today*. That was an especially important goal because the regular NBC sales personnel preferred to sell prime-time programs that sold more easily. Richard Pinkham, then executive producer of *Today*, hired Matthew J. (Joe) Culligan to direct the sales program for *The Today Show*, and Culligan, in turn, hired three salesmen who sold only *The Today Show*: Bob Bonagura, Bill Asip, and Dick Sewell. Culligan had been the advertising director for Siff-Davis publications and had connections with several advertising agencies. Together, he and David Garroway made the presentations to the advertising agencies.[3] Culligan recalled those presentations: "When they all assembled, I would walk in with Garroway. He would lean on the podium and talk with such charm and literacy about what he was intending to do with *The Today Show* that we got our first nibbles."[4] *Today* sales executives were determined to sell the show by attracting the small advertiser. They felt that the show was particularly suitable for selling products designed for the specialized audience watching *The Today Show*. Food products and household items were ideal.

The second important *Today* advertising strategy was to have the host and panel members of *Today* actually do the commercials live. It was a practice that proved very attractive to advertisers but caused a great many practical problems in the early days. Later, when *Today* was produced under the News Department, it caused philosophical conflicts.

THOSE EARLY YEARS

In the early years of *Today*, having David Garroway do live commercials was a brilliant advertising idea that helped to establish a secure financial base for the program. That made it necessary, however, for Garroway and other panel members to arrive at the studio earlier than usual in order to familiarize themselves with the commercial copy and proper demonstration of any new product. Doing live studio commercials required close coordination between the advertising agencies and *Today* production staff. The NBC Sales Department distributed information to clients on *Today*'s policy regarding live commercials:

> *The Use of Garroway in Commercials:*
>   The producers reserve the right to determine how many commercials Dave Garroway will be available to do each day.
>   Dave Garroway will not taste advertising products, will not demonstrate any action which is out of keeping with his sex and personality. He will not for example, mix cake batter, beat eggs, wear funny hats, drink beverages, smoke cigarettes, cigars or pipes, etc.
>   No "test" type commercials will be accepted unless Dave Garroway is convinced of their credibility. We have learned through trial and error that the best method of procedure is to arrange a strategy meeting with the agency client and *Today* production people as soon after consummation of a sale as possible.
>   Dave Garroway will do live lead in to sight and sound films, and the voice over sight only films.

Commercials should not exceed one minute in their storyboard or script form. It may be that Garroway will occasionally run over the one minute, but we shall not accept any commercial script that "times out" at more than one minute.

General Commercial Information on Today:
Use of J. Fred Muggs in Commercials:
J. Fred Muggs is not available for use in commercials.
Commercial Rehearsals:
A minimum of ½ hour of camera rehearsal is required for each new client prior to the starting date of a campaign on *Today*.[5]

There were regulations concerning the use of promotional photographs that featured *Today* personalities. If a client wished to use them, it had to be accompanied by a phrase similar in meaning to "As featured by _____ on *Today*," and the word *"Today"* had to be the show's logo. Also, the client had to obtain permission from the producer if the picture was to be used in connection with a direct or implied testimonial. Because of the limitations imposed by the *Today* facilities, it was required that all scripts had to be cleared with the *Today* production staff: "Only hand props may be used in commercials. A hand prop may be described as anything that can be held easily in the two hands of the commercial announcer."[6]

The *Today* talent, conscientiously accepting their roles as pitchmen, were causing problems in the early days by extending the actual amount of commercial time allotted for a product. Since the commercial was live, it was easy for the talent to ad-lib about the qualities of the product for more than just a few seconds of excess time, but they caused problems by cutting into program feature time. A memo by Steve Flynn of the Participating Sales Department outlined the problem: "With the probability of an almost sold-out condition in the Fall, there will be very little of Dave Garroway and news left on the program if we're going to allow this amount of commercial to each customer." For example, regular advertiser Dial Soap was paying for only four fifteen-second spots but was averaging almost thirty seconds of airtime for each of those four spots. U.S. Rubber paid for one-minute spots but clocked in closer to a minute and thirty seconds. Squibb and Polaroid, paying for sixty-second spots, doubly benefited by getting as much as two full minutes of airtime, so the averages were highly significant and caused the show to lose both time and money.[7]

The *Today* sales staff had to deal with procedures and policies that were both new and unique to the program. Often, that meant they had to clarify and be very specific about the process to their clients and the stations that participated in the advertising. In the beginning, it was especially important for *Today* to maintain good relations with the advertising agencies in order to ensure future sales and for the *Today* salesmen to prove their reliability since it was difficult in the first place to sell *Today*. There were sales complications in the early years stemming in part from the salesmen failing to notify the agencies about changes or interruptions on the station lineup. Suggestions were made to the sales staff to first send written confirmation to the agency and then notify the agency immediately if any changes did occur.

By 1953, NBC, having worked out the major issues, sent the following memo to the *Today* sales staff in order to clarify the program's sales policies. The major points were as follows:

1. Advertisers purchase participations (the word segments has proved to be misleading) on desired days and in one or both of the two hours of the show. As a general rule we shall no longer permit the advertiser to name a specific time segment for his commercials.
2. We urge advertisers to rotate and stagger their commercial pattern to maximize exposure of the commercials to the greatest unduplicated audience.
3. We reserve the right to move an advertiser's commercial in the event of a late-breaking news story which forces a recasting of the show's schedule.
4. An advertiser who buys three or more participations per week for 13 weeks can gain exclusivity for the product advertised.
5. Special exclusivity arrangements will be made for advertisers who use *Today* five times per week or more for a family of products even though some of the products may not appear there three times per week or more.
6. The standard commercial pattern for *Today* shall be a combination of 20 second lead-in by Garroway, with bulk of commercial delivered by Lescoulie and/or other permanent members of *Today* staff. Dave will also do 20 second lead-ins to film commercials. Except for our present commitments for all-Garroway commercials, we will not accept new advertisers who insist on having all commercials delivered by Garroway exclusively. Each case should be studied on its individual merits for it is felt that a suitable formula can be developed for most new advertisers.
7. Fixed editorial features on *Today*, adjacencies to which we shall sell under the following conditions, are:

The *Today* Weather Map
   This feature is on twice daily, at 7:12 and 8:12 local time. General Mills has contracted for it five times per week, and Capital Airlines three times per week, alternate weeks, hence two adjacencies per week are available through fall 1953 and all of 1954.

Today Baseball Scoreboard
   This feature is seen twice daily at _____ and _____, local time. Adjacencies to it may be sold.

Today Front Page
This is the news package at 7:00–7:06; 7:30–7:36; 8:00–8:06; 8:30–8:36.

Conditions for sale of adjacencies to fixed editorial features:

1. Three per week or more participations for 13 weeks or duration of base-ball season, non-cancellable contracts.
2. Understanding that non-competitive advertisers may buy participations on other days, or other time periods.[8]

In order to meet the demands of the stations, the network sales execu-tives, and the sponsors, *Today* was forced to reconsider its advertising policies quite often. Originally, *Today* was offered to advertisers in seg-ments of five, seven and a half, ten, and fifteen minutes each. However, in October 1952, the structure was revised, and *Today* was sold in purchases of five minutes only. Harry Bannister, then vice president of NBC Sales, had requested the change to five minutes after determining the most common practice: "92% of all *Today* sales have been of that type. This has not been of our doing. Some of the smallest clients could afford no more than five minutes weekly. The others prefer it because they can distribute more commercial messages across the week or month, thus increasing both frequency of impression and cumulative audience."[9]

Although selling *Today* from the start was somewhat challenging, one thing that the sales staff did not have to consider was competition for sales dollars. Then, in 1954, *The Today Show* met its first major competitor when CBS programmed *The Morning Show* opposite *Today*. Of course, this was of paramount interest to the NBC sales staff because now they had to deal with a program that competed for ratings and hence advertising dollars. One encouraging note was that *Today* had clearly established that there was an audience in the early hours of the morning that provided enough viewers to make a profitable time period possible. However, they needed to size up their competition, so the sales staff analyzed the ben-efits of buying time on *The Morning Show* compared with *Today* and sent the results to Culligan, director of sales for *The Today Show*:

It is possible to buy 26 segments of the CBS show for $78,861 time and tal-ent. This represents 53 stations. Twenty-six segments of *Today* cost $111,306 time and talent. Therefore, the CBS package is cheaper by $32,445—approxi-mately $1248 per segment. Reportedly, CBS is granting any client who buys two segments a week for 13 weeks an extra 3 weeks without additional cost. The *Today* segments are 6½ minutes—the CBS segments are 5 minutes. A CBS segment cost $550 for program and $2,588 gross for time—or a total of $3,138 gross. A *Today* segment costs $394 for program and $3,887 gross for time—or a total of $4,281 time and talent.[10]

After the sales development staff had seen the memorandum, they issued the following points to the network sales staff on the advantages *Today* offered when compared to *The Morning Show*:

  a. *Today* has a star salesman.
  b. *Today* offers merchandising support.
  c. Time costs on *The Morning Show* are less because CBS has inferior coverage—offers substantial less potential homes.
  d. Because of its inferior coverage, *The Morning Show* will require a higher rating than *Today* to equal our low cost per thousand.[11]

There were problems in 1954 with those stations that carried *Today* from 6:00 to 7:00 a.m. during Daylight Savings Time. In order to protect their advertisers in terms of guaranteed audience, *Today* sales executives requested the Ratings Section to determine the difference in audience when *The Today Show* was carried normally from 7:00 to 8:00 a.m. Standard Time and when it was carried from 6:00 to 7:00 a.m. during Daylight Savings Time. The results showed a substantial loss of audience:

> A study of *Today* ratings in five of the thirteen markets where the program was carried from 6–7 AM, indicates that the ratings suffered substantially. Our best estimate is that the rating for the 6–7 AM portion was about 1/3 less than what it would have been if the program had been aired at its normal time.[12]

The *Today Show* sales department responded by offering special discount packages to advertisers who bought time on those stations that were reaching a smaller audience.

Another change affecting opportunities for advertisers occurred on February 28, 1955, when *Today* expanded its West Coast programming to two hours. Originally, *Today* fed the West Coast on a quick kinescope delay that aired only from 8:00 to 9:00 a.m. Pacific Standard Time. In 1955, it added the 7:00–8:00 a.m. hour and promoted the change to its advertisers:

> Starting February 28, 1955 regional network advertisers and national advertisers seeking Pacific Coast regional coverage will get a real commercial break. NBC-TV's famed *Today* will add 7:00 to 8:00 AM PST to its current 8:00 to 9:00 AM morning schedule. This totals up to two hours with the hottest salesman on the air today. . . . DAVE GARROWAY (if you have any doubts on that score, ask to see the long list of success stories Dave has racked up for his sponsors). . . . Dave Garroway, as emcee, is ably assisted by Jack Lescoulie and newsman, Frank Blair. Contact with the animal kingdom is maintained through J. Fred Muggs and Phoebe B. Beebe, champ chimps.[13]

The following year, *Today* again revised the West Coast programming and the sales policy. The new West Coast sales plan was to make the five segments available for sale on only a regional basis rather than sold locally. "The reasoning behind this position is that the network is investing substantial additional programming money in altering the entire repeat hour of *Today* to improve the show's audience position in the Coast area by inclusion of regional interest material, much of which will fall within the five minute segments."[14]

The implementation of participating advertising on *The Today Show* made it possible for the small advertiser to sell a product on a national basis for relatively low cost. It also made it possible to scatter the advertising message across different times and to reach a more diverse audience. This became very attractive to advertisers who wanted to buy even smaller amounts of time. In the early years, it was often requested of the Participating Sales Department that the sixty-second commercial spot be reduced to thirty seconds, but that request was consistently rejected by sales executives:

> The basic reason for our not wanting to entertain this kind of a sale is that, as you know, stations are extremely sensitive as to the sale of participating announcements on the network as a whole, and it continues to be felt unwise to attempt any fractionalizing of our current one minute base. In addition, you are, I know, familiar with the program problems inherent in additional commercial interruptions which such fractionalizing would obviously produce. Thirdly, by maintaining the one minute standard for all advertisers, our clients get theoretically equal viewer impression which would also not be the case if an advertiser for the price of a one minute participation was granted two split exposures within the program.[15]

Although that was the official *Today* procedure, it can be noted that when *Today* had difficulty attracting advertisers to the program, individual deals were made with the advertisers. For example, *Today* allowed Dial Soap, one of its earliest advertisers, to split their one-minute spots into four fifteen-second announcements. By 1976, the thirty-second spot became the advertising standard on *Today*.

PROGRAM AND ADVERTISING REORGANIZATION

After a somewhat shaky start, the *Today* ratings climbed considerably when J. Fred Muggs joined the show in 1953. When the ratings went up, so did interest from the advertising agencies, and *Today* became increasingly financially viable over the next few years. By 1958, however, *Today* was again in serious financial trouble, but it was not directly attributable to low ratings. Instead, the show needed—and got—a revision in the programming and sales organization. Losses on *The Today Show* in 1958 were estimated at two and a half million dollars. Those losses stemmed primarily from the daily three-hour production costs and an advertising policy that did not generate sufficient income to meet expenses. A plan was developed to reorganize the network and local sales time on the program. The new plan would provide the extra five-minute units for local news, weather, and service.[16]

The other major revision that saved a considerable amount of production cost for the show was the videotaping and tape replay of the first hour of *Today*. The third hour had been live.

When the new plan went into effect in October 1958, the *Today* Sales Department produced a new sales plan to induce advertisers to purchase the full-station lineup rather than buying only the required stations. The plan was to offer the optional stations at 50 percent of the rate currently being charged. William Storke, NBC sales executive, explained:

> With almost total dollar retention under the new *Today* plan I think if we were to offer the *Today* optional market package at a 50 percent rate, we could at least double the above percentages, strengthen *Today*'s media values making it more attractive to all advertisers, and finally keep to a minimum problems that conceivably will arise from unordered stations failing to cut away from network commercials.[17]

Within a short period of time after the affiliate stations approved the change, *Today* made minor adjustments in the new format. In an experiment, the Sales Department sent five salesmen to New York and three salesmen to Chicago to record their impressions of the program, including client and advertising agency reactions to the new format. The unanimous response was that *Today* was interrupted too often with cutaways. As a result, NBC sales executive James Hergen made recommendations to *Today* producer Robert Bendick, resulting in the following program change:

> Effective Tuesday, November 4th, *The Today Show* will operate on a new time schedule. This change is being made to reduce the number of cutaways and cutaway cues in order to smooth out the continuity of the show, and at the same time, leave an equal amount of time for local station programming and commercials.
>
> The new programming schedule will effect only the 1st and 3rd half hours—i.e., 7:00–7:30 and 8:00–8:30, EST.
>
> In brief:
>
> 1. The 5:00 co-op break away for local news and weather will be returned to its former position at 25 minutes after the hour.

2. The four 1:00 cutaways for local station commercials each ½ hour will be consolidated into two 2:00 breaks. For stations which don't cutaway, *Today* will fill with temperature crawl and recorded music.

This schedule repeats from 8:00–8:30, EST.

Please note each 2:00 break for local commercials actually runs for 2:10. *Today* telop will be carried by the network for five seconds preceding and following the 2:00 break to facilitate commercial cutaways and returns by local stations. These 2:00 breaks will be signaled by a network electronic cue approximately 1:00 before the break. A second network electronic cue will appear continuously for approximately fifteen seconds before the break. When cue mark disappears, the station cuts away for two minutes. The verbal switch cue is—"This is *TODAY* on NBC."[18]

Copies of the new format were sent to all program affiliates to keep them informed of the new sales opportunities and the switching cues for the breaks.

ADVERTISING PLANS AND RATES

Today advertising rates were determined by the Participating Program Sales unit of the NBC Sales Department and reflected how the advertising rates, station lineup, and types of advertising packages changed over the years. Records of advertising rates on *The Today Show* from 1955 to 1958 indicate that *Today* offered four basic advertising plans, which they called A, B, C, and D coverage. Each of the four coverage plans consisted of basic (required) stations and supplementary stations. For any plan, advertisers were required to buy the basic stations as a group. Supplementary stations were available for purchase in addition to the required stations as a group or individually. The basic stations were generally in the best markets, and the supplementary stations were available at much lower rates than the required stations.

All the coverage plans itemized the various charges that would be made to the advertisers on a "per participation" basis. The type of coverage was based on various combinations of *Today*'s broadcast hours. The required and supplementary stations varied with each plan. The amount per participation varied, too, according to the ratings for each hour of the program. The coverage also compared each hour of the program and compensated for the differences in time zones. In 1959, the coverage plans were reduced to an A or B option, each offering required stations and supplementary stations. That simplified plan was in effect from 1959 to 1976. Again, the basic plans, option A or B, were determined according to the hour of origination, and the advertising rates varied according to the ratings for each hour and the number of stations and market rankings offered in the plan. Information was added to the rate card that was useful to the potential advertiser, such as the "*Today* Percentage of U.S. TV Set Coverage." This information was supplied by the Nielsen Television Index and was taken into consideration for each type of coverage, with and without the supplementary stations. This made it possible for the advertiser to determine the best possible coverage for the product. In 1959, for example, an advertiser could reach 97 percent of the U.S. TV set coverage when the required lineup and all supplementary *Today* stations were purchased. There was little growth in the *Today* station lineup in the next three years, and it cost only about $600 more to purchase the required station lineup. In spite of the very low cost of adding the supplementary stations to the required station purchase, advertisers were reluctant to buy the full station lineup. As an incentive, *Today* initiated a 25 percent discount plan on the supplementary group. The result was that it was possible to purchase more stations in 1962 for a price that was lower than the cost in 1959 for fewer stations.

Over the next several years, there were only minor changes in the rate cards and advertising plans. By 1965, except for a rise in the number of available stations from 159 to 173 and the cost of the basic lineup rising to approximately $7,200, there were few changes in the rate cards. The full station lineup increased only about $1,300 from 1959. In 1968, the available station lineup for coverage B had increased to 197 stations. *Today* listed sixty-seven of those as required stations and charged approximately $8,200 for their purchase. The remaining 130 supplementary stations were available for an additional $3,000. Although the supplementary stations were offered as a group for that incredibly low rate, the advertisers were not buying them. In order to further encourage advertisers to purchase the full station lineup (the 25 percent discount plan was still in effect), NBC added a table in the rate card that directly compared the average A and B coverage required station cost of $8,211.25 to the full station lineup for each plan, which was only $10,447.64. The advertiser could clearly see the advantage of adding 130 stations for very little extra cost. This incentive was moderately successful, and after 1968, NBC included the direct comparison table in all the rate cards until 1976. Except for an increase in the available station lineup of 197 to 211 stations, there were few changes between 1968 and 1971. The cost per participation for the full station lineup increased by less than $500. Although it appears that in 1974 *The Today Show* changed its advertising policy, in fact it changed only the rate card form. The basic coverage plan was the same as it had been in 1959. The new form added information and made easier the direct comparisons between the A and B coverage plans.

In 1976, however, *Today* instituted a major change in its advertising policy. First, only a full station lineup was available to advertisers, and, second, the price per participation was based on a thirty-second spot. It had previously been priced according to sixty-second participations. Over the twenty-one years from 1955 to 1976, the advertising rates had gone up approximately $10,000 per minute, and the full station lineup had changed from eighty-seven stations in 1955 to 222 stations in 1976, providing 99 percent of U.S. TV coverage.[19] From then on, *Today* was available on a full station lineup basis only.

DISCOUNTS AND OPTIONS

In addition to regular advertising rates, the rate cards listed special discount and advertising plan options that were available to the advertiser. For example, advertisers could receive discounts based on the number of ads purchased during a specific time period.

The summer discount incentive plan had been in effect as early as 1955 and applied to *Today*, *Home*, and *Tonight*:

> Advertisers scheduling participations on the *Today* and or *Home* and or *Tonight* programs for telecast during the 14-week period beginning Monday, May 30, 1955 and ending Friday, September 2, 1955 will be allowed to schedule on a no-charge basis an additional number of participations. For example, after seven advertising spot purchases, the advertiser would receive one free, and with fifty would receive an additional fifteen, a strong incentive to make additional purchases and guaranteeing a strong revenue flow for NBC.[20]

The plans were typical of the discount incentive plan that was offered during the regular year, but other plans included a summer discount option. The discounts were called "dividend" plans, and many were generous packages:

> Advertisers ordering more than 40 paid participations during the term of this plan will be allowed 2 additional dividend participations for every 4 paid participations.[21]

One other discount plan was the station lineup incentive discount of 15 percent. This discount applied to those advertisers that bought the full station lineup:

> *Station Lineup Incentive Discount:*
> An advertiser ordering for any participation all available stations, and maintaining same in the event of station additions, will be granted for such participation a twenty-five percent (25%) discount on gross time charges for the aggregate value of all Supplementary stations.[22]

The Participating Program Sales rate cards for the *Today* program included general information on the advertising policies set by NBC. The 1976 Rate Guide outlines the following:[23]

Advertising Agency Commission
All gross billings are subject to an advertising agency commission of 15%. Such commission is allowed only if authorized by the Advertiser to the advertising agency of record whose financial responsibility is acceptable to NBC.

Integrated Networking Charge
A production facilities charge of $175 gross is applicable to each insertion which does not exceed 60 seconds in length. This charge covers the services as required for Transcontinental Transmission, and the Recorded Repeat Network Telecast(s). It also includes the insertion of film or tape commercials when originated from network control points at New York and/or Burbank.

Production Facilities Charges
Production charges are published in the current *Television Network Production Facilities and Services Rate Manual*. Commercial material for insertion into all network originated programs should be delivered at least 14 days prior to broadcast. Additional charges may be made for late delivery of commercial material in accordance with the *Television Network Production Facilities and Service Rate Manual*. It is suggested that the Commercial Producer of *Today* and Tonight be consulted in advance in reference to an Advertiser's specific requirements.

Station Orders
In order to serve the public interest in having NBC television programs available on a national basis and to maintain the network function as an effective national advertising medium, orders for NBC Television Network facilities are subject to acceptability of the station lineup ordered.

In connection with administering orders for participating or multi-sponsored programs, NBC may designate, for each such program individually, the basis of station order acceptability.

NBC will accept orders for regional advertising to be matched with other advertisers on a pool-participation basis. An outline of the basis on which such orders can be accepted will be furnished upon request.

Contracts
Participating Advertisers are required to make individual contracts (Participating Sponsorship Agreements) with NBC for their sponsorship arrangements.

Special Services
Arrangements may be made for the substitution of or addition to Advertisers' network commercial messages on a local or sectional basis to meet special product or service distribution requirements. Such arrangements must

be made through NBC Special Services unit. It is suggested that this unit be contacted sufficiently in advance of the dates on which such special services will be required in order that a complete outline of the basis on which orders can be accepted may be furnished.

Network Program Originations
Should NBC permanently alter the regular time period, the conditions of sales for the affected program would be subject to revision effective with the change of time period.

NEWS AND ADVERTISING PART WAYS

Another major advertising policy change also occurred in 1976 but had its roots in 1961 when NBC News revisited the practice of having the host participate in commercials. When *Today* was placed under the control of NBC News, it hired newsman John Chancellor to take over from Dave Garroway. Chancellor felt that it compromised journalistic integrity for a newsperson to participate in commercials, and he adamantly refused to do them. At the time, NBC agreed, but ultimately that practice caused the sponsorship to drop significantly. So, when Hugh Downs joined the show a year later, *Today* benefited once more by reinstating the old practice of having the host pitch commercials. Significantly, Downs did not come from a news background and happily accepted the responsibility. Subsequently, other hosts all agreed to sell commercial products until the search for a replacement host after Frank McGee's death in 1974, when many of the top contenders refused. Garrick Utley, candidate for the position, said, "I question whether a reporter does not lose his journalistic virginity by doing commercials. And can you recover that virginity later?"[24] In an article written for the *Washington Post*, journalist Sander (Sandy) Vanocur outlined the arguments against allowing journalists to do commercials:

> Advertisers are delighted when they can get television news people to peddle their wares. It lends a certain respectability and authenticity to their pitch. A number of commercials deliberately try to make the pitchman seem as if he or she is a reporter covering a story. Television news people who were trained as journalists are very sensitive about such hucksterism. A certain amount of bitterness was directed against the late Chet Huntley when he did American Airlines commercials after leaving NBC. Sadness was the more appropriate word to describe the reaction when NBC News allowed the late Frank McGee to anchor news specials after he started doing commercials as the *Today* show host. Television journalists take enough guff from their print media colleagues about being in show business. They are justifiably concerned when people who deal in the news also are permitted to handle commercials.[25]

According to Vanocur, NBC was the only network that allowed its news personnel to do commercials, and the exception was made only for *The Today Show*. Vanocur was not so much concerned with the *Today* host doing commercials as he was with "whether or not they should be allowed to go outside the confines of the program to act as journalists." In 1976, when *The Today Show* was again looking for a new host, NBC executives reconsidered and revised their policy once more in order to hire Tom Brokaw. Under the new policy, the host was not required to do commercials.

NETWORK-AFFILIATED STATION RELATIONS

NBC fed *Today* over the network to its owned and operated stations and also to the local stations that affiliated with the network through a renewable contract. The network relied on its lineup of stations to provide an outlet for national network advertising that would allow them to reach the largest potential audience. Since the affiliates had the opportunity to reconsider their relationship with a particular network on a regular basis (usually every two years), networks worked very hard to keep their "outlets" satisfied. Cities all over the United States (particularly the top one hundred markets) usually had two or three viable VHF stations (channels 2 to 13) that could be received over the air via antenna in homes. Cable or satellite were definitely not part of the program distribution system that would prevail decades later. By the early 1970s, generally NBC and CBS competed somewhat evenly, while ABC tended to be a distant third. Those two or three local stations would have a strong network identity, as "CBS" or "NBC," and few viewers understood the difference between what was a network or a local feed, so the local audiences tended to strongly identify with the programming broadcast over their local station and were very vocal about any changes that might occur. Both the network and the local stations were responsive to their viewers because advertising rates are based on ratings, which are based on the number of people watching. The more stations a network had in its lineup, the larger the potential audience. So the goal for networks and those local stations was to attract the most eyes to their programming and then to keep them tuning in. Local stations received a certain prestige by being associated with a particular network, but they also shared in the advertising revenues provided by network advertising and local participation. It was the promise of that financial reward that first attracted local stations to carry *The Today Show* in 1952:

> To secure the best possible lineup of stations, the web obviously has patterned the ambitious two-hour morning spread so it can be used by the local

plants as a lure for hometown revenue. . . . For instance, WNBQ, the Chi [Chicago] NBC-TV operation can rack up a hefty maximum of $9,500 weekly on *Today* hitchhikers. That's the potential weekly tab on the four daily five-minute news segments and the 12 daily stations breaks that are being offered for station sale.[26]

For many local stations, despite the financial incentive, carrying the *Today* program required an extra production burden. In 1977, for example, station WILX-TV in Jackson, Michigan, was a typical one of NBC's 221 network stations that carried *The Today Show*. WILX-TV is a medium-market affiliate station that produced a five-minute news segment during the regular *Today* cutaway at twenty-five minutes after the hour. But not all stations took advantage of the local cutaway because it was not required by NBC and also because *Today* continued to feed the network during the break. In 1963, Carl Lindemann Jr., then NBC executive in charge of *Today*, requested a breakdown of the stations that cut away for local programming during the five-minute block created for that purpose. The results of that study indicated that in the 7:25 a.m. break, thirty-four stations took the network service and that 127 stations cut away for local programming. In the 8:25 a.m. segment, thirty-three stations took the network feed, and 122 cut away for local programming. NBC still fed the *Today* program during those breaks by continuing an interview, promoting future events on the show, or generally filling with relatively unimportant content. If a significant number of local stations elected to stay with the network during the break, it would have made a difference in the type of programming placed into that time period. Therefore, it was Steve Flynn's suggestion that "it should certainly be satisfactory to all concerned if an interview is 'lightly' wrapped up before the 25-minute point which you see service the majority of stations, in both cases and then return for more from the same personality for the less than 30% of the network which stay with us."[27] Over the years NBC monitored the number of local stations that broke away for local programming and those that remained with the network feed. In 1972, another survey indicated that forty-one of the 197 NBC stations used the network feed rather than breaking away. In 1977, of the 221 NBC stations, 64 percent provided two local newsbreaks, 23 percent did not provide any breaks, and 13 percent provided one break in one of the hours.

REPRESENTATIVE-AFFILIATED STATION WILX-TV

NBC affiliate station WILX-TV in Jackson, Michigan, was one of the stations that provided local news in 1977 during the local cutaway break.

Their production staff described the special arrangements and production that were necessary to do a live newsbreak: WILX station logs were prepared by the continuity staff and were distributed to the operations manager, news director, and engineers. Since *Today* aired early in the morning, all break materials with the exception of the news segment were prepared the night before. All commercial breaks were clearly marked as to network or local origination. WILX-TV's day began at 6:12:20 a.m. with the test pattern, national anthem, station sign-on, "thought for the day," and two short programs: *Operation Second Chance* and *Today's Women*. In this way, the station could make sure it was functioning properly, allow for late staff arrivals, log public service program time, and check local break material well before the large *Today* audience tuned in at 7:00 a.m.

The news segment fell under the responsibility of both the operations manager, Stuart Hazard, and the news director, John Tallerico. Both men indicated that their news day began earlier because of *The Today Show*, when normally their services would not be necessary until later in the day. This was particularly true in the news director's case because the bulk of news activity would usually come in the afternoon.

Steve Wright was WILX-TV's anchorman during the local newsbreak for *The Today Show*. In addition, he anchored the 6:00 news that evening. In order to do both, Wright accepted a split-shift working day that began at 5:00 a.m. to 9:00 a.m. and resumed from 2:20 p.m. to 6:30 p.m. Since he was responsible for gathering and writing the news for both segments, his day began by checking the police logs before going to the station. There, he would read through the AP wire overnights for national, international, and local news; sports; and weather for the Jackson and Lansing, Michigan, areas. The newscast was organized to meet local needs, and Wright explained that it was the policy of WILX to give priority to news in the Lansing area over Jackson, unless the story was of paramount importance. Weather was also very important and was given two slots during the five-minute newscast: once at the open and then a recap before returning to the network. Since many viewers expressed interest in the local sports results, they were usually included whenever available. Wright was also responsible for selecting standard slides and visuals to accompany each of the stories. Occasionally, it was possible to use film footage that may have been run the night before during the 6:00 or 11:00 news. Generally, the stories were kept short, usually not running over one minute in length. Wright was also responsible during his morning shift for the five-minute newscasts broadcast over WILX's radio station, WJCO-AM.

Taking the two-hour *Today* feed from the network was no more complex than the normal network feed during the broadcast day, except for the longer newsbreak periods, which were locally produced by WILX and many other affiliates. Those breaks occurred at 7:25 a.m. and 8:25 a.m. and ran five minutes in length including commercial breaks. Because WILX cut away for the local news, there was a director assigned specifically to direct the two news segments, and the regular engineer, Dave Bjorling, was required to throw a master switch changing the network feed over to the local studio "switcher." That gave director Durwood Carn local control of the broadcast. The show was shot with one fixed, unmanned color camera that was framed to position the newscaster on the left side of the screen. Slides and other graphics were then chroma-keyed into the area behind the newscaster and to the empty space on the right. There was a commercial break immediately before the news and again following the news. The commercials were usually voice-overs with slide, film, or videotape. One staff person was responsible for the loading and cuing of commercial material. Before air, there was a quick walk-through rehearsal in which the director switched rapidly through the support graphics to check the correct order and positioning. It was not a difficult segment to direct since the newscaster picked up his cue from the on-air light on the lone studio camera. In addition, time cues were not necessary because the newscaster had a clock mounted out of camera range atop the news desk, where he could easily time the show himself. To allow a smooth transition from network to local and back, *Today* fed its logo and theme for several seconds, allowing stations to "break" without exact timing required.

Although many local stations such as WILX used the break for local news, NBC did not require that the segment be used exclusively for news. For a local station, however, it was a good opportunity to demonstrate local community content to the FCC at license renewal time.

To keep local stations informed, NBC's News Department sent out weekly program reports that detailed the types of segments that would be covered in the following week. It was basically an outline breakdown for each show. In addition, NBC informed the affiliate stations of major network plans, program changes, or changes in personnel.

Generally, the management at WILX felt that *The Today Show* was an excellent show to carry. The ratings for the time period attracted substantially more viewers than the competing networks. It was especially true in Jackson, Michigan, where there was no "broadcast" ABC affiliated station at the time. This lack of competition made it possible to sell the local commercial breaks as an attractive time slot. The *Today* segment was listed on the WILX rate card as $50 per minute and $40 per minute preemptable. That compares with the normal daytime cost per minute of $45 and $35 preemptable. The weekend morning rates were higher for Saturday by $5 per minute, and on Sunday, rates were $15 per minute less than the weekday comparable period.

The WILX-TV staff felt that the changes in host or on-air talent did not significantly affect the local audience during the *Today* time slot. They were aware, however, that *Today* seemed to be slipping in the overall national ratings against the recent ABC competitor, *Good Morning America*. They mentioned that the ABC program was attracting a significant audience in Detroit, Michigan, where the nearest local ABC station was located. They also stated that it was an additional financial and programming burden to do a local newsbreak but that they were committed to doing local news during that time since it served the public interest. "Serving the public interest" was a significant requirement for FCC station license renewal in 1976.

Although it was not widely known at NBC, it was permissible under a plan developed in 1958 for stations not to carry the local half-hour segments of *The Today Show*. Carl Lindemann Jr., NBC executive in charge of *Today*, questioned the practice in a memo to Steve Flynn, then director of station relations for the NBC Sales Department. On a trip to Omaha, Nebraska, Lindemann watched *The Today Show* and saw, according to the memo, "a local news operation running from 8:00 to essentially 8:10 local time. They joined *Today* clean with the first feature and apparently do not carry our opening news segment. They also cut away for local news at 8:25. Do they have the right to do this, and does it happen in other markets?" Flynn replied that they did have the right to join *Today* at any time during those half-hour segments. He further stated, "Three other stations do not carry any of either the 7–7:30 or 8–8:30 half-hours which is also acceptable to us, although not particularly good programming."[28]

NETWORK–STATION COMMUNICATION

The Station Relations staff was often in contact with the local stations for a variety of reasons. It was especially necessary for the network to contact the stations to inform them if there was to be a change in the regular *Today* feed. A typical wire sent to the stations was similar to the one sent on November 20, 1968. It informed the stations that *The Today Show* was to be preempted in the Central and Mountain time zones in order to prevent the competition from "stealing an audience lead on coverage of the Macy's Thanksgiving Day Parade." NBC programmed a special called "On Parade," which filled the hour prior to the parade. The following wire was sent to the stations to clarify the commercial break time and sales:

> The commercial format for this hour special program will be essentially the same as the *Today* show with the exception that no five-minute cutaway for local news will be provided at 9:25 AM NYCT. Thus, between 9 and 9:30 AM

NYCT there will be two two-minute ten-second cutaways available for lcl sale; a 72-second stn break at 9:30 AM; four network commercials for Central and Mountain time zones in the 9:30–10 AM segment which substitute for the *Today* commercials which would have been sked in that time segment on that date. There will also be a 32 second stn break at the mid-point of the 9:30–10 AM pgm portion with a 72-second stn break, as normally sked at 10 AM NYCT. Eastern time zone stns only may sked lcl co-op commercials in all eight, one-minute positions within the hour at the normal daytime co-op fee. For Central and Mountain time zone stations the regular co-op/ network commercial exchange arrangement applicable to the *Today* show between the first and second half hours of the pgm will apply.

We will assume that all Central and Mountain stns which carry the *Today* show in this time segment will accept "On Parade" unless advised to the contrary. Eastern time zone stns are asked to advise George Stella of NBC, New York, of their acceptance.[29]

When the network carried a special advertising campaign, often there was a possibility that the local stations could "tie in" with the national campaign. However, there were conditions and restrictions that varied with each campaign. Therefore, if there was any question about a tie-in, the local stations were advised. For example, *Today* featured a promotion for the Annual U.S. Savings Bond Drive and sent the following wire to the NBC stations:

Some stations may be approached by lcl bond officials requesting a lcl tie-in. You should know, however, that the network feed will not provide for a cut-in of any kind for this purpose. Therefore, if you desire a lcl tie-in it will have to be accomplished in either the lcl co-op position in the segment or in the adjacent stn brk.[30]

It was the responsibility of the Station Relations Department to advise local stations about last-minute changes in the *Today* line feed, particularly if the situation could not be resolved by airtime and special arrangements had to be made. This was the case when *Today* was to pick up a live direct satellite feed from Great Britain for the investiture of the Prince of Wales, which was to take place July 1, 1969. On June 30, 1969, the following information was wired to all stations advising them of technical problems and of the possible programming alternatives:

Have just been advised by COMSAT that INTELSAT III is in trouble, thereby jeopardizing our ability to deliver as planned live coverage of the investiture of the Prince of Wales from Caernarvon Castle tomorrow morning. We are desperately working with COMSAT on alternate transmission routes, even to the extent of obtaining circuits using ground stations and satellites via India and Japan to the West Coast.

Should no pictures at all be available, it will obviously be announced on the air by the *Today Show* and the *Today Show* will program with its normal format 7–9 am NYCT for Eastern stations, 8–10 am NYCT for Central zone stations, with normal programming for all stations at 10 am NYCT. If, however, partial satellite transmission is received but less than enough to provide 7–11:30 am NYCT programming originally contemplated, the *Today Show* will program live for all stations 7–10 am NYCT. Since it will not be practical to advise you of this alternative by teletype, your control room personnel should be guided by the *Today Show* on air announcement.[31]

Programs that involved satellite transmission were considered to be special on *The Today Show* and were certainly more costly in terms of production. Therefore, whenever *Today* used a live satellite feed, it was certain to communicate all necessary information to their stations. Since live events were not generally staged for television, they rarely followed the strict time demands for commercial broadcasting. When *The Today Show* decided to transmit a live feed, it usually made special arrangements for the program to be aired for extended periods of time and to disrupt normal commercial breaks. When *Today* covered the signing of the treaty between the United States and Japan that returned jurisdiction of Okinawa to Japan, there was a possibility that the local stations might lose their local newsbreaks. The stations were notified by wire:

You should be warned that the preliminary timings that we have received from the state dept indicate that our coverage of these impt ceremonies may extend beyond the start of the normal 8:25 am NYCT lcl news cutaway point. Accordingly, you should be prepared to shorten yr lcl news segment or lose it entirely. You are assured that we will endeavor not to runover if at all possible.[32]

Another live satellite event of an unusual nature occurred in 1972. *Today* expanded its normal program to cover the arrival of the bodies of the slain members of the Israeli Olympic team at Tel Aviv Airport. Stations were advised as to the program changes:

The nature of the program dictates that some commercials and local cutaways and breaks will almost undoubtedly have to be eliminated. We cannot advise in more detail because no schedule is available from Tel Aviv. Israeli pictures only will be in black and white.[33]

That case was different because of the solemn nature of the event—it would have been in extremely bad taste for NBC to interrupt coverage to cut away to a commercial.

Another instance of irregular programming was on December 7, 1972, when stations had to be notified of possible cancellation of break periods due to a late-breaking news event:

Due to the planned covg of Apollo 17 and fact that former President Harry S. Truman is in critical health situation, there may be alterations of regular pgm format tomorrow involving loss of coop positions, five-min cutaways and network commercial positions. There is no way to indicate to you now how show will be programmed so suggest your director on duty be warned that he will have to cope with variable network feed.[34]

Some of the correspondence between NBC and its stations dealt with programming changes other than break information, and *Today* kept its local stations informed when a major change in format or personnel took place. For example, in 1974, NBC wired the stations when *Today* hired Jim Hartz to cohost the program:

Delighted to advise you that NBC will be announcing today that Jim Hartz will be joining Barbara Walters as co-host on the *Today* program effective Monday, July 29. His selection from a number of attractive candidates results from Jim's unusual combination of qualities which suits him so well for this unique broadcasting assignment and on which the unanimous judgment of the NBC News and management officials concerned was confirmed by audience research. Each of the other NBC newsmen who were considered was highly qualified and each has an important future with NBC in other assignments that will advance his news career. It is particularly fitting that Jim Hartz, who was Frank McGee's protégé and very close personal friend now succeeds him in an assignment which he is eager to take on. Thanks to many of you for your own helpful observations and suggestions on the program and co-host.[35]

That was a special case since the stations had participated to a limited extent in the selection process of the new cohost.

In 1976, the stations were again notified of a new panel member. This time it was Jane Pauley, and the message was to inform the stations of a special closed-circuit presentation in which Pauley would be introduced to the stations.

Next Monday, October 11, at 4:30 pm NYCT, I hope you can make time to view a brief closed circuit presentation during which Dick Wald, President of NBC News, and members of *Today* would like to introduce to you personally Jane Pauley who has joined them as a permanent member of the pgm staff. The presentation will be apx 15 minutes in length. If it is not convenient for you to view at the network feed time, I hope you will make arrangements to record for later screening.[36]

It was often necessary to relay special information to the *Today* stations. For example, stations that subscribed to the NBC News Service had the right to record certain portions of *The Today Show* that could be used later in their local news programs. However, there were occasional exceptions:

> During the program tomorrow, Thurs. July 10, we will use film footage of this past Sunday's tragic race at Belmont between Ruffian and Foolish Pleasure. Because our acquisition rights to this film footage are for one-time network use only, you are advised that even though an NPS subscriber you may not, repeat may not, excerpt this portion of the *Today* show for later local origination.[37]

Occasionally, a technical problem would occur during transmission of *Today* from the network to the local stations. This was not generally a problem that needed further explanation from the network, but when Edwin Newman interviewed Dusko Popov, the international spy, a technical problem caused embarrassing consequences. In order to clarify the situation, NBC sent the following wire to local stations:

> This morning at 9:52:30–9:53:00 NYCT at the conclusion of an Ed Newman interview with Dusko Popov, the international spy, some stns, principally west of Toledo, experienced an ATT audio failure which resulted in hum and distortion. Because this occurred at a critical point in the interview, it apparently created in the minds of some viewers the idea that we had censored the audio portion of the interview. This of course was not the case but I thought that you would want to have this information to answer viewer complaints. We are currently examining the possibility of repeating the interview as an NPS special feed this afternoon.[38]

SPECIAL EVENT ADVERTISING

The Participating Program Sales unit of the NBC Sales Department was responsible for securing the advertising for *The Today Show*. Once an account was arranged, the details were turned over to the commercial producer, Win Welpen. Most commercials were preproduced on film and only needed to be scheduled into the appropriate time slot. However, many commercials, particularly prior to 1976, used the *Today* personalities as the commercial talent. After 1976, *Today* policy did not allow either the host or the principal panel members to do commercials. As a result, special talent had been hired in addition to Lew Wood to perform the large number of live commercials. Unless a personality was specifically requested, Welpen chose the appropriate talent for the commercial that was most suitable to the product. Advertisers liked the close product identification with the host and other panel members, but according to Welpen, the lack of host participation had not caused advertising to diminish.

Even for the most successful programs, the sales staff would try to get the best possible sales lineup. In the case of *The Today Show*, it sold best during the winter months when television viewing in general was up. Other times, when *The Today Show* was less attractive, sales packages were combined with sales incentive plans, dividends from multiple purchases, and packages that included the purchases of other participating programs such as *Tonight*, *Tomorrow*, or *Saturday Night*. Those usually resulted in sales contracts that were mutually profitable for NBC and the advertisers.

Although *Today* was fully sponsored, the show occasionally aired without commercials. This occurred generally when there was a major news event of significant importance or solemnity that commercial interruption would have been incompatible with good taste or public service. At those times, special news events tended to be live and unstructured so that breaking away for commercial announcements would have been awkward or not feasible. Such programs were generally more costly than normal studio production, and increased advertising rates or additional advertising minutes could not compensate for those extra expenses. Therefore, the cost of that special programming, which usually involved an extended *Today* program, was often absorbed by other advertising profits from the normal *Today* programming.

Not all major news events were unsuitable for advertising, of course. In fact, some events were enormously profitable, as *Today* executives discovered as early as 1961, when the Sales Department developed an idea to take advantage of the special news events on *The Today Show*. Unexpected and important events usually gave *The Today Show* an increase in ratings that could justify a special packaging of advertising rates. For example, special news events from September 1960 to July 1961 often showed a significant increase in ratings, which at the time averaged about 4.0. When *Today* producers planned to cover a significant event, such as the wedding of Great Britain's Princess Anne, or a major national election, the sales staff arranged for special rate packages based on anticipated increases in the ratings. Some of the special programming that caused delightful spikes in ratings included election returns that could go as high as 20.4. Others included the inauguration of John F. Kennedy and coverage of the space program Project Mercury, both attracting a 7.7 rating.

Ratings deliver significant advertising rates, and programming that attracted high ratings was especially attractive to NBC executives who relied on its advertising revenue in order to meet the expenses of the production of the program and to provide a profit for NBC. Although NBC did not reveal its profits, it was estimated that *Today* profits in the mid-1970s were approximately $10 million a year, making it one of the most profitable NBC programs. The advertising rates were the highest charged for that time period by any of the networks, and the ratings from which advertising rates are determined were higher than those of either ABC or CBS.

The most important aspect of any commercial program is to secure adequate and, whenever possible, profitable advertising. It was the intention of Pat Weaver that the sale of advertising would cover the production costs of *Today* and also make a profit for NBC. The early advertising policy grew out of a need for *Today* to attract advertisers to a program that was unproven in format and that suffered from low audience ratings. As an incentive to advertisers, *Today* advertising policy offered a wide range of attractive features. *Today* adopted the newly developed participating advertising plan that allowed even very small advertisers the opportunity to advertise on network television for very low rates. NBC also made the *Today* talent available to perform live commercials. That practice appealed to advertisers because of the close product identification that resulted when the program talent endorsed its product. *Today* promoted the early morning hours as an untapped market in which the advertising of morning food products and household products would appeal to the prime advertising market: women.

Another important aspect of the early advertising plan was to make the program attractive and profitable for local stations through the commercial minutes and co-op time that were available for local advertising. That made it necessary for close coordination and cooperation between the network and its owned and affiliated stations. NBC had demonstrated that it could maintain excellent relations with its stations through constant and reliable communication.

Except for a major change in the advertising structure that came about because of the reorganization of the program in 1958, there were few changes in *Today*'s advertising policy during those first twenty-five years. The newer structure after 1958 very successfully divided the available commercial minutes into "network" and "local" advertising half hours.

Besides a brief period from 1961 to 1962, NBC finally relieved the *Today* talent from the responsibility of doing commercials in 1976. Although *Today* executives feared that because of this change advertisers would desert the program, their fears were unfounded. Instead, they affirmed that the single most important factor in attracting advertising to a program was the ratings since advertisers want to reach the most people in their target audience for the lowest possible cost. For their advertisers' money, *Today* was also able to provide an excellent "cost per thousand" purchase with its attractive sales incentive plans that made its less attractive markets a profitable buy. When stronger competition entered the field in the early 1970s, it forced *Today* to become more responsive to its advertisers. More important, however, it forced *Today* to concentrate on maintaining strong ratings so that advertisers would not be tempted to stray toward the competition.

6

+

Watching *Today*

A Look at the Audience

Originally, *Today* pioneered early morning television broadcasting by carving out an audience from regular radio listeners and newspaper readers. The American public had to be persuaded to watch television in the early morning hours and, once attracted to the set, had to be persuaded to stay. In order to succeed, *Today* had to attract and retain a large enough audience to make the show a viable purchasing option for advertisers. *Today* needed to generate enough revenue to not only continue broadcasting but also implement the ambitious plans of its creator, Pat Weaver. Although time has verified *Today* as one of the most successful concepts in broadcast history, those early months were risky for NBC. In most instances in commercial broadcasting, a program is considered successful if it receives high ratings and a large share of the audience. In some instances, a program can be considered successful if it receives low ratings or a small share of the audience as long as it also receives good critical reviews and it adds to the overall prestige of the network. In rare instances, a program can receive high ratings, a large share of the audience, *and* good critical reviews. And in that case, the program is generally considered to be a smash hit. Such was the case for *The Today Show* for most of its first twenty-five years on the air.

In 1952, the networks were not convinced that there was a marketable audience during those early morning hours, and there was very little attempt to provide programming other than some sporadic children's cartoons provided by a local station. Initially, there was only a small audience watching *Today*, but many who did watch wrote favorable comments to the network. In fact, in the first two weeks, *Today* received 65,000 unsolicited letters. Those letters were used by NBC to convince advertisers that *Today* was a good product and had potential as an advertising market:

> At meetings between *Today* executives and ad agency account executives, NBC page boys would march in and, with dramatic flair, dump postal sacks full of unopened *Today* mail on a large conference table. The *Today* people then passed out letter openers and let the advertising men slit the envelopes and read for themselves. They were told that if they didn't like what they read, they could forget *Today*.[1]

A very compelling reason *Today* had been successful, particularly in those first twenty-five years, was that producers and NBC executives were very sensitive to their viewing audience. One explanation for *Today*'s consistently high ratings is that for other networks, it was difficult to establish a competitive program. Viewers were reluctant to "dial around" to see what was offered by other networks. In its earliest years, there was no programming opposite *Today* that attracted large numbers of adult viewers, although children preferred to watch the popular children's show *Captain Kangaroo*, which aired opposite *Today* during one of its two hours. But over the years, adult viewers made watching *Today* a habit. In 1976, *New York Times* writer J. Anthony Lukas explained the audience's phenomenal addiction:

> The show has become a habit for millions of Americans—as much a part of the day as brushing their teeth, eating their flakes, or drinking their coffee—and they deeply resent changes in that routine. A flip through the program's recent mail suggests just how sensitive such viewers are to the slightest alterations in their matinal rhythm. Commenting on recent cast and format changes, they use words like "appalled," "horrified," "shocked," and "disgusted."[2]

Getting accurate information about *Today*'s viewing audience depended on demographics, which attempted to describe the nature of the audience itself. Determining the exact number of viewers who watched the two-hour early morning program and ascertaining when they were actually watching was the job of the A. C. Nielsen Company, an outside company that provided audience measurement in terms of ratings and audience share. Ratings are based on the total number of television households tuned to a particular program and are important because they determine the advertising rates for the program. Because there were fewer people available to watch morning television, ratings were generally much lower than evening prime time. Share is the number of people actually watching that are "tuned" to a particular show. In particular, share described how many people were tuned to *Today* compared to the competition. What makes the ratings numbers so critical is that the ratings are used to determine the advertising rates that stations charge advertisers. Even a slight rise or drop in ratings can mean a significant gain or loss in revenues for a network or individual station. Ratings were determined by two types of viewing: total audience viewing and average audience viewing. The average number of viewers watching over a fifteen-minute time period determined the average audience rating. Those fragmented viewing habits made programming the two hours a problem. When ABC network vice president Edwin Vane looked at the way audiences watched early morning programming, he described the problems that ABC faced when it decided to air *A.M. America* and later *Good Morning America*:

> The format is largely determined by the viewing pattern and there is nothing you can do about it. The average viewer stays with the program for less than 30 minutes and then goes off to work or school or whatever. So you couldn't sustain a straight show if you wanted to. We tried to mix in some musical numbers with the news presentations, but apparently television viewers aren't up to listening to music early in the morning. It boils down pretty much to some kind of mix of talk, interview and information.[3]

Stuart Schulberg, executive producer of *Today* from 1968 to 1976, described the *Today* audience as one that "ranges between 4 million and 6 million people during an average minute [and] is particularly heavy outside major urban centers. At least half of the viewers are over the age of 50, and, especially in the second hour, are women."[4] He also said that *Today* did not program strictly to a New York audience. *Today's* largest audience was in the rural areas and primarily in the South. A description of the viewing demographics released in 1974 indicated some surprising results:

> [*Today* does] only about half as well in New York, Chicago, and Los Angeles as it does in the nation as a whole. According to the latest available rating breakdowns for local markets from the American Research Bureau, if *Today's* average national audience is defined as 100, *Today* attracts listeners in New York at only 54 percent of that rate. In Washington, D.C., a middle-sized city, where politics is the major industry, it achieves a respectable but unspectacular 97. But in Oklahoma City, the figure is 192 percent, double the show's average. This big city-small town opposition occurs partly because there is serious competition for *Today* in the bigger markets.[5]

Schulberg explained his approach to programming for the diverse audience problem. "'We don't produce programs for New York City that's for sure,' he says. In fact he has recently increased the number of news features from the local NBC bureaus to 'give the show more of a regional feeling.'"[6] However, *Today*'s audience was also described as sophisticated and well educated, with high income levels. Doug Sinsel, producer of *Today* in 1976, said that the audience was very similar in makeup to the readership of *Time* magazine. It was most important for *Today* to compete effectively in the major market areas because of the large number of viewers as compared to the smaller markets. It was an added burden to program to such a diverse audience, a burden that *The Today Show* had continually faced.

Because of its excellent news segments over the years, many of the *Today* viewers had been political officials. Congressmen and several U.S. presidents had been devoted viewers of *Today*. For example, not only did President Lyndon B. Johnson watch the program, but he frequently called *Today* to offer praise or criticism of a guest or interview. In 1967, *Time* reported on the president's viewing habits and those of others:

> The President watches the program from his bed turning the volume up during the Washington sequences. Across town, 70% of the Congress and most Cabinet members are regular viewers. Secretary of State Rusk has gone so far as to position his bedroom TV so that he can see *Today* in his shaving mirror. Beyond the Potomac, *Atlanta Constitution* Publisher and Syndicated Columnist Ralph McGill watches "with great frequency." TV Chef Julia Child does her morning calisthenics by it. On the West Coast, Danny Kaye and Pat Brown are fans. In Manhattan, *Today* is one of the two programs (the other: the *Huntley-Brinkley Report*) that RCA Boss David Sarnoff watches regularly, and even William Paley, board chairman of rival CBS is said to find *Today* irresistible.[7]

A survey conducted for NBC by the Applied Management Sciences research firm in the early 1970s indicated that government officials were enthusiastic viewers of *Today*. Personal interviews and mail questionnaires were used to obtain results. Sixty-six percent of U.S. senators, 66 percent of the members of the House of Representatives, and 267 officials in the cabinet and independent government agencies were contacted for the survey. The results were as follows:

> From one-half to two-thirds of Congressmen interviewed report watching *Today* frequently—once a week or more often. When traveling, government officials rarely miss watching *Today*. More than three out of four viewers report watching *Today* in their hotel or motel room when on a trip. These officials have a high regard for the program. More than four out of five rate *Today* favorably in terms of presenting worthwhile guests dealing with topics of national interest.[8]

When producer Paul Friedman took over control of *Today* in 1976, he made changes in the program that affected the viewing habits of the audience. His most significant innovations were to make the feature segments shorter and to make the program more visual. He increased the use of the minicam in order to feature live remote pickups from around the nation. He hoped that even though doing the remote pickups added expenses, the results would be effective in terms of increased ratings and overall better programming. But there was criticism of Friedman's efforts:

> Friedman could be miscalculating. *Today* has been described by some as "visual radio," capable of being absorbed without actually watching it. An increased load of features (or segments) could demand closer watching and thereby alienate part of the traditional *Today* audience.[9]

When *Good Morning America* aired opposite *The Today Show*, it was estimated that within a year, it attracted 1.5 million former *Today* viewers. The host of *Good Morning America*, David Hartman, explained the makeup of the ABC audience during an interview. He was asked about the audience that the program was attempting to reach, whether it was to attract disaffected *Today* watchers or to reach a totally new audience:

> Both. But we hope the disaffected *Today* watchers are disaffected because they have tried us and would rather watch our show. Although all three networks said there was no new audience available in the morning, the ratings indicate that we are tapping younger people who never watched morning television before.[10]

An NBC survey conducted in 1976 compiled information about the makeup of the early morning audience in general: the audience was approximately two-thirds female, half of whom were over fifty years old. Viewers generally appeared to be community oriented, news and television oriented, and politically involved. They also held the impression that *Today* was approximately in the middle of the hard-news/soft-news continuum. As for programming, the audience wanted more segments on health and science, more use of the minicam, more local news and weather, more consumer information, and more human interest features. The major criticisms of *Today* included that the news segments were too repetitive, that book reviews were too narrow in interest scope, that there were too many commercials, that interviews were too short, and the "cold personalities of the talent."[11]

AUDIENCE REACTION: *THE TODAY SHOW* MAIL

One way *The Today Show* had of monitoring audience preference was through the mail received by the program. A special staff member was responsible for categorizing all incoming mail. In the mid-1970s, *The Today Show* received approximately four thousand letters per month, depending on the programming. Most letters complained about a specific segment on the program, but there were a substantial number of letters that praised some aspect of the program. The mail was divided into several categories: Approvals, Disapprovals, Requests for Further Information, Program Suggestions, and Miscellaneous. After the mail was sorted and categorized, it was synthesized into the "*Today* Mail Report," which was generally written and distributed on a monthly basis, although occasionally two months were reported together. *Today* program writers put together the "Mailbag," which was an on-air feature of *The Today Show*. Because it was a useful and critical gauge of audience approval, the official *Today* Mail Report was distributed to all of the New York *Today* staff, the Washington staff, the Legal Department, NBC Audience Service, Program Analysis, the Sales Department, and News Research. In general, the audience wrote and commented on remote location trips, especially citing the ones to Hawaii, London, and Chicago. Other popular topics that received great volumes of mail were consumer segments, mandatory retirement, nutrition, most of Dr. Art Ulene's health segments, and a special filmed report on *Roots*, which was hosted by Jim Hartz. Election coverage and the bicentennial series elicited a large audience response. Segments that did not receive many responses were the entertainment features, but those few tended to be somewhat favorable.[12]

Although the most favorable mail received was strong approval of the yearlong bicentennial series, there were a few letters from the southern audience complaining that the southern states were reported from a northern viewpoint. However, nearly all the mail praised the series. One writer said,

Thank you kindly for the bicentennial state-to-state tour. It was inexpressibly beautiful and rewarding. Each state has its own special charm, and interesting and concerned people with a story to share. More than ever, "see America first" bestirs my thankfulness of living in America.

The *Today* Mail Report gave the highlights of the mail for the given month(s) and a complete breakdown as to type of mail response.[13] An example follows:

Total Today *Mail for October 1975*
Total: 4,508
Approvals: 669
Program / Cast: 364
Guests / Issues: 304

Disapprovals: 2,899
Program / Cast: 351
Guests / Issues: 2,548
Requests for Further Information: 875
Program Suggestions: 41
Miscellaneous: 24

One reason for the high disapproval response in October 1975 was that viewers were very critical of an interview with John Dean. The response was summed up in the Mail Report that served as a representative example of the types of letters received by the *Today* program:

> The three-part interview with John Dean received one of the largest responses in recent memory. Mail was directed to Tom Brokaw, Carl Stern, in Washington, John Dean and the *Today* program. The total response was approximately 2500 pieces of mail, and they were mostly unfavorable to the program for having Mr. Dean appear, and more so for allowing him three days to "slander the Presidency and all but ruin President Ford's chances for re-election." Many viewers claimed that "this more than ever points out the liberal bias of the northeastern establishment press, which will stop at nothing to see that a Democratic [*sic*] is elected to the White House."

Fortunately, during the summer, the Mail Report for July and August 1976 reflected more approval than disapproval from the audience by approximately three to one at a time when *Today* was in the process of selecting a new host and new female panel member. Although the show was in turmoil, viewers responded to the "parade" of candidates that were auditioned for the permanent positions. A summary of the mail revealed that "more than 75% of *Today* mail received during the summer of 1976 has been related to the changes in cast. . . . In general, there seems to be some confusion as to whether or not the program will continue with the same format, in view of all the cast changes."

Some of the comments about the female guest hosts helped NBC executives make a decision to hire Jane Pauley for the permanent position. Although the mail on Pauley was overwhelmingly favorable, critical comments by viewers were also included in the report:

> "Let's have more of Pauley!"
> "I think you have a worthy replacement for Barbara Walters in Jane Pauley."
> "We vote for Jane Pauley for Barbara's replacement. The others you have paraded before us did not have the 'pizazz' that Jane showed during her brief tour on the Today show."
> "Refreshing and charming."
> "Just another pretty face. Does not have the knowledge or background to fill one of the most important jobs in TV broadcasting."

"Madison Avenue, kewpie doll. She does not appear to have any real sub-
stance."

The Mail Report also listed comments for the other female guest panelists: Catherine Mackin, Betty Rollin, Betty Furness, and Linda Ellerbee.
Other cast changes that had already been made prompted viewers to
express their sentiments, which were summed up in the report: "In addition to the comments received about cast changes on the distaff side of
the program. . . . We have received wide ranging comments from people
who said they had nothing against either Tom Brokaw or Floyd Kalber as
news personalities, but at the same time were upset to find that neither
Messrs. Hartz nor Wood would not be continuing in the same position
on the program":

> I just thought I would write and tell you how much I like Jim Hartz and how
> sorry I am that he will no longer be the host of the *Today* show. He has such
> a nice personality. I am afraid I do not feel that way about Tom Brokaw. In
> regard to other changes on your show, they seem to be change for the sake of
> change. I can't see what great improvement Floyd Kalber is over Lew Wood
> in reading the news.

One viewer was able to succinctly sum up the general feeling expressed
in three months of mail:

> The *Today* show has become an unfamiliar, unfriendly, uncoordinated and
> relatively uninformative program. There was a time when the unity of co-
> hosts between Barbara Walters, Gene Shalit and Jim Hartz made this pro-
> gram a familiar, and comfortable viewing experience, done with intelligence
> and care. Now it is a mishmash that is very easy to turn off.

In addition to the large number of mail responses, *Today* received
phone calls in which viewers made basically the same types of comments
or requested information. All guests that appeared on *Today* were asked
to fill out an index card that contained information that *Today* made available to viewers on request. All mail that was marked "personal" or that
was personally addressed to the *Today* talent was given directly to the talent. It was impossible given the volume of mail to write personal replies;
therefore, *Today* sent form letters that in essence thanked the viewer for
any comments or suggestions with an assurance that the remarks would
be forwarded to the appropriate personnel.

THE TODAY SHOW COMPETITION

Once *Today* had established that there was an early morning audience, the
competition was anxious to share in the advertising profits.

The Morning Show

The earliest competition that *Today* faced was *The Morning Show* on CBS, hosted by Walter Cronkite. It premiered in March 1954 as a two-hour news-variety program that aired between 7:00 a.m. and 9:00 a.m. Monday through Friday. It was nearly an exact replica of *Today*'s program format, consisting of news, weather, feature pieces, and, for the kids, the Bill and Cora Baird puppets. One of Cronkite's duties was to engage in light bantering conversation with puppet Charlemagne the Lion, who was the CBS answer to J. Fred Muggs. His contribution as host of *The Morning Show* was summed up in a review by *Variety* shortly after the premiere:

> Walter Cronkite is the relaxed, smooth-as-silk salesman operating in the anchor spot as the centrifugal force from which the proceedings stem. He defies pindown definition; it's sufficient that one feels his presence without intrusion.[14]

Cronkite was supported by regular panel member Will Rogers Jr. and newscaster Charles Collingwood, whose responsibility was similar to the one performed by Frank Blair on *Today*. Carol Reed was responsible for the weather segments, which featured an animated electronic map, and her role was similar to the one performed by the first *Today* girl, Estelle Parsons. Among other obvious similarities, *The Morning Show* studios overlooked the Central Terminal at Grand Central Station, which provided the same "window to the people" approach used by *Today*. The breakdown of the program was also very similar to the *Today* program in that there were two local five-minute segments sold on a participating basis and even a sales incentive discount package that was identical to *Today*'s. Although it received very favorable reviews when it debuted, all critics noted the striking similarities between *The Morning Show* and *Today*:

> CBS's answer to NBC's going-on-three-years-and-past-the-critical-point, *Today*, is quiet "good morning" to you between 7 and 9 a.m. Devoid of any extra-special gimmicks with the possible exception of a fluent, animated weather map, *The Morning Show* represents the web in peak form as to news, entertainment and interview facets. . . . Judged off the first outing, *Morning Show* is a winning entry in the wake-up sweepstakes, but its format, granting a couple of departures, is too close in general complexion to that of *Today* for the comfort of clientele who might want to see both in the limited time imposed by ayem customs and habits.[15]

Although the program was able to impress critics, the morning audience was indifferent. A comparison of their ratings indicate the failure of *The Morning Show* in attracting viewers as successfully as *Today*. Prior to the competition offered by *The Morning Show*, the *Today* ratings had averaged 3.9 with an audience share average of 63.1. The average *Today* rating against *The Morning Show* dropped to 3.62 with a 51.6 share. The rating ranged from 5.5 in January–March 1954 to a 2.2 rating in July–September 1954. *The Morning Show* for the same period of time had an average rating of 1.9 and an average share of 26.7. Thus, *Today* outdistanced its competition by scoring on the average twice as much in both ratings and share of audience. The highest average rating and share obtained by *The Morning Show* was a 3.0 in January 1954 with a 28.3 share. Although *The Morning Show* made a dent in the *Today* audience, it was not able to sustain it and was therefore unable to compete successfully. CBS dropped the program from its schedule in July 1955.

Captain Kangaroo

Although *Captain Kangaroo* premiered on CBS in October 1955 and, with only minor changes, remained on the air until December 1984, it was not considered to be a serious threat to the *Today Show* audience. That was because the target audience for *Captain Kangaroo* was children, and it therefore attracted a different type of advertiser. NBC did not even keep competitive ratings on the program until 1956. Those first records in 1956 indicated that *Captain Kangaroo*, which aired from 8:00 a.m. to 9:00 a.m., was slightly behind *The Today Show* in average share of audience: 42.7 compared to *Today*'s 43.6. However, the ratings tended to favor *Captain Kangaroo* with a 4.3 compared to *Today*'s 2.8. The difference was accounted for in terms of average audience ratings over the longer *Today* program compared to the average audience rating for *Captain Kangaroo*, which aired for approximately half the time and was aimed toward a very specific audience. The half hours of *Today* that were available for network advertising were the ones in which *Today* was most interested for purposes of revenue rates. The ratings on *Captain Kangaroo* continued to outdistance *Today* by an average rating and slightly better share, but *Today* executives who monitored the situation were not overly concerned with the *Captain Kangaroo* competition. *Captain Kangaroo* had been moderately successful against *Today* because it had been programmed to a specific audience (children) and for a limited time period each morning. More important, it provided an alternative to *Today*, not a replica of its format.

CBS Morning News

CBS tried various programs to compete against *Today* in the early morning time slot. In 1957, CBS tried a more direct approach with *The Jimmy Dean Show* against *Today* from 7:00 a.m. to 8:00 a.m. The show lasted only a few months before CBS decided to remove it from the air. Shortly after the show was dropped, an article in *Variety* suggested that perhaps CBS had been too hasty in its decision and speculated that the program had the potential to compete successfully with *Today* if given more of a chance:

> Despite the old adage about hindsight, CBS-TV may have reason to regret its axing of the *Jimmy Dean Show* and the darkening of the network in the 7 to 8 a.m. period after four years of trying to top the Dave Garroway competition. Just a few days after the network decided to swing the axe on Dean, the Second October Nielsen reports came out and gave CBS-TV its highest ratings ever for the 7–7:45 Dean slot. Show averaged out to a 3.9 AA rating, a full point ahead of *Today*'s 2.9. Those of the web's execs with misgivings about the cancellation feel that perhaps the show would have been kept in a little longer, in light of the fact that Dean has been able to top *Today* in a few months whereas the web hung on previously for four years despite never having been able to approach the Garroway rating before.[16]

In spite of this "hindsight" advice, CBS did not put the program back on the air. It did, however, continue to search for morning vehicles to compete with *Today*. It returned to news in the morning but offered it on only a very limited basis, expanding and shortening the morning network news from fifteen minutes to thirty minutes at various times. CBS resumed serious programming competition in 1968 with the debut of *CBS Morning News* with Joseph Benti. *CBS Morning News* kept the same program title over the years, although it occasionally changed host and format. It was never a serious threat to *Today*, but NBC kept a wary eye on its progress and monitored its ratings on a regular basis.

During that time, the *CBS Morning News* format was considered to be substantially more hard-news oriented compared to *Today*, which relied on a mixture of short hard-news segments and several soft-news features. Despite the low audience viewership, CBS stuck with its commitment to news but in 1969 changed anchors when John Hart was brought onboard. Still, for the next four years, the program did not do well in the ratings. Then in May 1973, CBS announced a major change in the program and began by replacing anchor John Hart and Washington, D.C., anchor Nelson Benton. In addition, Lee Townsend replaced executive producer Dick Clark. It seemed that CBS was serious about taking on *The Today Show*. "At the time he told the affils of the planned changes, CBS News president Richard S. Salant admitted that the *Morning News* had not met the ratings challenge of NBC-TV's *Today* show and clearances were falling off. However, he indicated that the network was committed to keeping the a.m. news on the air."[17] The change was not to occur until the late summer of 1973, causing much speculation in the industry as to the exact nature of the change: "One strong possibility is that a woman will sign on as co-anchor. Present thinking is that she will be a hard news type, rather than just another pretty talking head. Too, Townsend is given high marks by CBS staffers as a newsman, and it isn't considered likely that he would consent to sit in on the softening of the early news show to a gimmick dispenser."[18] However, CBS was to realize its worst fears. It hired former *Washington Post* reporter Sally Quinn to coanchor with Hughes Rudd, who had been the CBS news correspondent in Moscow and Germany. Quinn was expected to give serious competition to *Today*'s Barbara Walters "both in attracting audiences and top politicians as interviewees." In anticipation of the new program and as a sign of their determination to commit to the new format, CBS changed its policy with its affiliated stations. The new edition of *CBS Morning News* would no longer be available in half-hour form as the old edition had been. CBS also launched a heavy publicity campaign designed to attract at least the curious and then hoped to provide programming that would persuade them to become steady viewers. *CBS Morning News* with Rudd and Quinn debuted on August 6, 1973, at 7:00 a.m. The critics were not impressed with Quinn's performance:

> Just in case all the advance publicity didn't raise audience anticipation to a fever pitch for the debut of *CBS Morning News*, Sally Quinn came up with a fever of her own . . . it must have had an effect on her performance. It was said that she wasn't able to write her own lines. It may also have been that her chitchat with Rudd was limited by her indisposition too, for she seemed lagging in the kind of responsiveness one might expect from a woman who has spent years around the top drawer Washington set. Unfortunately, it didn't affect her voice. It came over as the same limp instrument, which has been cajoling CBS viewers to watch the show on numerous web promo spots.[19]

Hughes Rudd was considered to be an asset to the program, but overall reviews indicated that Sally Quinn was a disappointment, particularly in light of the heavy press buildup: "Whether or not the show will click against the heavy *Today* odds is largely a matter of Quinn's adaptation to the medium and to Rudd. He is there, but she seems to have a way to go, with or without the flu."[20]

Over the months, the show was a disappointment in the ratings, and Sally Quinn did not improve. Rumors circulated in December 1973 that she would be asked to leave the show. Finally, after four months as coanchor, CBS dismissed her in January 1974. "When Sally Quinn and the *CBS Morning News* parted company in January 1974, the sighs of relief were almost of hurricane force," wrote one critic.[21] Quinn was bitter about the experience and blamed CBS for allowing her to make so many mistakes and to go on the air with no previous television experience: "Quinn discovered that her executive producer, Lee Townsend, 'had never produced anything in his life. I thought it was kind of funny. There was Lee with no experience, Hughes who had never been an anchorman and I who had scarcely been on television. They must know what they are doing, I thought.'"[22]

A look at the ratings over those past few years showed little change despite CBS's best attempt. The *CBS Morning News* with Hughes Rudd remained on the air but without Sally Quinn. "The Quinn-Hughes Rudd show had been chugging along at about the same 1.4 rating its predecessor achieved. CBS would be happy with a nice steady 2.5, still well under NBC's *Today* ratings but 'enough to make it worthwhile putting a show on,'"[23] said a CBS News executive. A comparison between the *Today* ratings and those of the *CBS Morning News* from 1968 to 1976 indicates that changes on the program had virtually no effect on either improving the average rating at 1.6 for CBS or lessening *Today*'s average rating of 4.7.

A.M. America

ABC did not attempt to compete seriously with *The Today Show* until it developed *A.M. America*, which premiered on January 6, 1975. Like the first CBS attempt, *The Morning Show*, ABC decided to try a *Today* show replica. That was not its original intention but rather one that was suggested by its consulting agency, Frank M. Magid, Associates. Magid was retained to do research on the early morning audience currently watching NBC or CBS:

> One thing the researchers found was that the answers held both good news and bad. The good news was that only 10% or less were "loyal" to the CBS morning show. The bad news was that 33% of them seemed wedded to NBC in the a.m. But, . . . that left more than half the morning viewers with no hard-and-fast rule for morning dialing.[24]

The research was said to have been the most extensive ever done for a single program, according to ABC.

Up until that time, morning programming offered by ABC affiliate stations had been primarily local. Therefore, ABC needed to present the idea of a morning news show in an attractive enough way to get them to "clear" for the program. Initially, the affiliates were reluctant, in part because of the uncertainty of a new program and one that required two hours of clearance. Also, in many two-network markets, ABC was only a secondary affiliation. And in some markets where ABC was the primary affiliate, the stations carried *Today* because of a secondary affiliation with NBC. This left, on the whole, fewer affiliate stations available to carry the proposed new program.

Affiliates were also reluctant to commit themselves to a significant change in morning programming without knowing who was going to be hosting the show. Although the program plans had been announced to the affiliates in May 1974, the actual selection of hosts did not occur until September. Bill Buetel was named as the host, and Stephanie Edwards and Bob Kennedy became the new cohosts. Buetel had been coanchor for *Eyewitness News* on WABC-TV in New York. Edwards was a former actress who was cohosting *Ralph Story's A.M.*, the morning news program in Los Angeles, and Kennedy was the host of talk show *Kennedy and Co.* on WLS-TV in Chicago.

Dennis Doty, director of morning program development at ABC, hoped that the three hosts would appeal to the eighteen–forty-nine-year-old age group. He also felt that the looks, style, warmth, and wearability of the hosts were the key ingredients that would bring success to the show:

> He said the web studies have shown NBC's *Today* show and CBS' morning news have a heavy appeal to older groups. He said that in markets where successful local rivals to those programs have been mounted, the emphasis always has been on youth appeal, gaining audiences that had not been morning TV viewers before, according to researchers.[25]

A.M. America, with a format that was nearly an exact replica of *The Today Show*'s, was given a budget of $8 million for the first year, and there was the familiar advertising revenue share incentive for the ABC affiliated stations:

> Stations will get six commercial minutes in the first half hour and four in the second, with the same pattern repeated in the second hour. There will also be options for five minutes of news at 7:30 and 8:30. The show will provide a minimum of 42 minutes per program of news and public affairs and slightly more for entertainment segments and instruction.[26]

Alas, even with diligent research guiding the ambitious ABC attempt to program successfully against *Today*, a comparison of ratings from January to November 1975 clearly revealed that *A.M. America* did not live up to its expectations. The average audience rating for *The Today Show* during that time was 4.9 compared to the 1.4 of ABC's *A.M. America*. *Today* outdistanced its newest competitor three and a half times in average share of audience, with a share of 36 versus *A.M. America*'s average share of 10 for the same nine-month span.

By the end of February, the faltering program already underwent major changes. Chris Dyerly and Ken Livesay, producers of *A.M. America*, were fired and replaced by Bob Cuniff, who had been a writer-producer for *Today* and a writer for Dick Cavett. He was given the title "managing editor," and his primary responsibility was to supervise the on-air written material. By August, the program had lost cohost Stephanie Edwards, executive producer Jules Power, and director of morning programming Dennis Doty. In September, ABC announced to its affiliates that the morning program was going to be considerably revised, including the acquisition of a new principal host.

Although it was prudent of *The Today Show* to take their latest competition seriously, it was not long before they were able to relax. *Today*'s executive producer Stuart Schulberg wrote a humorous article that mocked the ratings battle between the networks. *Today* was the network "champion," and *A.M. America* was the challenging new "contender." The article demonstrated Schulberg's excellent writing background and also highlighted the vital statistics on the two rival programs:

And coming into the ring now, the scrappy challenger from the upper West Side, weighing in at 186 stations, a game contender at $3,000 per minute, a fighter who really knows his ABC's, Goldenson's Golden Boy—*A.M. America*, accompanied by his corner persons, Bill Buetel and Stephanie Edwards. . . . And now, ladies and gentlemen and network researchers, here comes the champion, at 214 stations, $12,000 per commercial minute, none other than *Today* itself, that bruising battler who's held the early morning title for 23 years—your favorite and mine, or as manager Julian Goodman calls him so affectionately, "Rocky of Rockefeller Center." . . . Doing the living color for us tonight here at Nielsen Square Garden is Hughes Rudd at CBS, familiar to all you TV fight fans as that wily boxer who staged such a game contest with *Today* his last time out. 'Hughes, it's a privilege to have you with us and how do you see the outcome?' . . . Well, it's got to be youth versus experience, the classic confrontation that makes all our ratings beat a little heavier. . . . Personally, I'm pulling for *A.M. America* because I think the morning news game needs new blood, not to mention better station lineups for us contenders. I look for *A.M. America* to jab away at *Today* through the early rounds, stick and move and hope the champ's legs give out before he can deliver that combination of his—the Shalit jab, the Hartz right hand and the Walters left hook. . . . Lad-eez an' gentle-mun and TV critics, we come now to a solemn moment. Please rise and stand in silent tribute to a good lady who departed this world of ours since our last championship bout. Let us dedicate one minute of media meditation to the blessed memory of Sally Quinn.[27]

As it turned out, there was no contest. *A.M. America* lasted only a few months. The next contender must have gone through better training because it had the chops over the long haul to give *Today* a serious fight. Most encouragingly, there was enough indication that the stalwart *Today* audience was willing to check around for other alternatives that the idea of presenting a competitive two-hour morning show was still feasible. The right combination of program content and appealing talent was all that was needed. One important reason for *Today*'s success over the years had been its strong, consistent talent.

Good Morning America

During the early 1970s, after ABC had begun to improve its ratings in prime-time programming, they decided to reexamine other programming time slots more seriously and turned their attention to the morning. Edwin Vane, then network vice president and national program director, explained, "It was very important for us to be able to tell our affiliates, as well as the communications industry in general, that ABC had become a complete-service network that was in full operation right from the start of the day."[28] In response to the failure of *A.M. America*, the network knew it had an expensive flop on its hands but was determined to keep trying. Vane felt that having a morning news program was important for many reasons. "It helps our news staff in their contact work when major political figures can see a valuable forum becoming available on ABC in the morning. It provides greater flexibility for potential advertisers. And it is vital in providing our affiliates with the public service programming they need to fulfill their requirements for FCC licensing. We have the responsibility as a network to inform the public, and an extended morning program goes a long way toward meeting that responsibility."[29] In November 1975, after completely revising its approach to the morning program, ABC premiered *Good Morning America*.

Among the many major changes from *A.M. America* to *Good Morning America* was the change in host. Because *A.M. America* and, subsequently, *Good Morning America* were produced under ABC's Entertainment Department rather than its News Division, ABC executives did not feel any responsibility to secure a host with a news background. The ultimate selection was an actor who had appeared on two prime-time television series: *The Bold Ones* and *Lucas Tanner*. Vane explained their choice: "'We definitely did not want a newsman. But the man we were looking for had to be believable, articulate, intelligent, warm and likable—a man very much in control of himself who could work well under stress.' The man who best met these qualifications was David Hartman."[30] The new principal female, Nancy Dussault, was also a performer without a news background. ABC cast a large group of engaging regular specialists who contributed to the program at various times, including Jack Anderson, Rona Barrett, Erma Bombeck, John Lindsay, Bruce Jenner, Geraldo Rivera, Helen Gurley Brown, Sylvia Porter, Lendon Smith, F. Lee Bailey, and Sandy Hill.

One of the reasons *A.M. America* failed was that it was so much like *The Today Show* that it did not provide the morning viewer with an incentive to switch from *Today* to the ABC competitor. *"Today* had been doing an excellent job for a long time and we didn't give the viewer sufficient reason to come over to us," explained Vane. When ABC was in the process of producing a new morning program, it decided to give the set a "living room" appearance, with comfortable chairs and a couch, hoping to create a more informal atmosphere and to attract a different audience to its program. David Hartman explained the difference between *Today's* sterile atmosphere and the warm, comfortable set used on *Good Morning America*:

> Whenever politics, government or economics is discussed on television, we're conditioned to expect a stark and cool setting as background. That's the way it's always been. But our set is warm and homey with a flowered couch, plants and bookcases.
>
> Although our background is disarming, it suggests that world affairs can be and, in fact, are treated every day in such an environment by the Secretary of State as well as by ordinary citizens. Perhaps that's why people can relate to our programs so well.[31]

The *Good Morning America* format (see table 6.1), while basically retaining the same concept as *Today*, was different in many significant ways. The program was heavily feature oriented and faster paced than *Today*. Individual segments adhered to strict time limitations. The local stations were allowed to cut away from the network to do local weather inserts during the opening news sequences at 7:00 and 8:00 a.m. Also, there were more breaks within the half hour than there were on *The Today Show*. The available advertising slots were not limited to specific half-hour blocks as in the *Today* program but were integrated with the network breaks.

Good Morning America became a significant threat to *Today* by cutting into its audience. Even more important, it began to attract viewers that advertisers most wanted to reach. The new ABC morning show was specifically designed to attract viewers in the prime advertising target, women eighteen to forty-nine years old, and the demographic studies showed that *Good Morning America* had succeeded in doing exactly that. It also co-opted the advertising practice that originally attracted sponsors to *Today*—the close product identification that benefited the advertiser when the *Today* talent did the commercials. But beginning in the summer of 1976, the *Today* hosts no longer did commercials. *Good Morning America*, on the other hand, required talent to do them, thus creating yet another incentive for advertisers to defect, particularly when it was combined with the incentive of a young female audience. By September 1976, many former *Today* sponsors had bought time on the ABC program, including Bristol-Myers, Campbell Soup Company, Colgate-Palmolive Company, and General Foods.

Table 6.1. *Good Morning America* Format

Time	Sequence
7:00 AM	1. Part I (Includes Program Open and News with Local Cutaway Weather Segment)
	2. Title Art Work (Music Over) :05
	3. Commercials #1 and #2 (Local) 2:00
	4. Part II (No Announce first :05)
	5. Title Art Work (Music Over) :05
	6. Commercials #3 and #4 (Local) 2:00
7:25 AM (exactly)	7. Part III (First :05 generic shot—no announce)
	8. Title Art Work (Music Over) :05
7:29 AM (exactly)	9. Commercial #5 (Local) 1:00
7:30 AM	10. Part IV (No Announce first :05—Includes maximum of two (2) :05 Billboards—supered)
	11. Commercial #6 (Network) 1:00
	12. Commercial #7 (Local) 1:00
	13. Part V (No Announce first :05)
	14. Commercials #8 and #9 (Network) 2:00
	15. Part VI
	16. Commercial #10 (Network) 1:00
	17. Commercial #11 (Local) 1:00
	18. Part VII (No Announce first :05—Includes close)
	19. Net Ident :18
7:58:47 AM	20. Station Break 1:13
8:00 AM	21. Part VIII (Includes Program Re-Open and News with Local Cutaway Weather Segment)
	22. Title Art Work (Music Over) :05
	23. Commercials #12 and #13 (Local) 2:00
	24. Part IX (No Announce first :05)
	25. Title Art Work (Music Over) :05
	26. Commercials #14 and #15 (Local) 2:00
8:25 AM (exactly)	27. Part X (First :05 generic shot—no announce)
	28. Title Art Work (Music Over) :05
8:29 AM (exactly)	29. Commercial #16 (Local) 1:00
8:30 AM	30. Part XI (No Announce first :05—Includes maximum of two (2) :05 Billboards—supered)
	31. Commercial #17 (Network) 1:00
	32. Commercial #18 (Local) 1:00
	33. Part XII (No Announce first :05)
	34. Commercials #19 and #20 (Network) 2:00
	35. Part XIII
	36. Commercial #21 (Network) 1:00
	37. Commercial #22 (Local) 1:00
	38. Part XIV (No Announce first :05—Includes Close and Credits)
	39. Net Ident :18
8:58:47 AM	40. Station Break 1:13

Source: NBC Affiliate Relations Department Files.

Good Morning America had the distinction of being the first program to make serious inroads against *Today*, although *Today* remained ahead in the overall national ratings. That was primarily because *Today* was carried by 221 network-affiliated stations compared with the ABC lineup of just 177 stations. According to David Hartman, in those early days the station difference was even greater, and ratings for the ABC program were strong and gaining in the major market areas. "When I began hosting the show, we had a rating of 1.7 and now we're averaging between 2.5 and 3.2. In terms of certain key markets, we are beating *Today* in Los Angeles, San Francisco, Chicago, Detroit, and lately in New York and Washington. Nationally, *Today* beats us on overall audience because NBC has about 80 more local outlets in its network."[32] ABC continued to make gains. In April 1977, *Broadcasting* magazine mentioned the surprising success of the *Good Morning America* program. According to their figures, *Today* came in first in five of the top ten TV markets during March and April 1977. In 1976, *Today* had swept all ten markets. Those figures from research conducted by ABC and Arbitron indicated that

> the five markets where *Good Morning* led the early morning network race this year, according to ABC, were Chicago, San Francisco, Detroit, Washington, and Dallas-Fort Worth. *Today* retained the lead in New York, Los Angeles, Philadelphia, Boston, and Cleveland. CBS-TV's *CBS Morning News*, according to the ABC analysis, is carried in nine of the top ten markets and placed third in all but Cleveland, where *Good Morning* is not carried. *CBS Morning News* also was shown as having lost audience since last year in seven markets and gained in two, while *Good Morning* gained in seven and lost in one, and *Today* gained in five, lost in four and held even in one.[33]

NBC kept early comparative ratings between *Today* and *Good Morning America*, and an examination of the ratings in table 6.2 reveals that *Good Morning America* began to make steady gains after September 1976.

Comparisons for the year 1976 between *Today* and *Good Morning America* indicated that *Today* averaged a rating of 4.2 compared to 2.3 for *Good Morning America*. The average share on *The Today Show* was a 29, while *Good Morning America* was only able to draw an average share of 16. The figures also suggested that *Good Morning America* was steadily gaining on the *Today* program. In fact, early 1977 showed even greater gains, up to as much as 3.5. For a time, the ratings leveled off, suggesting that *Good Morning America* may have reached its peak.

Table 6.2.   Nielsen Ratings for *Today* and *Good Morning America*

	Today		Good Morning America	
Date: 1976	A.A. Rating	Share	A.A. Rating	Share
January	4.4	31	1.8	13
February	4.6	29	2.1	14
March	4.8	28	2.3	14
April	4.7	28	2.4	14
May	4.1	28	2.5	17
June	4.1	30	2.3	17
July	3.2	27	2.0	18
August	3.9	31	2.0	16
September	4.0	29	2.4	18
October	4.0	29	2.5	18
November	5.0	30	2.7	17
December	4.6	29	2.8	18

Note: Ratings apply to 7:30–8:00 a.m. and 8:30–9:00 a.m. segments.
Source: NBC Ratings Department based on Nielsen Television Index figures.

A RATINGS PERSPECTIVE

In 1976, for the first time since it aired in 1952, *Today* had to compete seriously with another program. All indications suggested that *Good Morning America* would continue to attract morning viewers, although its numbers were not likely to actually surpass those drawn by *Today*. *Good Morning America*'s ability to attract new viewers to morning television broadened the total morning audience, which at the time numbered approximately 10 million people. So although *Today* was concerned, they were not panicked. In an attempt to respond to the success of *Good Morning America*, *The Today Show* made some format changes that executive producer Paul Friedman hoped would combat the sliding ratings and make *The Today Show* more attractive to young viewers. Tom Brokaw and Jane Pauley were refreshingly young talent, feature segments were shortened, and more consumer, health, and sports features were added. The *Today* set was also redesigned using brighter, warmer colors, although it was still far from the "homey" set used by *Good Morning America*.

All those changes seemed to stem the worst of the ratings drain. Jerry Jaffe of NBC's Ratings Department made several observations about the *Today* ratings in general. He explained that the ratings had been fairly consistent throughout *Today*'s twenty-five years on the air. An occasional drop in the ratings for a short period of time was not a significant worry for NBC. In fact, Jaffe explained that it was impossible to determine what

Jane Pauley and Tom Brokaw.

may have influenced the ratings on a short time basis since so many vari-
ables are possible and that only long-term averages can be a reliable index
to viewing patterns.

For example, one pattern that emerges from long-range figures is that
viewing tended to drop significantly in the summer months so that July–
September averages were always lower than the other months. That also
coincided with the overall viewing pattern for prime-time and daytime
viewing during those months. NBC kept regular biweekly rating records
on *Today,* and also special ratings were kept on special programming. For
example, one of the highest average ratings ever recorded for *The Today
Show* was during the 1973 coverage of Princess Anne's "Royal Wedding"
from Great Britain.

NBC averaged a 7.3 rating for the two and a half hours of commercial coverage. This is more than double the audience obtained by CBS for the four
hours of their commercial coverage (3.3) and ABC's two hours of coverage
(3.2). The two regular *Today Show* half hours averaged a 9.8 rating on the
14th. This is 72% higher than the average rating for the *Today Show* this fall
(5.7).[34]

Separate ratings were also kept for most special remote broadcasts, although not all remotes attracted a higher average rating than the normal

rating. Special ratings were kept on election days and particularly for the day following a major election when large numbers of viewers were likely to tune in for election results. On November 3, 1976, for example, *Today*'s average audience rating was 12.7. Special ratings were also kept on the Fridays that were devoted to the state salutes during the bicentennial tribute. The average audience rating for those Fridays was a 4.4 rating, slightly higher than the average rating for the entire year, which was 4.3. Since the bicentennial Friday ratings were included in that yearly average, the actual difference is probably somewhat greater. According to the ratings, the most watched state salute was West Virginia with a 5.3, and the least watched salute was Maine, which was the last state to be honored in the bicentennial tribute and attracted an audience rating of only 3.1.

Special ratings were also kept for the days when the guest hosts were being auditioned between April 15 and July 26, 1974, to replace Frank McGee. The best rating for a particular host was difficult to determine because the ratings rapidly declined from an average of 6.0 the week of April 15 to a low of 4.1 on July 26, 1974. The guest-host rating seemed to coincide with the steadily decreasing program ratings; therefore, each successive guest host had a lower rating than the previous guest host. There was only one significant rise, and that occurred the week of July 8, 1974, when Jim Hartz was the guest host. The rating prior to his appearance had been a 4.5, and after his appearance it was a 4.1. The "Jim Hartz Week" received a 4.7. NBC felt that this indicated audience approval and made Hartz the prime candidate for the position.

Those short-term, special ratings could not be considered to be very accurate. As Jaffe explained, the only reliable ratings are those that reflect viewing patterns over a long period of time. Very often, the ratings were extremely low with no obvious explanation. Those extremes tended to even themselves out over extended periods. Jaffe also observed that *Today* had enjoyed an unusually long span of time virtually untouched by competition, which was an unnatural event in television, and it was therefore just a question of time before *Today* faced a significant competitor.

Conclusion

Today in History

It is worth revisiting those opening lines of the NBC film that first promoted *Today* in 1952 to see just how prophetic Pat Weaver's vision was and to understand just how brilliantly the men and women of *Today*, both in front of and behind the camera, carried out that vision:

> *Today* is a program that must through its entertainment and its news become a national habit. It must stir imagination. It must create an informed listener public. A program like this is a magnificent view of the tool of television and its ultimate social responsibility. John Smith, American, on this program will meet the people that he must know to be an informed citizen of a free society. He will hear the voices that count in the world. He will listen to word that echoes the story of history. He will see the places of peace and the places of war. His horizons will be limited by neither time nor place. John Smith will be there. He will know. This is the real secret weapon of free men: To know, to understand, so that John Smith is ready for today, whatever it may bring.[1]

Despite the sexist language, those visionary words were predictably true in 1952, proven true by 1977, and enduringly true more than sixty years later.

A RECIPE FOR SUCCESS

There are several factors that have contributed to the initial success of *Today* and that in most cases still contribute to its current success:

1. Today *was a unique and original concept: Today* was created as primarily a news program. It gave the audience a sense of being "up-to-the-minute" informed as the day began, and the contemporary nature of the program made it responsive to the current social and political issues of the day. During those first twenty-five years, the demand for more news increased substantially and steadily as evidenced by the expansion of the network evening news, more local news, and the popularity of such programs as *60 Minutes*. It was a trend that grew exponentially over the years, and *Today* contributed significantly to the appetite for news that would eventually be available 24/7.

2. Today *had large amounts of time available:* When the majority of Americans were rising and preparing for work or other activity, *Today* provided two hours of daily programming. Viewers were able to "tune in" anytime because of the repetitive nature of the programming format and to watch as their morning routine allowed. More important, time allowed some topics to be covered in depth and for a broad range of topics to be covered every day.

3. Today *was broadcast live:* Almost all television was live until the mid-1950s when videotape was perfected and made prerecorded programming possible. With the exception of a short period of time, *Today* has always been broadcast live. That gave the program flexibility in broadcasting late-breaking news events and gave the audience a sense of immediacy and participation in a program that was taking place at that moment.

4. Today *was designed to both inform and entertain its audience:* Pat Weaver felt that news and information should be delivered in an interesting or entertaining way. In addition to a wide variety of news, *Today* covered in-depth topics, including social and political issues, art, sports, and entertainment.

5. Today *developed a reputation for credibility and reliability:* The audience felt that *Today* was a reliable source for information. Presidents, congressmen, cabinet members, world leaders, renowned authors, and social and political experts were a regular part of the programming. The ratings were significantly higher during major news events, such as an international or national crisis, elections, and space flights, or whenever Americans felt a particular need to be informed.

6. Today *established successful advertising policies:* The establishment of participating "magazine"-style advertising set *Today* soundly on the road to financial success. Talent participation in commercials attracted advertisers to the program by providing a strong connection between host and product. Those practices made it possible for NBC to pay for the expensive daily production costs and eventually made *Today* highly profitable.

7. Today *established excellent relations with its affiliated stations:* Establishing good relations with its stations was critical to the early success of the program and continued to be important over the years. The more stations that "cleared" for broadcast each morning, the higher the potential *Today* audience and ratings. Excellent communication with the stations also made complex program arrangements feasible for special or extended programming. NBC also offered attractive opportunities for local stations to share in the advertising revenues.

8. Today *used technology to provide a "window to the world":* As Pat Weaver anticipated, when technology was developed or perfected, it would be incorporated into the programming. Gadgetry gave way to critical technological advances that were effectively used to deliver on the Weaver promise to bring world events to the average viewer.

9. Today *talent related easily and comfortably to the audience:* The personalities and duties of the *Today* talent were carefully considered to provide a balance of professional competence with warmth. For eighteen of its first twenty-five years on the air, David Garroway and Hugh Downs represented the ideal host qualities that contributed to their popularity with the audience. Viewers not only expected to trust the panel members but also wanted to like them.

10. Today *became a habit with millions of American viewers:* For many years, the morning audience came to depend on *Today* because there was no attractive competitive programming alternative. Watching *Today* provided a sense of continuity, familiarity, and security for viewers that eventually evolved into a habit. As a network program, it was available to all areas of the country so that *Today* was heavily viewed by people even while on vacation and was popular with traveling businessmen and politicians. *Today* was loyal to its viewer expectations and responsive to criticism.

11. Today *launched the career of Barbara Walters and paved the way for women to be regarded as journalists on par with men:* Today provided the opportunity, but women provided the competence to cover news events and other content that was not defined by its relevance

to women. Walters developed a reputation for excellent interviewing skills that served her well as she met and talked with world leaders.

12. The Today *concept was always fresh and contemporary: Today* was (and is) contemporary. Each day is a new day, with news and world events providing the content. *Today* was reinvented every day while maintaining solid reliability and familiarity. The content was fresh because *Today* was always new and relevant.

More than sixty years later, Pat Weaver would be proud of his enduring creation, *Today*, and would certainly recognize the format in hundreds of successful imitations all over the world.

Notes

CHAPTER 1

1. NBC News Press Release, December 9, 1976.
2. Interview with Sylvester L. (Pat) Weaver, *Today*'s Twenty-Fifth Anniversary Program, January 14, 1977.
3. Film excerpt, *Today*'s Twenty-Fifth Anniversary Program, January 14, 1977.
4. Robert Metz, *The Today Show* (Chicago: Playboy Press, 1977), 93.
5. George Rosen, *"Today,* TV's Top Grosser," *Variety,* September 23, 1953, 27.
6. Interview with Sylvester L. (Pat) Weaver, *Today*'s Twenty-Fifth Anniversary Program, January 14, 1977.

CHAPTER 2

1. *Variety,* January 16, 1952, 25.
2. NBC Program Analysis File: Show Format Records, 1952.
3. Robert Metz, *The Today Show* (Chicago: Playboy Press, 1977), 36.
4. NBC Program Analysis File: Show Format Records, 1952.
5. Metz, *The Today Show,* 38.
6. *Variety,* January 16, 1952, 25.
7. Giraud Chester, Garnet R. Garrison, and Edgar E. Willis, *Television and Radio,* 4th ed. (Englewood Cliffs, NJ: Prentice Hall, 1971).
8. NBC Affiliate Relations File, 1952.
9. *Variety,* January 16, 1952, 36.
10. Metz, *The Today Show,* 25.
11. Thomas Thompson, *"Today,"* *Life,* December 10, 1971, 67.
12. Metz, *The Today Show,* 40.

13. Sylvester L. Weaver, Memo: Program Analysis File, 1952.

14. Metz, *The Today Show*, 42.

15. NBC Program Analysis File: Show Format, 1954.

16. NBC Program Analysis File: Anniversary, 1953.

17. Ibid., 1952.

18. Metz, *The Today Show*, 58.

19. Frederic A. Birmingham, "Everything Happens on the *Today* Show," *Saturday Evening Post*, September 10, 1973, 62.

20. Metz, *The Today Show*.

21. NBC Program Analysis File: Show Format, 1964.

22. Ibid., 1953.

23. Ibid., 1954.

24. Ibid.

25. NBC Program Analysis File: West Coast Programming, 1955.

26. Ibid.

27. NBC Program Analysis File: Colorcasts, 1955–57.

28. NBC Program Analysis File: Show Format, 1956.

29. Ibid.

30. *Today: The First Fifteen Years* (an NBC Promotional Booklet, 1967), 9.

31. Ibid., 6–12.

32. NBC Program Analysis File: Anniversary, 1957.

33. NBC Program Analysis File: *Today* Girls.

34. NBC Program Analysis File: Show Format, 1955, 1956, 1957.

35. Ibid.

36. NBC Affiliate Relations: New Format for the *Today* Show, Booklet (distributed to affiliate stations), September 1958.

37. NBC Program Analysis File: Show Format, 1958, 1959.

38. *Today: The First Fifteen Years*, 18.

39. NBC Program Analysis File: Show Format, 1959.

40. Metz, *The Today Show*, 135.

41. "Man-of-*Today* Honored by Network in Renaming of Early-Morning Show," *St. Petersburg Times*, September 15, 1960.

42. "Let Me Out," *Newsweek*, June 11, 1962, 88.

43. *Today: The First Fifteen Years*, 17.

44. Ibid., 20.

45. Ibid., 1963.

46. NBC Program Analysis File: Show Format, 1963.

47. *Today: The First Fifteen Years*, 35.

48. NBC Program Analysis File: Show Format, 1963.

49. NBC Affiliate Relations Memo: June 19, 1962.

50. Ibid., January 25, 1963.

51. Ibid., February 4, 1963.

52. NBC Program Analysis File, 1962.

53. Ellen Kay, *The Five-Million-Dollar Woman: Barbara Walters* (New York: Manor Books, 1976), 64.

54. NBC Program Analysis File: Show Format, 1963.

55. Ibid., 1964.
56. NBC Affiliate Relations File: Interdepartment Correspondence, September 17, 1965.
57. *Today: The First Fifteen Years*, 51.
58. Ibid.
59. NBC Program Analysis File: Show Format, 1965.
60. *Today: The First Fifteen Years*, 58.
61. NBC Program Analysis File: Show Format, 1966.
62. NBC Program Analysis File: Card 5813–5815.
63. Ibid.
64. NBC Program Analysis File: Show Format, 1967.
65. Ibid.
66. NBC Program Analysis File: Show Format, 1968.
67. "*Today*, Tote-Up on 1968," *Variety*, March 5, 1969, 37.
68. NBC Program Analysis File: Show Format, 1969.
69. Ibid., 1970.
70. Ibid., 1971.
71. Ibid.
72. NBC Press Release, June 17, 1971.
73. Ibid., January 14, 1972.
74. Ibid., January 18, 1972.
75. NBC Program Analysis File: Show Format, 1972.
76. Ibid.
77. NBC News Press Release, September 27, 1972.
78. NBC News Press Release, February 20, 1973.
79. NBC Program Analysis File: Show Format, 1973.
80. Ibid.
81. Ibid.
82. NBC Program Analysis File: Show Format, 1974.
83. Ibid.
84. NBC Press Release, December 9, 1974.
85. NBC Program Analysis File: Show Format, 1975.
86. NBC News Press Release, March 26, 1975.
87. Ibid., April 4, 1975.
88. Ibid., March 6, 1975.
89. Ibid., June 12, 1975.
90. Ibid., June 9, 1975.
91. Ibid., January 21, 1975.
92. J. Anthony Lukas, "What Does Tomorrow Hold for *Today*?," *New York Times*, August 22, 1976, 1.
93. NBC Ratings Department.
94. Lukas, "What Does Tomorrow Hold for *Today*?," 20.
95. Ibid.
96. Ibid., 21.
97. Ibid.

CHAPTER 3

1. NBC Program Analysis File: History, Producers.
2. Robert Metz, *The Today Show* (Chicago: Playboy Press, 1977), 27.
3. Ibid.   `
4. Raymond A. Sokolov, "The *Today* Show," *Atlantic Monthly*, August 1974, 11.
5. Ibid.
6. NBC Program Analysis File: Regular Cast.
7. Metz, *The Today Show*, 64.
8. Ibid., 67.
9. Ibid., 47.
10. NBC Program Analysis File: History, Producers.
11. Metz, *The Today Show*, 116.
12. Ibid., 118.
13. NBC Program Analysis File: History, Producers.
14. Metz, *The Today Show*, 121.
15. Sydney Head, *Broadcasting in America* (Boston: Houghton Mifflin, 1972), 341.
16. NBC Program Analysis File: Show Format, 1958.
17. Metz, *The Today Show*, 133.
18. NBC Program Analysis File: History, Producers.
19. NBC Program Analysis File: Show Format, 1961.
20. NBC Program Analysis File: Regular Cast.
21. Metz, *The Today Show*, 143.
22. NBC Program Analysis File: Show Format, 1962.
23. Metz, *The Today Show*, 149.
24. NBC Program Analysis File: History of Origination.
25. Ellen Kay, *The Five-Million-Dollar Woman: Barbara Walters* (New York: Manor Books, 1976), 65.
26. Ibid.
27. Ibid., 89.
28. Metz, *The Today Show*, 193.
29. Ibid., 201.
30. Ibid., 199.
31. Metz, *The Today Show*, 201.
32. Sokolov, "The *Today* Show," 12.
33. NBC Program Analysis File: History, Producers.
34. Metz, *The Today Show*, 47.
35. NBC Program Analysis File: Production Credits.
36. Interview and material from Barry Solomon, NBC, New York, June 1977.
37. Ibid., August 6, 1975.
38. Ibid.
39. NBC Press Release, December 4, 1973.
40. NBC Press Release, January 29, 1973.
41. Ibid.
42. Frederic A. Birmingham, "Everything Happens on the *Today* Show," *Saturday Evening Post*, September 10, 1973, 62.
43. Sokolov, "The *Today* Show," 13.

44. Ibid.
45. Ibid., 14.
46. Interview and material from Barry Solomon.
47. Sokolov, "The *Today* Show," 14.
48. Ibid.
49. Metz, *The Today Show*, 47.
50. Interview and material from Barry Solomon.
51. Ibid.
52. Kay Gardella, "New Producer for *Today* First in Revamping," *New York Daily News*, May 18, 1976, 66.
53. Ibid.
54. Ibid.
55. Personal observation of production, June 30, 1977.
56. NBC Audience Research Department, "*Today* Monitoring Study," November 1976.
57. Gardella, "New Producer for *Today* First in Revamping," 80.
58. NBC Program Analysis File: History, Theme Music.
59. NBC Program Analysis File.

CHAPTER 4

1. Robert Metz, *The Today Show* (Chicago: Playboy Press, 1977), 17.
2. *Today Show* interview with Sylvester Weaver, January 14, 1977.
3. Metz, *The Today Show*, 17.
4. Ibid., 52.
5. Ibid., 75.
6. Ibid., 78.
7. "Why Garroway Signed Off," *Life*, June 30, 1961, 102.
8. Ibid.
9. "Television, Professor Garroway of 21-Inch U.," *Time*, December 28, 1962, 35.
10. "Rule Daly Out as *Today* Host: NBC News in Control," *Variety*, June 21, 1961, 25.
11. "John Chancellor Hosts *Today*," *Variety*, July 5, 1961, 34.
12. "John Chancellor," *Variety*, July 26, 1961, 24.
13. Ibid.
14. "Let Me Out," *Newsweek*, June 11, 1962, 88.
15. "John Chancellor," *Variety*, July 26, 1961, 24.
16. Ibid.
17. Metz, *The Today Show*, 147.
18. Ibid., 150.
19. Ibid., 152.
20. "McGee Will Not Shun Ad Duties as Downs' Successor on *Today*," *Advertising Age*, October 11, 1971, 16.
21. NBC Press Release, April 27, 1971.

22. Ibid.
23. Arthur Unger, "Frank McGee, Host of *Today*, Not Running Scared," *Christian Science Monitor*, March 4, 1973, 8.
24. Ibid., 9.
25. Metz, *The Today Show*, 227.
26. Ibid.
27. NBC News Press Release, July 30, 1973.
28. Ibid.
29. Ellen Kay, *The Five-Million-Dollar Woman: Barbara Walters* (New York: Manor Books, 1976), 95.
30. Barbara Walters, "Barbara Walters by Barbara Walters," *Ladies Home Journal*, September 1976, 28.
31. NBC Award Department File.
32. "*Today*'s Woman," *Newsweek*, May 19, 1969, 73.
33. Metz, *The Today Show*, 5.
34. Ibid., 7.
35. Ibid., 8.
36. Jeff Greenfield, "The Showdown at ABC News," *New York Times Magazine*, February 13, 1977, 32.
37. Walters, "Barbara Walters by Barbara Walters," 26.
38. NBC News Press Release, July 1, 1974.
39. "The Great Host Hunt," *Time*, July 15, 1974, 95.
40. Ibid.
41. Ibid.
42. Les Brown, "NBC Will Replace McGee by July 31," *New York Times*, July 19, 1974, 70.
43. Val Adams, "*Today* Co-Host Hunt Narrows," *New York Daily News*, July 16, 1974, 31.
44. "Morning Star," *Newsweek*, August 5, 1974, 76.
45. Ibid.
46. "The Great Host Hunt," *Time*, July 15, 1974, 96.
47. "Brokaw to Become Host of *Today* Next August," *New York Times*, June 19, 1976, 75.
48. Ibid.
49. NBC News Press Release, August 30, 1976.
50. Kay Gardella, "*Today* with Tom Brokaw's Off to a Sedate Start," *New York Daily News*, August 31, 1976, 62.
51. Ibid.
52. Metz, *The Today Show*, 154.
53. Ibid., 150.
54. Bob Williams, "On the Air," *New York Post*, August 11, 1966, 63.
55. Metz, *The Today Show*, 218.
56. Ibid., 217.
57. Ibid., 218.
58. Frederic A. Birmingham, "Everything Happens on the *Today* Show," *Saturday Evening Post*, September 10, 1973, 98.
59. NBC Press Release, January 4, 1973.

60. "Critic as Quipster," *Newsweek*, December 2, 1974, 53.

61. Kay Gardella, "Miss Furness in NBC Wings to Open *Today Show* Door," *New York Daily News*, April 29, 1976, 140.

62. NBC News Press Release, October 4, 1976.

63. Bettelou Peterson, "New Look Keeps *Today* on Top of the Morning," *People*, January 14, 1977, 8.

64. "On the Air," *The New Republic*, February 4, 1952, 22.

65. NBC Program Analysis Files: *Today* Girls; also Appendix D.

66. Marvin Kitman, "Blair Leaves the Air," *The New Leader*, April 14, 1975, 25.

67. Ibid.

CHAPTER 5

1. NBC Memo, Sylvester L. Weaver Jr. to Harry Bannister, October 10, 1952.

2. Giraud Chester, Garnet R. Garrison, and Edgar E. Willis, *Television and Radio*, 3rd ed. (New York: Appleton-Century-Crofts, 1963), 59.

3. Robert Metz, *The Today Show* (Chicago: Playboy Press), 61.

4. Ibid.

5. Affiliate Relations File: NBC Sales Department Memo, October 15, 1953.

6. Ibid.

7. Affiliate Relations File: Steve Flynn to Richard Pinkham, July 9, 1953.

8. NBC Memo, George H. Frey to Network Salesmen, July 2, 1953.

9. Ibid.

10. NBC Memo, Roy Porteous to George Frey, March 11, 1954.

11. NBC Memo, Sales Department to TV Network Sales, March 16, 1954.

12. NBC Memo, Robert D. Daubenspeck to Roy Porteous, October 8, 1954.

13. NBC Sales Release, February 1955.

14. NBC Memo, Steve Flynn to Henry Maas, April 23, 1956.

15. NBC Memo, Steve Flynn to James Hergen, June 21, 1956.

16. NBC Memo, Hugh Belville Jr. to Robert Kinter, August 5, 1958.

17. NBC Memo, William Storke to James Hergen, September 9, 1958.

18. NBC *Today* Memo, Robert Bendick to NBC Sales Staff, October 31, 1958.

19. NBC Participating Program Sales, Rate Guides 1976.

20. NBC Participating Program Sales, Rate Guides 1955.

21. Ibid.

22. Ibid.

23. NBC Participating Program Sales, Rate Guides 1976.

24. "The Great Host Hunt," *Time*, July 15, 1974, 95.

25. Sander Vanocur, "Split Personalities," *Washington Post*, February 11, 1976, 21.

26. *Variety*, January 16, 1952, 36.

27. NBC Memo, Steve Flynn to Carl Lindemann Jr., April 9, 1963.

28. Ibid.

29. NBC Wire, Steve Flynn to All NBC Owned and Affiliated Stations, November 20, 1968.

30. Ibid., April 16, 1976.
31. NBC Wire, Steve Flynn to All Stations, Managers, and News Directors, June 30, 1969.
32. NBC Wire, Steve Flynn to All NBC Owned and Affiliated Stations, June 16, 1971.
33. Ibid., September 6, 1972.
34. Ibid., December 6, 1972.
35. NBC News Wire, Don Mercer, Vice-President Station Relations to All Stations, July 24, 1974.
36. NBC Wire, Steve Flynn to All NBC Owned and Affiliated Stations, October 8, 1976.
37. Ibid., July 9, 1975.
38. Ibid., May 15, 1974.

CHAPTER 6

1. Robert Metz, *The Today Show* (Chicago: Playboy Press, 1977), 56.
2. J. Anthony Lukas, "What Does Tomorrow Hold for *Today?*," *New York Times*, August 22, 1976, 1.
3. Peter Andrews, "With a Folksy Flavor . . . ," *TV Guide*, February 26, 1977, 27.
4. John J. O'Connor, "The *Today* Show 6,500 Mornings Later," *New York Times*, January 9, 1977, 25.
5. Raymond A. Sokolov, "The *Today* Show," *Atlantic Monthly*, August 1974, 15.
6. Ibid.
7. "Bright and Early: *Today* Show," *Time*, January 20, 1967, 55.
8. NBC News Press Release, October 7, 1975.
9. O'Connor, "The *Today* Show 6,500 Mornings Later," 25.
10. Philip Nobile, "Talk with ABC Host David Hartman," *Detroit News*, January 30, 1977, 26.
11. NBC News Audience Research Survey, 1976.
12. Interview with Barbara Lapidus, Coordinator, *Today* Mail, July 1977.
13. *Today* Mail Report, October 1976.
14. "*The Morning Show*," *Variety*, March 17, 1954, 27.
15. Ibid.
16. "Dean Plug Pulled Too Soon?," *Variety*, November 27, 1957, 61.
17. "It's Quinn-Rudd vs. Walters-McGee, as CBS Tries Again to Dent *Today*," *Variety*, June 27, 1973, 38.
18. "*CBS Morning News* in for a Shakeup," *Variety*, May 9, 1973, 231.
19. "*CBS Morning News*—Review," *Variety*, August 8, 1973, 32.
20. Ibid.
21. "Avenging Angel," *Newsweek*, July 7, 1975, 43.
22. Ibid.
23. "CBS Weighs Quinn Anchor," *Variety*, December 19, 1973, 23.
24. "ABC's 'Son of *Today*' Ready: Web Pitches for Clearance," *Variety*, January 8, 1975, 89.

25. "Buetel, Edwards and Kennedy to Host *A.M. America* for ABC," *Variety*, September 4, 1974, 53.

26. "ABC's 'Son of *Today*' Ready," *Variety*, 89.

27. Stuart Schulberg, "*Today* vs. *A.M. America*," *Variety*, January 8, 1975, 89.

28. Andrews, "With a Folksy Flavor . . . ," 26.

29. Ibid., 27.

30. Ibid.

31. Nobile, "Talk with ABC Host David Hartman," 26.

32. Ibid.

33. "It's a '*Good Morning*' Rating for ABC-TV," *Broadcasting*, April 11, 1977, 49.

34. Interview with Jerry Jaffe, NBC Ratings Department.

CONCLUSION

1. Film excerpt, *Today*'s Twenty-Fifth Anniversary Program, January 14, 1977.

Index

Note: *Page references for figures are italicized.*

Steinman, Ron, 39, 58
Stempel, Herbert, 50–51
Stern, Carl, 151
Storke, William, 126
studios. *See Today* origination
Swayze, John Cameron, 1, 57

Tallerico, John, 134
tape. *See* videotape
technology, 6–7, 11–12, 19, 22, 23, 43–44, 65, 74, 75, 76, 169; Pat Weaver on, 6, 169. *See also* color, transition to; minicam; remote origination; satellite transmission; videotape
Today, criticism of, 12, 14, 23, 24, 35, 85, 101–2, 132, 145, 149, 153, 155; of hosts, 77, 78, 82, 87, 92, 101, 105, 107, 111, 114, 151–52; from viewers, 43, 149–51, 169
Today advertising, 7, 15, 49, 52, 53, 78, 86, 88, 117–43, 145–47, 154, 163, 169; compared to *The Morning Show*, 123–24; discounts and options, 129–31; host pitches, 13, 42, 53, 66, 69, 70, 73, 82, 97–99, 113, 120, 131–32, 140–41, 142, 161, 169; local affiliate advertising, 2–3, 72, 117, 126–27, 135, 137, 142; "participating" structure of, 4, 12–13, 119, 121–23, 125, 142, 153, 169; scheduling commercials, 11, 13, 68–70, 71–73, 121–25, 126–27, 136–37, 138, 141; special event advertising, 140–41. See also *Today* audience; *Today* ratings
Today audience, 1, 2, 5, 7–8, 9, 13–14, 15, 18, 24, 27, 29, 38, 43, 44, 45, 47, 48, 49, 60, 70–71, 79, 82, 87–88, 97, 99, 102, 103, 105, 110–11, 112, 113, 114, 123, 132, 145–66, 167, 168, 169; demographics of, 29, 61, 79, 97, 146–47, 148, 149, 158, 161; live audience, 22; politicians in, 8, 35–36, 148; viewer mail, 43, 51, 145–46, 149–52; women in, 13, 21, 79, 108, 142, 147, 149, 161

Today credits, 76–77
Today competition, 8, 39, 41, 43, 64, 67, 79, 95, 96, 114, 123–24, 132, 136, 143, 146, 147, 148, 149, 152–66, 169. See also *A.M. America*; *Captain Kangaroo*; *CBS Morning News*; *Good Morning America*; *The Morning Show*
Today girls, 5–6, 15, 20, 27–28, 34, 54, 92, 107–10, 114–15. *See also individual names*
Today hosts, 81–102. *See also individual names*
Today name, 9
Today origination, 20–21, 22, 26, 29–30, 32, 33, 35, 37, 38, 39, 54, 59, 65, 71, 72, 74–75, 76, 130, 131. *See also* Florida Showcase Studio; RCA Exhibition Hall; remote origination
Today panel, 5, 15, 43, 52, 53, 66, 85, 101, 102–7, 110–15; live commercials by, 13, 42, 53, 66, 69, 70, 73, 82, 97–99, 113, 120, 131–32, 140–41, 142, 161, 169; women on, 5, 27–28, 42, 99, 105, 107–10, 115
Today programming, 9–45; changes to, 19, 22, 23, 24, 43, 44–45, 64, 65, 79, 126, 148–49, 164; entertainment segments and comedy skits, 52–53, 62, 85, 102, 147; guests and interviews, 20, 25, 28, 31, 32, 35, 40, 60–61, 72, 89, 93, 168; and politics, 6, 19–20, 22, 26, 28, 32, 33, 36, 43, 45, 58, 59–60, 141, 151, 166; recurring segments, 17–19, 22, 28, 30, 32, 33, 38, 60, 104, 114, 150; special features and events, 19, 20, 22–23, 28–34, 36–39, 53, 59–60, 89, 93, 137–139, 141, 150, 165–66
Today ratings, xii, 5, 35, 49, 78, 88, 92, 99, 119, 124, 125–26, 127–28, 132, 135–36, 141–43, 145–48, 164–66, 168; compared to competition, 41, 142, 153–55, 157, 158, 159, 163–65; ratings slumps, 14, 41, 43, 52–53, 64–65, 91, 95, 99, 136, 164–66
Today schedule, 2, 9, 10, 11, 18, 20, 44, 124, 126–27, 133, 134–35; and

About the Author

Cathleen M. Londino earned her PhD from the University of Michigan in radio, TV, and film and is currently a New Jersey university professor of media and film. She has served for more than thirty years in higher education as faculty, chair of the Media and Film Department, and dean of the College of Arts, Humanities, and Social Sciences. Her writing interests involve film, production, and digital media. She combines her teaching with professional activity, serving as producer, director, writer, and talent for a number of video and film projects. Dr. Londino lectures internationally on a variety of media topics.